Managing Diversity in Organizations

Herausgeber
Jr.-Prof. Dr. Barbara Beham
Ass.-Prof. Dr. Caroline Straub
Prof. Dr. Joachim Schwalbach

Springer Gabler

ZfB-Special Issues

3/2009 Operations Research in der Betriebswirtschaft – Neue Anwendungsgebiete und Ergebnisse
Herausgeber: Heinrich Kuhn/Hartmut Stadtler/Gerhard Wäscher
144 Seiten. ISBN 3-8349-1723-0

4/2009 Rational Inefficiencies
Herausgeber: Günter Fandel
136 Seiten. ISBN 3-8349-1856-3

5/2009 Entrepreneurial Finance
Herausgeber: Wolfgang Breuer/Malte Brettel
132 Seiten. ISBN 3-8349-2005-3

6/2009 Management von kleinen und mittleren Unternehmen
Herausgeber: Peter Letmathe/Peter Witt
180 Seiten. ISBN 3-8349-2139-4

1/2010 Corporate Social Responsibility and Stakeholder Dynamics
Herausgeber: Joachim Schwalbach
100 Seiten. ISBN 3-8349-1995-0

2/2010 Internationale Aspekte der Unternehmensbesteuerung
Herausgeber: Norbert Krawitz
136 Seiten. ISBN 3-8349-2006-1

3/2010 Rechnungslegung, Kapitalmärkte und Regulierung
Herausgeber: Ralf Ewert/Hans-Ulrich Küpper
164 Seiten. ISBN 3-8349-1999-3

4/2010 Mixed Methods – Konzeptionelle Überlegungen
Herausgeber: Thomas Wrona/Günter Fandel
120 Seiten. ISBN 3-8349-1998-5

5/2010 Mixed Methods in der Managementforschung
Herausgeber: Thomas Wrona/Günter Fandel
140 Seiten. ISBN 3-8349-2521-7

6/2010 Jubiläumsheft zum 80. Jahrgang
Herausgeber: Günter Fandel
184 Seiten. ISBN 3-8349-2000-2

1/2011 Unternehmensethik in Forschung und Lehre
Herausgeber: Hans-Ulrich Küpper/Philipp Schreck
94 Seiten. ISBN 3-8349-1997-7

2/2011 Kundenmanagement
Herausgeber: Oliver Götz/Ove Jensen/Manfred Krafft
94 Seiten. ISBN 3-8349-1996-9

3/2011 Human Resource Management Issues of Foreign Firms in Japan
Herausgeber: Ralf Bebenroth/Werner Pascha
142 Seiten. ISBN 3-8349-3125-X

4/2011 Beiträge zur Theorie der Unternehmung. Horst Albach zum 80. Geburtstag
Herausgeber: Günter Fandel
152 Seiten. ISBN 3-8349-3172-1

5/2011 Kundenintegration 2.0
Herausgeber: Günter Fandel/Sabine Fliess/Frank Jacob
178 Seiten. ISBN 3-8349-3392-9

6/2011 Entrepreneurial Marketing
Herausgeber: Dietmar Grichnik/Peter Witt
136 Seiten. ISBN 3-8349-3448-8

1/2012 Real Estate Finance
Herausgeber: Wolfgang Breuer/Claudia Nadler
132 Seiten. ISBN 978-3-8349-3449-9

INHALTSVERZEICHNIS

1   Managing diversity in organizations
    Barbara Beham, Caroline Straub, Joachim Schwalbach

3   Diversity research—what do we currently know about how to manage diverse organizational units?
    Eric Kearney, Sven C. Voelpel

19 Getting tuned in to those who are different: The role of empathy as mediator between diversity and performance
    Sebastian Stegmann, Marie-Élène Roberge, Rolf van Dick

45 Managing demographic change and diversity in organizations: how feedback from coworkers moderates the relationship between age and innovative work behavior
    Stefan Schaffer, Eric Kearney, Sven C. Voelpel, Ralf Koester

69 Gender and nationality pay gaps in light of organisational theories. A large-scale analysis within German establishments
    Elke Wolf, Miriam Beblo, Clemens Ohlert

95 Women on German management boards. How ownership structure affects management board diversity
    Jana Oehmichen, Marc Steffen Rapp, Michael Wolff

GRUNDSÄTZE UND ZIELE

IMPRESSUM/HINWEISE FÜR AUTOREN

HERAUSGEBER/EDITORIAL BOARD

Eberhard Ulich / Bettina Wiese
Life Domain Balance
Konzepte zur Verbesserung der Lebensqualität
2011. 330 S. Geb. EUR 49,95
EUR 49,95
ISBN 978-3-8349-1403-3

Gegenstand dieses Buches ist das Balancieren wichtiger Lebensbereiche, zu denen neben der Erwerbsarbeit auch Partnerschaft, Familie, Hobbys, gemeinnützige Arbeit und die Gesundheit gehören. Es werden Konzepte für Einzelpersonen, für Personal- u. Organisationsentwickler sowie sozialpolitische Entscheidungsträger ausgearbeitet. Besondere Schwerpunkte bilden dabei die kritische Auseinandersetzung mit den Auswirkungen moderner flexibilisierter Arbeitsstrukturen für die Life Domain Balance sowie eine lebensspannenpsychologische Betrachtung der verschiedenen relevanten Handlungsfelder. Ergebnisse empirischer Untersuchungen und Fallbeispiele aus der Praxis ergänzen die Ausführungen der Autoren und veranschaulichen die dargestellten Lösungen.

Der Inhalt
- Vom Work Life Balance Konzept zum Life Domain Balance Konzept
- Prekäre Arbeitsverhältnisse
- Persönlichkeitsförderliche Arbeitsgestaltung
- Lebensfreundliche Arbeitszeiten
- Familiennahe Arbeitsorte: Telearbeit
- Arbeit außerhalb der Erwerbsarbeit
- Erholung
- Zusammenspiel der Generationen im Berufskontext
- Betriebsspezifische Maßnahmen
- Corporate Social Responsibility und weiter reichende Initiativen
- Lessons learned

www.wirtschaftslexikon.gabler.de
Jetzt online, frei verfügbar!

Einfach bestellen: buch@gabler.de   Telefon +49(0)611. 7878-626

KOMPETENZ IN SACHEN WIRTSCHAFT

GABLER

ZfB-SPECIAL ISSUE 2/2012

Managing diversity in organizations

Barbara Beham · Caroline Straub · Joachim Schwalbach

Diversity management has recently attracted a lot of attention in both academia and practice. Globalization, migration, demographic changes, low fertility rates, a scarce pool of qualified labor, and women entering the workforce in large scales have led to an increasingly heterogeneous workforce in the past twenty years. In response to those ongoing changes, organizations have started to create work environments which address the needs and respond to the opportunities of a diverse workforce. The implementation of diversity policies and practices and the creation of an organizational culture that values heterogeneity have been the focus of recent organizational initiatives. Likewise, research on workplace diversity and its management has gained importance in management sciences. Academic scholars have started to examine the positive and negative effects of workplace diversity on employee well-being, team performance and on overall organizational effectiveness. However, the findings of empirical studies are often ambiguous since relationships between diversity measures and outcomes are complex and based on a variety of contingencies. Further empirical studies as well as theory development is required to clarify these complex relationships. Scholars are only beginning to build theoretical frameworks regarding the impact of workplace diversity and programs on various workplace outcomes. This special issue aims at shedding light on some of these open research questions by including both theoretical and empirical contributions.

The first paper by Eric Kearney, Leibniz Universität Hannover/GISMA Business School and Sven Voelpel, Jacobs University Bremen provides an extensive review of the literature on team diversity and its effects on work group performance and group member satisfaction. Guided by a research framework that includes the two main theoretical perspectives that are usually cited to explain diversity's effects—the information-elaboration

---

© Gabler-Verlag 2011

Jr.-Prof. Dr. B. Beham (✉)
Department of Management, Humboldt-Universität zu Berlin,
Spandauer Str. 1, 10178 Berlin, Germany
e-mail: barbara.beham@wiwi.hu-berlin.de

Ass. Prof. C. Straub, Ph.D.
Department of People, Organizations and Society,
Grenoble Ecole de Management, Grenoble, France
e-mail: Caroline.Straub@grenoble-em.com

Prof. Dr. J. Schwalbach
Institut für Management, Humboldt-Universität zu Berlin,
Spandauer Str. 1, 10178 Berlin, Germany
e-mail: schwal@wiwi.hu-berlin.de

and the social categorization perspective—a complex model of direct effects, mediating and moderating effects of team level diversity on team performance is examined. The authors conclude with suggestions for future research and practical recommendations for managers involved in leading diverse work groups.

The second paper by Sebastian Stegmann and Rolf van Dick, both from Goethe University Frankfurt and Marie-Élène Roberge, Northeastern Illinois University proposes a theoretical model of the processes that mediate and moderate the team diversity-performance relationship that complements the well-established cognitive perspective (as documented in the first paper of this special issue) by adding an emotional perspective. They introduce the concept of empathy to team diversity research, an emotional state which arises from the comprehension and apprehension of fellow group members' emotional state. The authors propose that empathy may enhance the performance of diverse teams through within-group member and between-group member processes. A complex theoretical framework that identifies a mediating effect of empathy on the diversity-performance relationship and specifies moderating conditions for this relationship provides a rich avenue for future research.

The third paper by Stefan Schaffer and Sven Voelpel, both Jacobs University Bremen and Eric Kearney and Ralf Koester, both from Leibniz Universität Hannover/GISMA Business empirically investigates the role of feedback from coworkers on the level of innovation in age diverse teams. Given demographic change and the aging of the workforce of many organizations, their findings broaden the still fragmentary knowledge of the conditions under which aging is likely to have more or less positive effects on innovative work behavior.

The forth paper by Elke Wolf, the University of Applied Sciences Munich, Miriam Beblo, the Berlin School of Economics and Law, and Clemens Ohlert, the University of Hamburg analyses wage inequality with respect to gender and nationality within German establishments. Their findings are based on a large-scale analysis based on linked employer-employee data from the Institute for Employment Research (LIAB). Drawing on organizational theories the authors inquire as to how firm characteristics are related to the variation of intra-firm pay gaps and derive hypotheses about which establishments have a greater incentive and/or are more able to pursue wage equality in their workforces.

The final paper by Jana Oehmichen and Michael Wolff, Georg-August-University Göttingen, and Marc Steffen Rapp, Philipps-University Marburg, empirically discusses the role of different types of ownership concentration on the percentage of women on management boards. The authors thereby distinguish between institutional and individual owners and national and foreign owners. The analysis is based on 15,976 management board member positions from 2000–2007 in approximately 600 German-listed companies. With their paper they contribute to the current public discussion on diversity in companies' boardrooms.

Diversity research—what do we currently know about how to manage diverse organizational units?

Eric Kearney · Sven C. Voelpel

Abstract: Diversity with respect to demographic variables such as gender, age, and cultural background, as well as directly job-related characteristics such as tenure, educational specialization, and functional background is both a challenge and an opportunity. We review the extant literature on how best to manage diverse organizational units. We discuss the definition and conceptualization of diversity, its direct effects on team performance and team member satisfaction, as well as the mediating variables that explain these effects and the moderating variables that determine when the positive effects of diversity are likely to prevail over the negative effects. We conclude by offering managerial suggestions on how to leverage diversity's potential.

Keywords: Team heterogeneity · Demographic diversity · Job-related diversity · Team performance · Team member satisfaction

JEL Classification: M10 · M12

© Gabler-Verlag 2011

Prof. Dr. E. Kearney (✉)
GISMA Business School, Leibniz Universität Hannover,
Goethestraße 18, 30169 Hannover, Germany
e-mail: ekearney@gisma.com

Prof. Dr. S. C. Voelpel
Also Adjunct Professor at EBS Business School, Jacobs University Bremen,
Campus Ring 1, 28759 Bremen, Germany
e-mail: s.voelpel@jacobs-university.de

1 Introduction

Over the past decades, the population in Germany and other Western European countries as well as North America has become more and more diverse. This is increasingly reflected in the workforce of most organizations (Hays-Thomas 2004). Moreover, the percentage of women entering the labor force has risen substantially. On the one hand, greater diversity is inevitable due to enhanced mobility, which is driven by both political developments such as the E.U. expansion and less restricted labor markets as well as by economic developments such as the internationalization of business practices and markets (Stockdale and Cao 2004). Moreover, immigration is touted as a necessary antidote to the vacuum that is being created in many countries whose populations are projected to decline in the coming decades due to low birth rates. Thus, increasing diversity is a reality that societies and organizations must deal with and attempt to make the most of.

The topic of diversity in organizations can be viewed from two different perspectives. One perspective is primarily concerned with fairness (Agars and Kottke 2004). The U.S. has been one of the first countries that, with its Civil Rights Act and other legislation from the 1960s and beyond, passed laws intended to prevent discrimination in society and in the workplace. Other countries—most notably those within the E.U.—have followed suit and have either passed or are in the process of passing such laws. In Germany, for example, the AGG (Allgemeines Gleichbehandlungsgesetz) has been in effect since 2006. Indeed, there are studies indicating that unfair treatment and downright discrimination on the basis of demographic attributes such as age, gender, and national or cultural origin may still be widespread in many organizations (Hays-Thomas 2004; Kaas and Manger 2010).

The other perspective is premised on the idea that diversity constitutes a potential for enhanced performance, which one might call the business case for diversity (Williams and O'Reilly 1998). It is based on the rationale that in an increasingly competitive environment, innovation is key to retaining or bolstering one's competitive position and that diversity, under certain conditions, is conducive to fostering innovation and performance on complex tasks (Van Knippenberg et al. 2004). More diversity tends to entail a broader range of knowledge, experiences, and perspectives to draw on when developing or improving products, services, and processes. While we fully acknowledge the importance of the fairness perspective on diversity, in this review we focus on the view that diversity holds potential for improved performance.

The topic of diversity in organizations can be addressed at different levels of analysis. At the organizational level, one could examine how diverse an entire organization is with respect to particular diversity dimensions and then investigate how this diversity is associated with variables such as workforce satisfaction or company performance. At the dyadic level, one could study how the interaction and performance of two persons working together is affected by the degree to which these individuals are different with respect to a particular diversity attribute (Chattopadhyay et al. 2004). Finally, at the team or group level (we use the terms "teams" and "groups" interchangeably in this article), which stands between the organizational and the dyadic level of analysis, one can study the effects of heterogeneity among the team members on team processes and team outcomes (Jackson and Joshi 2011). In this review, we focus on team level diversity for a number of reasons. We do not focus on dyadic diversity (often referred to as relational demography) because it is a more distal and arguably less potent predictor of organizational performance than is team level diversity. And we do not focus on organizational diversity because just since people work in the same organization does not mean that there is a high level of interaction among them. This is especially true for large organizations in which many employees neither know the names nor would recognize the faces of most other persons working in their organization. Teams, by contrast, entail a high level of contact and interaction among its members. It is thus arguably the best context in which to study *how* diversity engenders its effects. Such an understanding is important to identify practical steps that managers can take to influence the outcomes of diversity. Finally, team diversity has received much more research attention than has organizational diversity and thus seems like a good vantage point to take stock of what we currently know about how to manage diversity (Jackson et al. 2003; Van Knippenberg and Schippers 2007).

Our review will begin by defining diversity. There are many different attributes with respect to which people in organizations differ from one another. Many taxonomies have been suggested, and we will attempt to identify the common thread underlying these different attempts to categorize the variable of interest. We will also address the question of how the level of diversity in an organizational unit could and should be measured to make it amenable to quantitative research. Based on the framework depicted in Fig. 1, we will then examine if, how, and when diversity engenders its effects. In this framework, diversity is the independent or predictor variable, while outcomes such as team performance and team member satisfaction serve as the dependent or criterion variables. After reviewing main effects, we will investigate mediators of the diversity-performance relationship. In

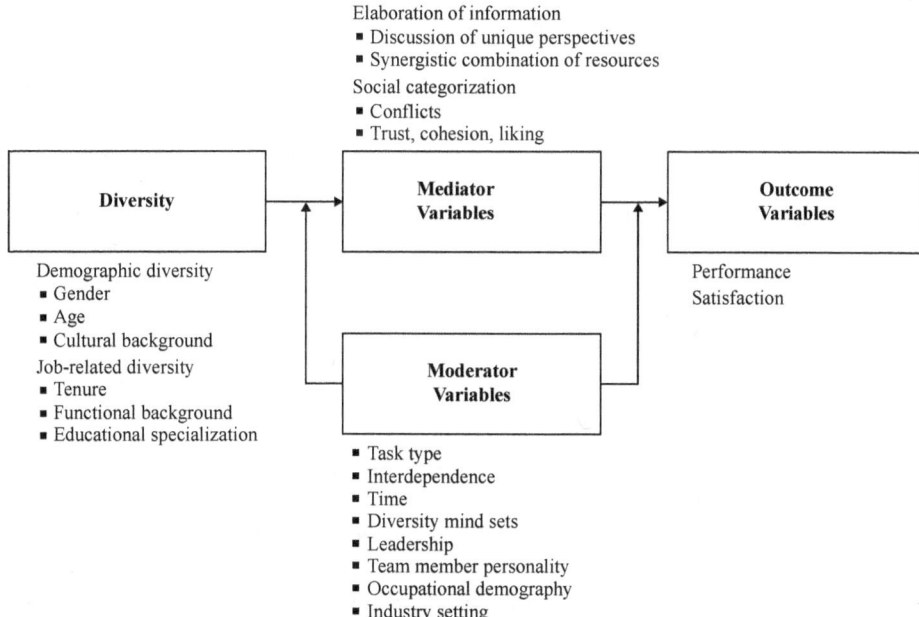

Fig. 1: The diversity-outcomes relationship including mediator and moderator variables

this section, we will delineate the two main theoretical perspectives that are usually cited to explain diversity's effects—the information-elaboration and the social categorization perspective, respectively (Williams and O'Reilly 1998). Next, we will review the extant literature on what determines the strength of the relationship between diversity and performance. In other words, we will focus on moderator variables.

Thereafter, we will look at more complex models of diversity that address the interactive effects of several diversity dimensions. Most prominent among these approaches is the faultline model (Lau and Murnighan 1998), which asserts that the effects of one diversity dimension depend on its degree of alignment with other diversity attributes. For example, the faultline approach suggests that the effects of age diversity would differ depending upon whether there is homogeneity or heterogeneity concerning nationality, educational specialization, and other diversity types. Finally, we will offer practical recommendations regarding what informed steps managers can take to ensure that diversity has positive, rather than negative, effects on performance.

2 What is diversity?

Scholars have defined diversity as the distribution of differences among the members of a unit with respect to a common attribute such as tenure, age, or ethnicity (Harrison and Klein 2007). Another definition states that diversity refers to differences between individuals on any attribute that another person is different from oneself (Van Knippenberg and Schippers 2007). Obviously, there are many attributes with respect to which people can differ from one another. Not all of these attributes are equally meaningful to organizations. Most research therefore only addresses differences that exist regarding directly job-related attributes such as educational specialization (i.e., the content of a person's education—e.g., engineering, business administration, sociology, etc.), educational level (i.e., the highest degree a person has attained), functional background (e.g., product design, finance, HR, marketing and sales, etc.), and tenure (the number of years a person has worked in an organization), as well as not directly job-related, demographic attributes such as age, gender, and nationality or cultural background (Jackson and Joshi 2011). Another frequently made distinction is that between surface-level and directly visible characteristics (such as gender and age) on the one hand and deep-level, not directly visible characteristics (such as personality and values) on the other (Harrison et al. 1998).

The preponderance of research has focused on easily measurable characteristics such as gender, age, nationality or cultural background, tenure, functional and educational background (Van Knippenberg et al. 2004). Some potentially important attributes such as religion or sexual preference have received little to no research attention because they are difficult to study and could easily be perceived by works councils or individual participants as an invasion of privacy. Still other diversity types such as level of physical ability (or disability) lend themselves better to an analysis from the fairness perspective on diversity, as opposed to the business perspective that we focus on here. Generally speaking, the term diversity appears to have a somewhat more restricted connotation in Germany and other Western European countries, where it tends to be mainly associated with demographic characteristics, than in North America, where diversity tends to refer to a broad range of demographic and non-demographic variables (Hays-Thomas 2004; Stockdale and Cao 2004).

3 Operationalizations of diversity

According to Harrison and Klein (2007), the theoretical conceptualization of diversity should determine its operationalization. These authors suggest that there are three types of diversity. First, diversity can constitute separation with respect to, for example, attitudes, beliefs, and values. The attribute shape at maximum levels of diversity would be a bimodal distribution, with half the team members at the highest and the other half at the lowest endpoints of a continuum. Suitable indexes to measure this type of diversity would be the standard deviation or the mean Euclidean distance, both of which assume an interval scale of measurement. Diversity as separation would tend to be a liability for a team and militate against attaining high levels of performance.

Second, diversity can constitute variety with regard to, for example, skills, knowledge, abilities, networks, and perspectives (Harrison and Klein 2007). A uniform distribution, with members spread out evenly across all possible categories of a variable, would be indicative of maximum levels of diversity. The appropriate indexes to measure this form of diversity would be Blau's index or Teachman's index, both of which assume a categorical scale of measurement. It is this conceptualization of diversity that is most in line with the business perspective of diversity, which assumes that heterogeneity entails a potential for enhanced performance (Harrison and Klein 2007). Most diversity variables discussed in this review (e.g., age, cultural background, educational specialization) could be conceptualized as either separation or variety. The choice of conceptualization could at times necessitate transforming a continuous variable into a categorical one and vice versa.

Third, and less pertinent to this review, diversity can constitute disparity concerning, for example, status, power and influence, income and prestige (Harrison and Klein 2007). The attribute shape at maximum levels of diversity would be a positively skewed distribution, where one person stands at the highest endpoint of a continuum, with all others at the lowest. Suitable indexes to operationalize this type of diversity would be the coefficient of variation or the Gini coefficient, both of which assume a ratio scale of measurement.

Biemann and Kearney (2010) have shown that the above measures (i.e., standard deviation, mean Euclidean distance, Blau's index, Teachman's index, coefficient of variation, and the Gini coefficient) are systematically biased whenever they are used in field studies whose samples include teams of varying sizes. These authors therefore offered slightly modified formulas that take into account the variability of team sizes within samples. To help researchers avoid obtaining biased results regarding the effect of team size and the diversity-performance relationship, Biemann and Kearney (2010) recommend that these slightly modified formulas be used whenever researchers study samples comprising groups of different sizes.

4 The diversity-performance relationship

Until the late 1990s, much of the diversity literature was focused on examining main effects of diversity (Williams and O'Reilly 1998). Researchers attempted to ascertain the association between, for example, age or gender or functional diversity with outcomes such as performance (i.e., the successful and efficient completion of assigned tasks) and satisfaction. This endeavor has proved rather disappointing. For nearly all demographic as well as job-related diversity types, there exist some studies that found positive, some that found negative, and some that found null relationships. While this may in part be due to different operationalizations of team performance, the inconsistencies of results occur even between studies that have utilized the same or at least highly similar outcome measures (e.g., Kearney and Gebert 2009; Kearney et al. 2009). Van Knippenberg et al. (2004) have concluded that all types of diversity can and often do have both positive and negative effects, and that instead of continuing the investigation of main effects, researchers should instead examine the conditions under which either the beneficial or the deleterious effects of diversity are more likely to prevail. In line with this conclusion, Van Knippenberg and Schippers (2007) have declared the bankruptcy of the main effects approach.

Indeed, a look at main effects in the extant literature could lead one to the (premature) conclusion that diversity isn't very important, given that there are so few consistent and generalizable findings (Stewart 2006). In their meta-analysis comprising 35 peer-reviewed studies, Horwitz and Horwitz (2007), report estimated population parameters (with weighted mean effect sizes in parentheses) of .13 (.12) between task-related diversity (i.e., functional expertise, education, and tenure) and the quality of team performance. The association between bio-demographic diversity (i.e., age, gender, and race/ethnicity) and the quality of team performance was -0.01 (with a weighted mean effect size of -0.02). In another meta-analysis comprising 39 studies, Joshi and Roh (2009) reported the following weighted mean r values between performance and different diversity types: gender -0.02; race/ethnicity -0.01; age -0.06; function .13; education -0.02; and tenure .03. In other words, functional background diversity was most strongly positively and age diversity was most strongly negatively correlated with team performance. Despite occasional statistical significance, the effect sizes of main effects are generally rather small. Moreover, the range of correlations examined in these and other meta-analyses (see also Bowers et al. 2000; Webber and Donahue 2001) is quite substantial, which underscores the need to move beyond simple direct effects to examine when (i.e., under what conditions) and how (i.e., through what processes) diversity engenders either positive or negative effects. Ever since the seminal work by Lawrence (1997) and Williams and O'Reilly (1998), respectively, the diversity literature has primarily focused on these moderators and mediators of the diversity-performance relationship (e.g., Roberge and van Dick 2010).

5 Mediators of the diversity-performance relationship

It is often claimed that diversity constitutes a potential for enhanced performance because heterogeneity entails a broader range of skills, knowledge, ideas, and networks (Jackson and Joshi 2011; Williams and O'Reilly 1998). Under the right conditions, this enlarged range of resources could yield ideas and solutions that are superior to those obtainable in groups with a more limited scope and more overlapping and redundant resources (Brodbeck et al. 2007). From this perspective, diversity as such is merely a potential. It is by no means certain that this potential will actually be leveraged and translated into enhanced performance. The process whereby this potential can be tapped is the elaboration of task-relevant information—that is, the exchange, discussion, and integration of ideas, knowledge, and insights that are germane to a team's task (Van Knippenberg et al. 2004). It is through this mediating variable of information elaboration—and the attendant team learning (Van der Vegt and Bunderson 2005)—that diversity can engender positive effects on team performance and/or team member satisfaction (Homan et al. 2008; Kearney and Gebert 2009; Kearney et al. 2009).

As many researchers have pointed out, however, diversity may be a "double-edged sword" (Milliken and Martins 1996). While it constitutes a potential for enhanced performance, as articulated in the information elaboration perspective, it simultaneously entails a higher likelihood for teams to derail and underperform (Williams and O'Reilly 1998). This downside of diversity is explained by the social categorization perspective, which posits that persons tend to prefer to communicate and work with persons who are similar to themselves (Van Knippenberg et al. 2004). Such "in-group" members are subsequently liked better and treated preferentially in comparison to those who are dissimilar and thus categorized as "out-group" members.

This line of reasoning is intuitively appealing. For example, when a person goes to a party where he or she knows no one, it is likely that, at the end of the evening, he or she will have spent the most time with and had the most fun talking to those persons with whom he or she shares some similarity—be it in terms of demographic characteristics such as age and cultural background or job-related attributes such as educational specialization. Thus, social categorization—that is, classifying other persons as "similar" and "like me" (in other words, as "in-group" members)—can foster trust, cohesion, and liking among those individuals belonging to the same social category. At the same time, however, classifying others as "different" and "unlike me" (in other words, as "out-group" members)—is likely to impede trust, cohesion, and liking and promote conflict among those persons belonging to different categories (Jehn et al. 1999; Pelled et al. 1999). Both demographic and non-demographic traits can be assumed to oftentimes correlate with other variables such as beliefs, attitudes, and values (Jackson et al. 2003). Van Knippenberg et al.'s (2004) categorization-elaboration model explains under what conditions diversity engenders social categorizations and under what circumstances such processes decrease trust, cohesion, and liking, and, ultimately, performance. For example, it is important whether differences among team members become salient and are regarded as meaningful. Diversity is unlikely to have any effect on team processes if the attribute with respect to which the team members differ from one another remains unnoticed or is regarded as irrelevant. Thus, neither social categorizations as such nor detrimental effects of social categorizations will inevitably occur in diverse teams (Van Knippenberg et al. 2004). Generally, however, the social categorization perspective focuses on the negative effects of diversity on team performance and member satisfaction (Williams and O'Reilly 1998).

Several researchers have suggested that in order to fully understand diversity's effects on important outcomes, both the information-elaboration and the social categorization perspective would have to be taken into account. In fact, Van Knippenberg and colleagues (Van Knippenberg et al. 2004; Van Knippenberg and Schippers 2007) have posited that negative effects resulting from social categorization processes (e.g., dysfunctional conflicts and/or a low quality of cooperation and communication) moderate the relationship between diversity and information elaboration, which in turn partly determines team performance. In other words, the extent to which heterogeneity leads to in-group/out-group effects, behavioral manifestations of prejudice and stereotypes, or simply the tendency to minimize contact and communication with dissimilar others affects the level of information elaboration in a team. Somewhat paradoxically, information elaboration is needed to leverage the performance potential inherent in diversity, yet it is diversity that, via deleterious social categorization processes, undermines the elaboration of task-relevant information. It should be noted, however, that detrimental effects of diversity must not necessarily be due to social categorization processes (Van Knippenberg et al. 2004). In many cases, heterogeneous teams may underperform simply because members frequently misunderstand each other—even if they like and are motivated to work with each other. For example, people with different educational specialization backgrounds inhabit different "thought worlds" (Dougherty 1992)—that is, different paradigms and models of the world and different ways of framing and addressing problems. Analogously, people of different age cohorts or cultural backgrounds may think differently and express themselves in ways that are easily misunderstood by dissimilar others.

Thus far, there are only few studies that, in attempting to explain how diversity engenders its effects on team outcomes, have simultaneously addressed both the information elaboration and the social categorization perspective (Kearney and Gebert 2009; Kearney et al. 2009). Yet even if we know *how* diversity may affect performance, we still would not know *when* either the positive or the negative effects of diversity are more likely to predominate. This leads us to the research on moderators of the diversity-outcomes relationship. (Many more recent studies examine both mediators and moderators).

6 Moderators of the diversity-performance relationship

In this section, we will review the literature on variables that moderate the association between diversity and team performance. Space does not permit a discussion of every single variable that has been identified as affecting the diversity-performance relationship. We chose to focus on those moderators that we feel are particularly important for both theoretical and practical reasons.

Task type. The last decade has yielded a vast literature on the contextual conditions that determine whether or not the performance potential inherent in diversity will be realized. One of the first and most frequently studied such moderators is the nature of the task. Mannix and Neale (2005) have argued that a team only stands to benefit from diversity on complex or explorative tasks. On these tasks, it is important to generate new and creative ideas and/or identify the best among many different ways of reaching a certain goal or devising a solution to a challenging problem. In such cases, a broader range of skills, knowledge and perspectives (i.e., diversity) obviously constitutes a potential. The elaboration of non-redundant, complementary information makes it possible to tap this potential. By contrast, simple, routine and exploitative tasks require teams to simply follow a defined course of action that tends to be the only avenue whereby a certain goal can be reached. An in-depth elaboration of information is typically not needed on such tasks.

Hence, it seems as though diversity is not beneficial to teams per se, but only constitutes a potential for certain types of teams—namely those working on complex, explorative tasks (Mannix and Neale 2005). There are several studies that confirm this assumption with respect to a number of different diversity attributes (e.g., Jehn et al. 1999; Pelled et al. 1999). For example, Wegge et al. (2008) found that age diversity was positively associated with performance only in groups working on complex tasks, whereas age diversity was positively related to health disorders in groups working on routine tasks. Moreover, Joshi and Roh (2009) reported that task-oriented diversity was positively related to performance in (complex) high-tech settings, but not in (arguably less complex) manufacturing and service settings.

Somewhat surprisingly, Horwitz and Horwitz's meta-analysis (2007) did not corroborate the hypothesis of a moderating influence of task complexity on the relationship between bio-demographic diversity (e.g., age, gender, and race/ethnicity) and performance. Nevertheless, this may be due to a restriction in range concerning task complexity in the studies included in Horwitz and Horwitz's (2007) study. Their meta-analysis comprised seven studies examining teams working on "high-complexity tasks", five studies investigating teams charged with "medium-complexity tasks", but no studies focusing on teams completing low complexity tasks.

Interdependence. Another moderator of the diversity-performance relationship is the degree of interdependence among the team members. Generally, there are two types of interdependence. Task interdependence is the extent to which individuals depend on their team members to do their jobs well (Van der Vegt and Janssen 2003). Goal or outcome interdependence is the extent to which individuals can reach their goals only when other team members also reach their goals (Van der Vegt and Janssen 2003). It could also be defined as the degree to which rewards are allocated on the basis of team performance, as opposed to individual performance in teams (Wageman 1995). Schippers et al. (2003) found that outcome interdependence moderated the effects of diversity on performance and satisfaction. Van der Vegt and Janssen (2003) examined three-way interactions among diversity and both types of interdependence. They found that interdependence had much greater effects in heterogeneous teams than in homogeneous teams. In diverse teams, both task and goal interdependence interactively affected innovative behavior, whereas the authors found no such effects in non-diverse teams. Thus, in diverse teams with high levels of goal interdependence, task interdependence was positively related to innovative behavior.

In examining the role of interdependence, a restriction of range may again pose a problem. For example, Horwitz and Horwitz (2007) were unable to test moderating effects of task interdependence in their meta-analysis because there was too little variability in task interdependence scores. None of the studies included in their sample investigated teams that were coded as being marked by "low task interdependence". Nevertheless, the meta-analysis by Joshi and Roh (2009) did confirm, albeit with a small effect size, that the relationship between task-oriented diversity and performance was more significantly positive when levels of task and goal or outcome interdependence were high. Somewhat surprisingly, however, these authors found that relations-oriented (demographic) diversity was positively associated with performance when interdependence was low, whereas this relationship was negative when interdependence was moderate or high. Once again, however, effect sizes were small.

Time. There are also several studies that examine how time affects the diversity-performance link. Research by David Harrison and colleagues (Harrison et al. 1998; Harrison et al. 2002) suggests that surface-level (demographic) diversity is important primarily in the early stages of interaction among team members, and that, over time, this type of diversity becomes less important, whereas deep-level (attitudinal) diversity becomes more important. According to Harrison et al. (2002), team reward contingencies (i.e., outcome interdependence) stimulate collaboration, which in turn weakens the effects of demographic and strengthens the effects of psychological diversity. Another way to look at time is to distinguish among projects of short duration and those of long duration. In this regard, the meta-analysis by Joshi and Roh (2009) revealed a positive performance effect of relations-oriented (demographic) diversity in relatively short-term teams, but a negative performance effect in more stable or long-term teams. These authors did not find an analogous moderating effect of time on the relationship between task-oriented diversity and performance.

Diversity mind sets. Another promising line of research has examined the effects of diversity attitudes, climates, or mind sets in organizations and teams. In a qualitative study, Ely and Thomas (2001) identified three different perspectives on diversity: the integration-and-learning perspective, the access-and-legitimacy-perspective, and the discrimination-and-fairness perspective. They found that only the integration-and-learning perspective provided a sound basis for continued efforts to attempt to benefit from diversity. This research illustrates that whether diversity turns out to be an asset or a liability may depend on how people view diversity and what they expect of it. If diversity is regarded as a nuisance that somehow needs to be accepted and dealt with, it seems unlikely that synergies resulting from unique combinations of non-redundant and complementary perspectives will emerge. Efforts towards attaining such synergies likely require that diversity is acknowledged and valued as a means to broaden the range of skills, knowledge bases, and ideas.

In recent years, there have been a number of studies that have examined what persons actually think about diversity and how attitudes, beliefs, and expectations related to diversity affect team functioning (e.g., Van Dick et al. 2008). Diversity mind sets can be viewed as shared cognitions among the members of an organizational unit with respect to how diversity affects teams and what team members must do to leverage the potential inherent in diversity (Homan et al. 2007). The underlying idea, which has received initial empirical support, is that diversity mind sets moderate both social categorization processes as well as information elaboration. In other words, positive mind sets about diversity help to prevent the negative and foster the positive effects of diversity.

Leadership. It is quite surprising that thus far only a few studies have examined how leadership affects the link between diversity and team outcomes. Possibly the first empirical study in this regard was conducted by Somech (2006), who found that in functionally heterogeneous teams, a participative leadership style was positively related to team reflection (i.e., the extent to which team members collectively reflect upon the team's objectives, strategies, and processes; West 1996). Team reflection, in turn, facilitated team innovation (i.e., going beyond routine work and generating new ideas), but not team in-role performance (i.e., doing exactly what is outlined in one's job description). By contrast, directive leadership enhanced team reflection in functionally homogeneous, but not heterogeneous teams.

The voluminous literature on transformational literature (Bass and Riggio 2006; Judge and Piccolo 2004) would suggest that this leadership style—which comprises the facets acting as a role model, articulating a compelling vision, and providing intellectual stimulation as well as individualized consideration—should be ideally suited to help tap the potential of team diversity. Indeed, Shin and Zhou (2007) found that educationally diverse (i.e., interdisciplinary) teams exhibited greater creativity when transformational leadership was high, rather than low. Moreover, Kearney and Gebert (2009) showed that, when transformational leadership was high, both nationality and educational diversity were positively related to team performance. Age diversity, by contrast, was not significantly associated with team performance when transformational leadership was high, but negatively associated with team performance when transformational leadership was low. Generally, however, our knowledge of how leadership affects the diversity-performance relationship is still fragmentary. In light of the fact that the topic of team diversity is often framed in terms of how best to "manage" diversity, the paucity of research in this domain constitutes a lamentable gap in the literature.

Mean team member personality. Recently, Kearney et al. (2009) suggested that the extent to which a team stands to benefit from diversity also depends on the personalities of the team members. For example, individuals differ in the extent to which they relish the opportunity to work with dissimilar others, think in-depth about alternative options, and like to view problems from multiple angles. Need for cognition (Cacioppo et al. 1996) is an individual difference variable that captures the degree to which people are motivated to engage in and enjoy effortful cognitive activities. Kearney et al. (2009) showed that the mean need for cognition in a team—which can be interpreted as the motivation to process diverse information—moderates the relationship of both age and educational specialization diversity with performance such that these types of diversity were positively correlated with team performance only when team need for cognition was high, rather than low. This research shows that, independent of technical skills and knowledge, it matters what types of personalities are assembled in diverse organizational units. Some persons are simply more open to working with dissimilar others and thus are much more likely to act constructively and strive for synergies in heterogeneous team settings (see also Homan et al. 2008).

Larger context. Organizational units such as teams and work groups as well as organizations themselves are always embedded in a larger context. For example, it can be assumed that national culture has an influence on the effects of diversity in organizational teams. While there now exist numerous studies on the effects of cultural diversity in teams and work groups (Stahl et al. 2010), there is a dearth of research on whether the findings of the extant diversity literature are generalizable across different cultures. In other words, it is not yet clear whether findings on the effects of different types of diversity obtained in, for example, the U.S. or Germany, would be replicable in, for example, Japan or Pakistan. Cultures differ substantially on attitudes concerning, for example, gender roles and the extent to which there exists gender equality. Moreover, cultures differ regarding the extent to which diversity per se is appreciated or even tolerated. Multi-level research is needed that examines how such cultural influences affect team processes and whether there are differential effects of diversity on team outcomes across cultures.

Also with respect to the larger overall context, there are a number of studies that have examined how occupational demography affects the diversity-performance relationship. Occupational demography addresses the relative distribution of, for instance, males and females (or members of a particular nationality or age group) within the population of persons in a particular occupation (e.g., software developers, accountants, teachers). This can be extended by examining how industry setting (e.g., manufacturing, retail, IT) influences links between diversity and outcomes.

Joshi and Roh's (2009) meta-analysis revealed that gender diversity was negatively related to performance in typically male occupational settings, whereas gender diversity was positively associated with performance in gender-balanced settings. Similarly, ethnic diversity was negatively correlated with performance in occupations with strong white majorities, whereas this relationship was positive in ethnically more balanced occupations. Moreover, the meta-analysis by Joshi and Roh (2009) showed that industry setting is an important moderator. For example, relations-oriented (demographic) diversity had a positive effect on performance in service industries, but a negative effect in the manufacturing industry. Somewhat surprisingly, demographic diversity had the strongest negative effect on performance in high-tech industry settings. By contrast, industry setting did not prove to be a potent moderator of the relationship between task-related diversity and performance.

7 Complex models of diversity's effects on performance

It makes sense to assume that the effects of, for example, gender diversity also depend on how this heterogeneity dimension is aligned with other diversity attributes. In other words, the diversity literature would be well advised not to focus exclusively on individual diversity dimensions, but rather examine numerous heterogeneity variables simultaneously (Jackson and Joshi 2011). The way in which diversity characteristics align can create "faultlines" (Lau and Murnighan 1998)—that is, hypothetical dividing lines that split a larger group into two or more subgroups. For example, if a new product development team with four members comprises two young Western European women with a background in marketing and two older Indian men with a background in product design, there exists a strong "faultline" that divides the team along the dimensions gender, age, cultural and functional background. Faultlines may undermine communication among all members of a team, foster conflicts between sub-groups and thus impede performance. Some studies have found that strong faultlines do indeed hamper performance (e.g., Li and Hambrick 2005; Rico et al. 2007). Lau and Murnighan (2005) showed that faultlines are associated with poorer communication among subgroups and lower expected performance. But the currently available evidence is far from conclusive. In the same study, Lau and Murnighan (2005) also found that faultlines were associated with less conflict and higher levels of satisfaction. Other researchers (e.g., Thatcher et al. 2003) have found curvilinear relationships such that moderate faultlines were associated with better outcomes than were either weak or strong faultlines.

Cross-categorization is another interesting concept that simultaneously examines several different diversity dimensions (Van Knippenberg and Schippers 2007). Cross-categorization occurs when, for example, a culturally diverse team includes two members who are much older than their team members, but belong to the same culture as the majority. In this case, there is a cross-cutting of culture and age. (If these two individuals belonged to the minority culture, this composition would constitute a faultline.) Some studies (e.g., Sawyer et al. 2006) indicate that cross-categorization within diverse teams may be more conducive to performance than are either homogeneity or faultlines. Generally, it seems logical and necessary to move beyond examining individual diversity attributes and instead examine a larger configuration of and interactions among traits. At this stage, the empirical research on these more complex models of diversity is still in its infancy, but rapid advances can be expected in the next few years.

8 Managerial implications

Based on the extant literature, it is fair to say that both demographic and job-related diversity constitute a potential for enhanced performance (Jackson and Joshi 2011). This potential seems to be somewhat larger for job-related than for demographic diversity, whereas the risk that diversity will engender negative effects seems to be somewhat greater for demographic than for job-related diversity (Joshi and Roh 2009; Horwitz and Horwitz 2007). However, all types of diversity can, under the right conditions, foster performance. The flip side is that, under the wrong conditions, all types of diversity can seriously impede performance. The often-quoted assertion that diversity is a "double-edged sword" (Milliken and Martins 1996, p. 403) thus still holds true. It is important that managers realize that diversity needs to be carefully managed. Positive effects should not be expected to emerge automatically. Such positive effects are possible via an elaboration of task-relevant information (Van Knippenberg et al. 2004). The potential for synergistic solutions and high performance on complex tasks is greater when the range of skills, knowledge bases, and perspectives is broad as opposed to narrow—in other words, when teams are diverse rather than homogeneous. At the same time, however, people tend to prefer to work and communicate with others who are similar to themselves. Differences with respect to meaningful social categories can undermine cooperation and hamper performance (Williams and O'Reilly 1998).

In order to foster the positive and prevent the negative effects of diversity, managers are well advised to take into account the nature of the task. When the task is complex and explorative, it makes sense to assemble a diverse unit (Mannix and Neale 2005). On simple, routine, and exploitative tasks, by contrast, diversity offers little promise for enhanced performance. Moreover, when managing diverse teams, managers should establish high levels of goal and outcome interdependence (Van der Vegt and Janssen 2003), which can serve to keep team members focused on commonalities, rather than differences. One of the most important steps that managers can take to facilitate positive effects of diversity is to foster an integration-and-learning perspective within their unit (Ely and Thomas 2001)—in other words, a positive diversity mindset that is based on the premise that diversity constitutes a valuable potential for enhanced performance (Homan et al. 2007).

A transformational leadership style that unites dissimilar persons in the effort to realize a common and shared vision seems particularly promising in this respect (Kearney and Gebert 2009; Shin and Zhou 2007). Furthermore, managers should take into account the personalities of those whom they assemble in diverse teams. Some individuals, especially those high in need for cognition and openness to experience, seem to be particularly likely to work well with dissimilar others (Homan et al. 2008; Kearney et al. 2009). Finally, managers should take into account the alignment of different diversity dimensions (Rico et al. 2007). If teams are diverse with regard to several different characteristics, efforts should be made to cross-cut these dimensions rather than to establish faultlines, which may divide a group into sub-groups and thus impede performance.

9 Conclusion

The last decade has seen a vast increase in the number of studies examining the effects of diversity in the workplace (Jackson and Joshi 2011). Most societies and organizations are likely to become even more, not less, diverse in the future. Thus, diversity research is important and will continue to flourish in the coming years. In this review, we have attempted to take stock of the current knowledge of the effects of diversity in organizational units. Naturally, we had to limit our review to a small portion of a by now expansive literature. We acknowledge that we did not address a number of interesting topics, such as the issue of perceived or subjective diversity, which may or may not coincide with objective demographic or job-related diversity (Jackson et al., 2003), or the issue of curvilinear effects, on which no clear and consistent picture has thus far emerged in the diversity literature (Van der Vegt and Bunderson 2005; Van Knippenberg and Schippers 2007). We also restricted our review to the business perspective on diversity and to the most commonly studied forms of demographic and job-related diversity. Nevertheless, we hope that the present review enables researchers as well as practitioners to gain a useful overview of what is currently known about the diversity-performance relationship. We recommend that researchers continue their efforts to shed further light on this relationship, particularly by developing and testing more complex models that include both mediators and moderators (sometimes spanning different levels of analysis) as well as interactions among different diversity dimensions. And we encourage managers to draw on solid research findings to inform their actions when assembling and leading diverse teams.

References

Agars MD, Kottke JL (2004) Models and practice of diversity management: a historical review and presentation of a new integration theory. In: Stockdale MS, Crosby FJ (eds) The psychology and management of workplace diversity. Blackwell Publishing, Oxford, pp 55–77

Bass BM, Riggio RE (2006) Transformational leadership. Erlbaum, Mahwah

Biemann T, Kearney E (2010) Size does matter: how varying group sizes in a sample affect the most common measures of group diversity. Organ Res Methods 13:582–599

Bowers C, Pharmer JA, Salas E (2000) When member homogeneity is needed in work teams: a meta-analysis. Small Group Res 31:305–327

Brodbeck FC, Kerschreiter R, Mojzisch A, Schulz-Hardt S (2007) Group decision making under conditions of distributed knowledge: the information asymmetries model. Acad Manag Rev 32:459–479

Cacioppo JT, Petty RE, Feinstein J, Jarvis WBG (1996) Dispositional differences in cognitive motivation: the life and times of individuals varying in need for cognition. Psychol Bull 119:197–253

Chattopadhyay P, Tluchowska M, George E (2004) Identifying the ingroup: a closer look at the influence of demographic dissimilarity on employee social identity. Acad Manag Rev 29: 180–202

Dougherty D (1992) Interpretive barriers to successful product innovation in large firms. Organ Sci 3:179–202

Ely RJ, Thomas DA (2001) Cultural diversity at work: the effects of diversity perspectives on work group processes and outcomes. Adm Sci Q 46:229–273

Harrison DA, Klein KJ (2007) What's the difference? Diversity constructs as separation, variety, or disparity in organizations. Acad Manag Rev 32:1199–1228

Harrison DA, Price KH, Bell MP (1998) Beyond relational demography: time and the effects of surface- and deep-level diversity on work group cohesion. Acad Manag J 41:96–107

Harrison DA, Price KH, Gavin JH, Florey AT (2002) Time, teams, and task performance: changing effects of surface- and deep- level diversity on group functioning. Acad Manag J 45:1029–1045

Hays-Thomas KM (2004) Why now? The contemporary focus on managing diversity. In: Stockdale MS, Crosby FJ (eds) The psychology and management of workplace diversity. Blackwell Publishing, Oxford, pp 31–52

Homan AC, Van Knippenberg D, Kleef GA, de Dreu CKW (2007) Bridging faultlines by valuing diversity: diversity beliefs, information elaboration, and performance in diverse work groups. J Appl Psychol 92:1189–1199

Homan AC, Hollenbeck JR, Humphrey S, van Knippenberg D, Ilgen DR, Van Kleef GA (2008) Facing differences with an open mind: openness to experience, salience of intragroup differences, and performance of diverse work groups. Acad Manag J 51:1204–1222

Horwitz SK, Horwitz IB (2007) The effects of team diversity on team outcomes: a meta-analytic review of team demography. J Manag 33:987–1015

Jackson SF, Joshi A (2011) Work team diversity. In: Zedeck S (ed) APA handbook of industrial and organizational psychology, vol 1, APA, Washington, pp 651–686

Jackson SE, Joshi A, Erhardt NL (2003) Recent research on team and organizational diversity: SWOT analysis and implications. J Manag 29:801–830

Jehn KE, Northcraft GB, Neale MA (1999) Why differences make a difference: a field study of diversity, conflict, and performance in work groups. Adm Sci Q 44:741–763

Joshi A, Roh H (2009) The role of context in work team diversity research: a meta-analytic review. Acad Manag J 52:599–627

Judge TA, Piccolo RF (2004) Transformational and transactional leadership: a meta-analytic test of their relative validity. J Appl Psychol 89:755–768

Kaas L, Manger C (2010) Ethnic discrimination in Germany's labour market: a field experiment. Discussion Paper Series IZA DP No. 4741

Kearney E, Gebert D (2009) Managing diversity and enhancing team outcomes: the promise of transformational leadership. J Appl Psychol 94:77–89

Kearney E, Gebert D, Voelpel S (2009) When and how diversity benefits teams: the importance of team members' need for cognition. Acad Manag J 52:581–598

Lau DC, Murnighan JK (1998) Demographic diversity and faultlines: the compositional dynamics of organizational groups. Acad Manag Rev 23:325–340

Lau DC, Murnighan JK (2005) Interactions within groups and subgroups: the effects of demographic faultlines. Acad Manag J 48:645–659

Lawrence BS (1997) The black box of organizational demography. Organ Sci 8:1–22

Li J, Hambrick DC (2005) Factional groups: a new vantage on demographic faultlines, conflict, and dis- integration in work teams. Acad Manag J 48:794–813

Mannix E, Neale MA (2005) What differences make a difference? The promise and reality of diverse teams in organizations. Psychol Sci Public Interest 6:31–55

Milliken F, Martins L (1996) Searching for common threads: understanding the multiple effects of diversity in organizational groups. Acad Manag Rev 21:402–433

Pelled LH, Eisenhardt KM, Xin KR (1999) Exploring the black box: an analysis of work group diversity, conflict, and performance. Adm Sci Q 44:1–28

Rico R, Molleman E, Sànchez-Manzanares M, Van der Vegt G (2007) The effects of diversity faultlines and team task autonomy on decision quality and social integration. J Manag 33:111–132

Roberge M-É, van Dick R (2010) Recognizing the benefits of diversity: when and how does diversity increase group performance? Hum Resour Manag Rev 20:295–308

Sawyer JE, Houlette MA, Yeagley EL (2006) Decision performance and diversity structure: comparing faultlines in convergent, crosscut, and racially homogeneous groups. Organ Behav Hum Decis Process 99:1–15

Schippers MC, Den Hartog DN, Koopman PL, Wienk JA (2003) Diversity and team outcomes: the moderating effects of outcome interdependence and group longevity and the mediating effect of reflexivity. J Organ Behav 24:779–802

Shin SJ, Zhou J (2007) When is educational specialization heterogeneity related to creativity in research and development teams? Transformational leadership as a moderator. J Appl Psychol 92:1709–1721

Somech A (2006) The effects of leadership style and team process on performance and innovation in functionally heterogeneous teams. J Manag 32:132–157

Stahl GK, Maznevski ML, Voigt A, Jonsen K (2010) Unraveling the effects of cultural diversity in teams: a meta-analysis of research on multicultural work groups. J Int Bus Stud 41:690–709

Stewart GL (2006) A meta-analytic review of relationships between team design features and team performance. J Manag 32:29–54

Stockdale MS, Cao F (2004) Looking back and heading forward: major themes of the psychology and management of workplace diversity. In: Stockdale MS, Crosby FJ (eds) The psychology and management of workplace diversity. Blackwell Publishing, Oxford, pp 299–316

Thatcher SMB, Jehn KA, Zanutto E (2003) Cracks in diversity research: the effects of diversity faultlines on conflict and performance. Group Decis Negot 12:217–241

Van der Vegt GS, Janssen O (2003) Joint impact of interdependence and group diversity on innovation. J Manag 29:729–751

Van der Vegt GS, Bunderson JS (2005) Learning and performance in multidisciplinary teams: the importance of collective team identification. Acad Manag J 48:532–548

Van Dick R, van Knippenberg D, Hagele S, Guillaume YRF, Brodbeck FC (2008) Group diversity and group identification: the moderating role of diversity beliefs. Hum Relat 61:1463–1492

Van Knippenberg D, Schippers MC (2007) Work group diversity. Annu Rev Psychol 58:515–541

Van Knippenberg D, De Dreu CKW, Homan AC (2004) Work group diversity and group performance: an integrative model and research agenda. J Appl Psychol 89:1008–1022

Wageman R (1995) Interdependence and group effectiveness. Adm Sci Q 40:145–180

Webber SS, Donahue LM (2001) Impact of highly and less job-related diversity on work group cohesion and performance: a meta-analysis. J Manag 27:141–162

Wegge J, Roth C, Neubach B, Schmidt K-H, Kanfer R (2008) Age and gender diversity as determinants of performance and health in a public organization: the role of task complexity and group size. J Appl Psychol 93:1301–1313

West MA (1996) Reflexivity and work group effectiveness: a conceptual integration. In: West MA (ed) Handbook of work group psychology. Wiley, London, pp 525–579

Williams K, O'Reilly CIII (1998) Demography and diversity in organizations: a review of forty years of research. In: Sutton RI, BM Staw (eds) Research in organizational behavior, vol 20, JAI Press, Greenwich, pp 77–140

Z Betriebswirtsch (2012) 82:19–44
DOI 10.1007/s11573-011-0543-y

ZfB-SPECIAL ISSUE 2/2012

Getting tuned in to those who are different: The role of empathy as mediator between diversity and performance

Sebastian Stegmann · Marie-Élène Roberge · Rolf van Dick

Abstract: We present a theoretical model on the processes that mediate and moderate the diversity-performance relationship. Past research on this topic—for example the categorization elaboration model (van Knippenberg et al. 2004)—has often focused on information elaboration as mediator. Complementing this cognitive perspective, we propose that group diversity can also stimulate group members to engage with each other emotionally, resulting in higher levels of empathy—an emotional state which arises from the comprehension and apprehension of fellow group members' emotional state. Empathy, in turn, is likely to enhance performance through processes within a single group member and through processes between group members. At the core of the model lies the proposition that group- as well as individual-level empathy mediate the relationship between diversity of organizational units and the performance of individual members and groups at large (multilevel mediation). Furthermore, we specify moderating conditions for the relationship between diversity and empathy. Diversity beliefs and diversity climates are introduced as second-order moderators.

© Gabler-Verlag 2011

Dr. S. Stegmann (✉) · Prof. Dr. R. van Dick
Department of Social Psychology, Institute of Psychology, Goethe University,
Kettenhofweg 128, 60054 Frankfurt am Main, Germany
e-mail: stegmann@psych.uni-frankfurt.de

Prof. Dr. R. van Dick
e-mail: van.dick@psych.uni-frankfurt.de

Prof. Dr. M.-É Roberge
Northeastern Illinois University,
5500 N. Saint Louis Avenue, 60625 Chicago, IL, USA
e-mail: m-roberge@neiu.edu

Keywords: Diversity · Empathy · Social categorization · Performance · Diversity beliefs · Diversity climates

JEL Classification: M54 · J10 · J79

The term diversity broadly covers all sorts of differences that exist within a given social unit such as a work team, a department or an organization as a whole (Harrison and Sin 2006). These differences can occur on many dimensions, for example ethnic background of employees, their age, functional background, abilities, personality, or religious beliefs. The reasons why modern-day organizations become increasingly diverse are also manifold (Jackson and Joshi 2011; Kochan et al. 2003). For example, organizations may become diverse as a result of demographic developments, or may actively strive to be diverse in order to increase their innovative potential, to access new markets, or to attract the most qualified employees. This increasing diversity is of great importance to organizations because diversity can have a range of positive as well as negative effects on organizations and their employees. Unfortunately, until now it is difficult to predict under which conditions what kind of diversity will have positive or negative effects (van Knippenberg and Schippers 2007). As part of this problem, reviews of the area reveal that the underlying mechanisms which translate diversity into individual and organizational outcomes, as well as the factors that moderate these relationships, are not yet sufficiently understood.

The aim of the present paper is to contribute to this understanding of both mediating and moderating processes. To that avail, we describe a theoretical model which focuses on emotional processes in diverse groups that underlie the effects of diversity. These effects have often been studied focusing on cognitive processes, such as, information elaboration (van Knippenberg et al. 2004). By emphasizing emotional processes, the model broadens the theoretical understanding of how diversity may increase group performance.

At the core of the model lies the proposition that diversity can not only draw group members' cognitive attention to the various differences between the group members, but that it can also stimulate them to get involved with each other emotionally through the experience of empathy. Empathy can be defined as "a state of emotional arousal that stems from the apprehension or comprehension of another's affective state" (Losoya and Eisenberg 2001, p. 22). Empathy, in turn, is proposed to have beneficial effects on individual and group performance. Therefore, we propose that empathy mediates the relationship between diversity and the performance of individuals or whole organizational units. Furthermore, we propose that the occurrence of empathy in diverse organizational units is contingent on a number of moderators. The model is depicted in Fig. 1.

Empathy has been studied by psychologists since the beginning of the last century (Davis 1994; McDougall 1908). However, only recently have researchers from the field of organizational behavior gained interest in empathy as a construct (Roberge and van Dick 2010). Studies that focused on empathy as a stable construct, found that empathy is positively associated with organizational citizenship behavior (Kamdar et al. 2006; Settoon and Mossholder 2002). Trait empathy also plays a role in resolving workplace conflicts and diversity-related problems such as sexual harassment or other forms of discrimination (Reiter-Palmon et al. 2008). In contrast to these developments, the present model includes

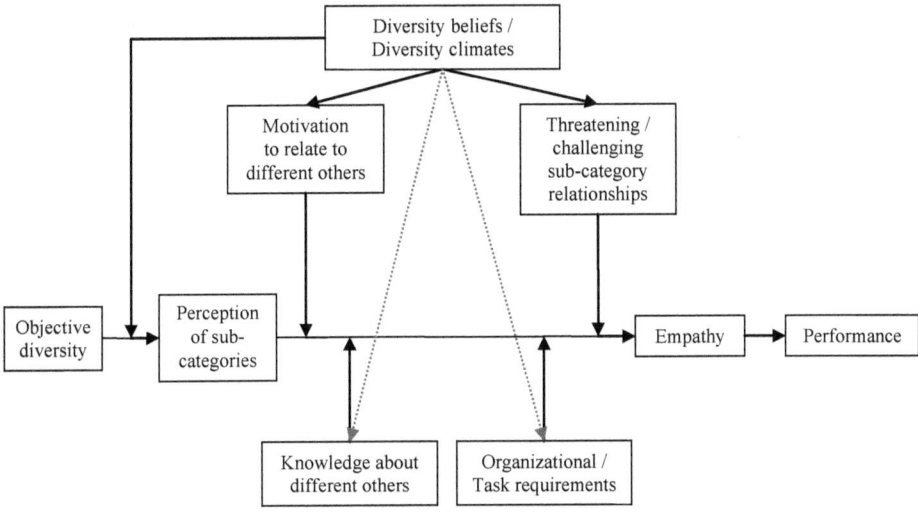

Fig. 1: The general model developed in this paper. Multilevel-relationships were omitted for easier interpretation

empathy as an affective state which opens up the possibility of examining its mediating role in the relationship between diversity and performance.

In the following sections, we will first define diversity and performance, emphasizing the multilevel-nature of each construct and, hence, of their relationship. Second, we describe the informational potential of diverse groups and the elaboration of information as the currently most prominently discussed mediating process underlying diversity's effects on performance. Third, taking this cognitive perspective as our point of departure, we introduce an emotional perspective on diversity and describe the emotional potential of diverse groups. Fourth, taking a similar view on the processes in diverse groups, we outline how empathy can mediate the diversity-performance link. Fifth, moderating factors influencing whether empathy will occur in diverse settings are introduced. Sixth, the relationship between social categorization and the processes described in the model is addressed in more detail. Finally, diversity beliefs and climates are introduced as second-order moderators of the relationship between diversity and empathy.

1 The relationship between diversity and performance

Diversity can be defined as "the collective amount of differences among members within a social unit" (Harrison and Sin 2006, p. 196). As such, diversity is a group-level construct. However, following Kozlowski and Klein (2000), it is not describing a "global unit property" (i.e. it does not originate at the unit level) but describes a "configural unit property" that emerges from lower level elements which are essentially different in nature (e.g., a group's age diversity emerges because the individual group members are of different age). Theoretically, there is a plethora of ways in which group members can differ from each other. This renders diversity a conceptually broad and complex construct.

Nonetheless, diversity is an important aspect of organizational life. First and foremost, this has been argued to be the case due to ethical, legal, or moral reasons. However, during the last decades, it has become more prominent in the scientific discussion that there are good reasons to assume that diversity is also affecting performance within organizations (Jackson and Joshi 2011). Thus, the primary outcome variable of interest in the present model is performance, which can refer to organizational performance, performance of smaller organizational units (departments, teams, etc.), or individual performance. On the individual level, performance has been defined as "the total expected value to the organization of the discrete behavioral episodes that an individual carries out over a standard period of time" (Motowidlo 2003, p. 39). This definition could theoretically be expanded to group and organizational-level performance by replacing "individual" with "group" or "organization".[1] This would mean conceptualizing group-level performance as a quasi-"global unit property" (Kozlowski and Klein 2000). Unfortunately, although such a conceptualization might be convenient from a measurement perspective, it neglects the fact that performance at a higher level necessarily emerges from lower level elements' performance. Groups do not have the ability to behave and perform independently of their members. Rather, group performance emerges through the combination of individual group members' contributions. Depending on the nature of emergence, group performance can be seen as shared unit property—in cases where individual performance contributions are similar in nature (e.g., in a tug of war). It can also be seen as configural unit property—in cases where individual contributions are dissimilar in nature (e.g., in interdisciplinary projects). Adding further to the complexity of the construct, group performance can be conceptualized with a wide range of dimensions or criteria in mind.

Partly stemming from this complex nature of the constructs, the relationship between diversity and (individual or group) performance is also of some complexity. As diversity is a group-level construct, its effects on individual performance are "contextual" or "top-down" processes (Kozlowski and Klein 2000). Group performance, in turn, is a construct that comes into existence through "bottom-up" processes or "emergence" (Kozlowski and Klein 2000), that is, individual efforts are combined according to a specific "compositional model" (Chan 1998) and form a super-ordinate, group-level construct. Hence, the effect of diversity on group performance involves both contextual effects of diversity on individual group members and emergent processes.

It is not surprising—given the numerous manifestations of diversity and performance, the multilevel-nature of their relationship, and the fact that each kind of diversity is embedded into a specific organizational context—that reviews (e.g., van Knippenberg and Schippers 2007; Williams and O'Reilly 1998) and meta-analyses (e.g., Joshi and Roh 2009; Stahl et al. 2010) revealed no consistent effects of diversity on performance. In some cases, positive relationships were reported, in others negative relationships have been found, and in yet others the relationship reported was not significantly different from zero. During the last years, promising results have been found regarding moderators that determine *when* diversity will affect performance positively or negatively, such as transformational leadership (Kearney and Gebert 2009), team members' need for cognition (Kearney et al. 2008), their openness to experience (Homan et al. 2008), or diversity beliefs and climates (Stegmann 2011). Nonetheless, these are but first steps towards a full understanding of the complex processes in diverse teams. Any understanding of *how* these moderating factors work, and of the effects of diversity on performance in general, necessarily hinges on the very processes that mediate the relationship between group-level diversity and individual- and group-level performance (van Knippenberg and Schippers 2007).

2 Information elaboration as mediator of the relationship between diversity and performance

From the beginning, two theoretical perspectives have dominated the discussion around these mediating processes: the information/decision making perspective and the social categorization/similarity-attraction perspective (Williams and O'Reilly 1998). When seen from the social categorization/similarity-attraction perspective, diverse groups are assumed to be prone to the formation of subgroups. This, in turn, has often been doomed to be the cause of all the downsides of diversity, because such social categorization is supposed to lead to conflicts, misunderstandings, and lack of cooperation between subgroups.

The understanding of social categorization that underlies the present article deviates from this traditional view. As we will elaborate on further below, objectively present differences between group members are likely to have any subjective relevance only if they are perceived by the people involved. Based on self-categorization theory (Turner et al. 1987), we propose that objectively present diversity is perceived as different group members belonging to different sub-categories within the overall group (see Fig. 1) and that this perception of sub-categories does not entail any negative effects per se. Rather, we propose that all effects of diversity that are based on conscious processing are necessarily mediated through the perception of diversity as sub-categories within the overall group. This is in contrast with the traditional social categorization perspective, according to which social categorization is seen as a process that is separate from the perception of diversity and that is inherently detrimental to group functioning.

When seen from the information/decision-making perspective, diverse groups are assumed to bear a unique *informational potential*: The different group members are supposed to contribute different perspectives, opinions, abilities, knowledge, skills and the like. This way, the group can utilize a larger pool of resources. Moreover, through contradicting perspectives, all members are required to process task relevant information more deeply. In other words, diverse groups are thought to be cognitively stimulating social environments. This informational potential of diverse groups has often been seen as the driving force behind the beneficial effects of diversity.

For a long time, social categorization/similarity-attraction and information/decision making perspectives coexisted as alternative theoretical approaches, with often conflicting theoretical derivations and predictions. More recently, van Knippenberg et al. (2004) combined both perspectives in their categorization elaboration model (CEM). In their view, diverse groups come to use their unique cognitive advantage over homogenous groups through a process of *elaboration of information*, which is defined as "the exchange of information and perspectives, individual-level processing of the information and perspectives, the process of feeding back the results of this individual-level processing into the group, and discussion and integration of its implications" (van Knippenberg et al. 2004, p. 1011)—a complex group phenomenon comprising contextual, within-person, and emergent processes. Consequentially, the CEM is based on the proposition that "the primary process underlying the positive effects of diversity on group performance is elaboration of task-relevant information" (Proposition 1, van Knippenberg et al. 2004, p. 1012). Social categorization processes, in turn, are supposed to disrupt and hinder this elaboration under certain circumstances.

Thus, according to the CEM, the main potential of diverse groups is their capacity to orchestrate a rich pool of different informational and cognitive resources. The process through which this potential is transformed into superior performance is assumed to be the elaboration of information. In principle, this could be conceived as a moderating process. However, the CEM—as well as past theorizing following the information elaboration perspective—includes the assumption that diversity directly stimulates the elaboration of information. Therefore, information elaboration is thought to mediate the effect of diversity on performance. This cognitive perspective currently dominates the discussion around the processes mediating the relationship between diversity and performance.

However, during the last years, other mediating mechanisms have been proposed to exist alongside this cognitive process of elaboration such as self-disclosure (Phillips et al. 2009) or identity confirmation (Milton and Westphal 2005). Contributing to this line of research, the aim of the present paper is to illuminate the processes in diverse teams from an emotional perspective. We postulate that diverse groups possess a unique emotional potential that can enable them to superior performance. Independent of this, we also postulate that diverse groups stimulate emotional responses in their members which can enable them to superior performance. We will attend to both these assumptions in the following sections.

3 The emotional potential of diverse groups

The more group members differ from each other, the more likely they will be to engage differently in any given situation—both from a cognitive, as well as from an emotional perspective. In other words, members of diverse groups are not only prone to *think* differently but they are likely to *feel* differently, too. As described above, the cognitive side of this effect has been discussed widely. Through the pooling of unshared information and differing perspectives, innovation is fostered and the team is better prepared to meet complex demands from dynamic environments. In addition to the pooling of this cognitive content, we propose that diverse groups can also pool a variety of different emotional states in any given situation.

On the group-level, one straightforward benefit of this emotional potential of diversity is that the group as a whole is less likely to become caught up in one particular emotion—that is, members do not feel the same all the time. In contrast, if members of a group share the same affective reactions there will be a homogeneous group-level emotional state or group affective tone (George 1990). A positive group affective tone is related to more prosocial behavior, less absenteeism, less conflict, more cooperation, and higher task performance (Barsade 2002; George 1990). Unfortunately, a positive mood is also associated with a tendency to use heuristic processing of information (i.e., fast processing, low effort), whereas negative affect leads to systematic processing (i.e., detailed processing, high effort; Bohner and Apostolidou 1994; Bohner et al. 1994; Forgas 1995). Consequently, Phillips and Lount (2007) propose that the negative feelings often elicited by being in a diverse group stimulate information elaboration, which is then assumed to lead to better group performance. Similarly, George and King (2007) propose that groups with a negative group affective tone, rather than a positive one, elaborate more, pay more attention to detail, and consider multiple perspectives. When seen from this angle, it is plausible to assume that both positive and negative affective tones have their benefits and pitfalls. In diverse groups these feelings are likely to be more balanced. Similarly, extreme optimistic or pessimistic moods of individual group members are likely to become balanced through group members who feel different. As a result the group may be, for example, less likely to bask in alleged achievements too early and, on the other hand, will also not be paralyzed by the shock of a severe backlash.

Similar benefits can be conceived on the individual-level of analysis. Through exposure to other group members who feel different, one's own emotional states might become more salient and a reflection of these states is stimulated—a contextual effect of group-level diversity on individual members' emotional experiences and their reflections on these. In this way, negative drawbacks of individual emotional states could be inhibited. Similarly, from an interpersonal perspective, it is more likely for diverse groups to have members who are in an emotional state optimal to support other members emotionally, since, for example, not all members will react to the same negative situation with the same amount of paralyzing negative affective states.

Research on these and other emotional processes in diverse groups is still in its infancy, with only little empirical results available (for an exception see Shemla et al. 2010). Whether or not future research will underscore the existence of such emotional synergy effects in diverse work groups, the thoughts outlined above draw attention to the fact that group members can relate to each other not only through cognitive understanding, but also on an emotional level. Indeed, if an emotional potential exists, it is likely to influence any group or individual process only if members become aware and appreciate each other's emotions—i.e. through empathy. Such empathy can also be helpful in harvesting the group's informational potential. We will now turn to these processes in more detail.

4 Empathy as mediator of the relationship between diversity and performance

As outlined above, the informational potential of diverse groups is often assumed to stimulate processes of information elaboration, which then transform the informational potential into beneficial performance outcomes. Essential here is the pooling and exchange of information among group members. In other words, diversity only exerts its full potential through communication and sharing of "who-knows-what" among the members—in the sense of a team mental model (DeChurch and Mesmer-Magnus 2010). This effect is in part contextual, because through it individual group members are able to integrate group-level diversity in cognitive content (e.g., different knowledge originating from different functional backgrounds) into their individual mental representation of the group. It can also be emergent, because these individual mental representations, again, can be subject to group communication and thus emerge as group-level constructs of various forms (DeChurch and Mesmer-Magnus 2010; Mesmer-Magnus and DeChurch 2009). Taking into account that group members are also able to get involved with each other on an emotional level, a similar process can be assumed.

Therefore, we suggest that diversity can stimulate a more holistic, enriching, and deeper process of engagement. Generally, diverse groups stimulate the perception of differences between the self and other group members. Unique aspects of the self and other group members become especially salient and attention is drawn to these aspects. They are experienced and members are stimulated to engage with each other on the basis of these unique aspects. Here we want to point out that this process of engagement can involve more than a mere cognitive realization of differences. Rather, group members engage with these differences by using the full range of human capacities, including emotional forms of engagement.

In particular, we are interested here in *empathy*, a term that refers to "feeling for" a person by being concerned for that person and that has sometimes been referred to as "empathic concern" (Batson 2010). Implicitly included in this definition is that the person feeling for someone has to have at least some cognitive understanding of the emotional experience of the other person. It also implies that the other person's feelings are accepted and valued. Empathizing with or "having empathy" for someone describes the extent to which one's feeling is congruent with the other's feeling (i.e. feeling positive when the other's state is positive or feeling negative when the other's state is negative). However, it is important to stress that affective empathy does not imply feeling the same emotion and is not to be confused with emotional convergence, which refers to two (or more) people coming to feel more similar (Anderson et al. 2003). As pointed out by Batson and Ahmad (2009), "you might, for example, feel sad or sorry for someone who is scared and upset" (p. 146). Thus, empathy is about "feeling for" someone and not about "feeling as" someone. Researchers from the field of organizational behavior have mostly studied "feeling as" or feeling similarity instead of studying "feeling for." Research from social psychology suggests that it is "feeling for" someone that directly affects prosocial behavior and not "feeling as" (Batson et al. 1997a). Interestingly, with regard to this distinction, research suggests that "feeling as" is neither a necessary nor sufficient precondition for "feeling for" someone (Batson and Ahmad 2009; Batson et al. 1997a). Moreover, despite the fact that most studies from social psychology have examined empathy as a negative state affect (e.g., "I feel for your pain"), empathy can also refer to positive state affects (e.g., "I am happy for you"). In the present model, we conceptualize affective empathy as an emotional state that can be both negative and positive.

We propose that the stimulating nature of diverse groups exceeds mere cognitive elaboration of information, but also includes group members' emotional responses to their experience of their fellow members' emotions—i.e. empathy. Evidence in favor of this proposition comes from a set of experiments in which participants were either primed to focus on differences or similarities between themselves and others (Todd et al. 2011). When focusing on differences, rather than similarities, people were more likely to adopt others' visual perspectives, were less likely to impute their own privileged knowledge to others, and communicated more efficiently with others. These results occurred when participants were directly primed to focus on differences/similarities. However, they also occurred when this focus was indirectly implied through the salience of group memberships—i.e.

if the other person was either German (similar to participants) or Turkish (different from participants). The results even occurred under minimal-group conditions—that is even if the group membership had no real meaning. In sum, these findings illustrate that diversity can stimulate taking the perspective of another person, which is a constituent part of empathy.

Empathy, in turn, can influence interpersonal encounters in work groups in a variety of ways and can, through this, lead to better performance. First, empathy is beneficial for interpersonal encounters in work groups because it evokes altruistic motivation (Batson 1991, 2010; Hoffman 2000) and increases concern for the welfare of a different other and the group as a whole (Batson et al. 1997b). Such altruism and concern is likely to produce organizational citizenship behavior directed at colleagues, which has been empirically proven to foster work group performance and is often considered as one form of individual performance (Podsakoff et al. 2009). Second, empathy increases moral judgment and helps to resolve conflicts between individuals or between people belonging to different (sub)groups (Batson et al. 1997b; Gibbs 2003). Meta-analytically, empathy has been shown to mediate the positive effect of intergroup contact on prejudice (Pettigrew and Tropp 2008). In other words, empathy is likely to help work groups to prevent or handle conflicts. This is likely to help work groups to perform better because conflicts are—by and large—detrimental to work group performance (De Dreu 2011). Third, empathy increases the likelihood of mutual identity confirmation between team members, which in turn fosters cooperation (Milton and Westphal 2005). Fourth, empathy also increases the likelihood of self-disclosure (Phillips et al. 2009) and, on the receiving end, the feeling of being understood by others may lead people to open up themselves and disclose valuable information (Marci et al. 2007). This is likely to lead to a better use of unshared information—a critical issue identified to determine the performance of decision making groups (Brodbeck et al. 2007). Fifth, empathy is also likely to foster team-learning behaviors, which have been proven to foster team performance (Gibson and Vermeulen 2003; van der Vegt and Bunderson 2005). Sixth, empathy toward specific social groups can positively influence their attitudes on organizational policies and programs aimed at reducing discrimination and on improving relationships between members of different social categories within the organization (Batson and Ahmad 2009; Harrison et al. 2006; Schur et al. 2005). Empathy can also directly reduce stereotyping and discrimination (Batson et al. 2002; Batson et al. 1997b). There is a multitude of reasons for why discrimination is bad for performance throughout the organization. Discrimination can damage an organization's reputation, limit the pool of qualified personnel to hire from, produce costs due to legal prosecution, lead to loss of organization-specific human capital, and, finally, discrimination decreases the job satisfaction of those being discriminated (Ensher et al. 2001), which will ultimately decrease their job performance (Judge et al. 2001).

In sum, these studies provide evidence that empathy can have important effects on cognitive, motivational, and behavioral processes of both the person feeling for someone and the other person. Ultimately, these effects place both persons and therefore the whole group in a better position to perform well.

In combination with the classic information-elaboration perspective, empathy opens up a richer and more complete way to engage with fellow group members. We propose that it is also through this emotional process of empathy that members of diverse groups come to realize the unique potential of diverse groups. This is plausible in the case of the above discussed emotional potential. In addition, through the processes described above, empathy provides a basis for interpersonal relationships marked not only by understanding but also by mutual acceptance. Based on such positive relationships, the various informational resources can be pooled and elaborated effectively. Therefore, empathy also helps to utilize the informational potential of diverse groups.

4.1 Individual-level empathy

As with the classic information elaboration approach, the processes here are multilevel in nature. So far, we have argued that empathy is a process through which group members of diverse groups come to realize each other's feelings and, therefore, gain a more complete and emotionally enriched understanding of the group, together with a felt acceptance of other group members. It is through this process and its cognitive and motivational consequences that group members are in an optimal position to use both the group's informational and emotional potential to foster individual and group performance. Empathy has mostly been studied as an individual emotional phenomenon (Batson 2010). As we have argued above, empathy is the process through which people relate to their fellow group members in a specific and holistic way. It is by this process that the emotional states of all the group members resonate in every individual group member—a contextual process linking group level diversity with what might be called an emotional resonance of the emotional setup of the group within every single group member. Nonetheless, this kind of empathy is still a construct on the individual level.

This *individual-level empathy* is of importance whenever effects of empathy occur *within* a single group member. Emotionally relating to other group members is a vital part of familiarizing oneself with the colleagues one has to work with in order to fulfill one's tasks. This emotional familiarity with other group members bears valuable input which can be used to adapt one's own actions accordingly and, hence, increase their effectiveness. For example, we have argued above that empathy is likely to reduce prejudice towards dissimilar others. Without these negative sentiments, a particular group member might be more likely to approach a dissimilar other member and use this other's knowledge to fulfill his or her own task in the group (i.e. to foster his or her individual performance and, through this, the performance of the group). To depict these processes, individually felt empathy would be the mediator of choice.

Proposition 1: The relationship between diversity and (individual and group) performance is mediated through individual-level empathy.

4.2 Group-level empathy

This contextual process leading to individual-level empathy can be complemented by emergent processes. As in the case of information elaboration, members can communicate their empathic experiences, learn how others' experiences might be similar or different and, as a consequence, develop an understanding of the level of empathy of the group as a whole. Therefore, empathy may also be considered at the group level. There are many ways and patterns of emergence that might be of relevance to group-level empathy. For the present purpose, we restrict ourselves to the simplest version. Thus, *group-level empathy* can be defined as the collective amount of empathy existing between the members of a group in a particular situation. According to multilevel theory such a process is best described as compositional emergence through pooling elements that are similar in nature (Kozlowski and Klein 2000). As such, it describes an emotional state of the group which designates the total availability of empathic relationships within a group.

This *group-level empathy* is of importance wherever the effects of empathy do occur *between* group members. Based on our above arguments, it is plausible that empathy can mediate the diversity-performance relationship through processes occurring between group members—that is one group member feels empathy and another group member is affected through this. For example, we have argued that empathy will increase the likelihood of support for fellow group members, leading to better performance of these group members. In this case, the degree of empathy experienced by all other group members is the mediator between the group's diversity and the performance of the group member in question, because it describes the availability of such supportive relationships.

Moreover, the group members' knowledge that their personal experience of empathy for the other group members is likely to be reciprocated by other members experiencing empathy for them is likely to create additional effects. Such knowledge—reflected in a perceived high level of empathy within the group—is, for example, likely to create interpersonal affiliation (cf. Haslam et al. 2005). It could also encourage members to voice deviating concerns or ideas, contributing to a "participative safety climate" (Anderson and West 1998; Edmondson 1999). Again, it is plausible that both affiliation and psychological safety climate will be beneficial for group functioning and performance. In a similar vein, research on group emotional intelligence revealed that both confrontation and caring for each other are optimal norms for successful collaborative work. When these norms are in place, confrontations can be seen in a positive light and interpreted as positive criticism (Druskat and Wolff 2001a). This line of research also unveiled that group effectiveness increases when groups regulate their emotions effectively (Druskat and Wolff 2001a, 2001b). It is easy to recognize the crucial role that group-level empathy might play in this context. To depict these processes, group-level empathy would be the mediator of choice.

Proposition 2: The relationship between diversity and (individual and group) performance is mediated through group-level empathy.

5 Moderators of the relationship between diversity and empathy

So far, we have suggested that individual and group empathy mediate the effects of diversity on group and individual performance. However, empathy does not necessarily and automatically occur within all diverse teams. Rather, it depends on a number of moderating factors, whether group members will feel for each other.

5.1 Organizational and task requirements

According to the categorization elaboration model, diversity should be related to information elaboration if the task requirements imply that the informational potential of diverse groups can be of use—that is, if the task requires a certain level of information elaboration (Proposition 2, van Knippenberg et al. 2004). In case of empathy, a similar argument is readily conceivable for work environments in which emotions play a key role. For example, many workplaces in the service sector require employees to monitor their emotions and to follow certain display rules with regard to emotionally intensive service encounters (i.e. emotional labor, see Hochschild 1983). In such environments, it is certainly obvious for employees that emotions are an important aspect to consider. Given this attention, feeling for co-workers might occur more easily and naturally in these settings.

However, as discussed above, also purely intellectual, creative and innovative tasks—such as those addressed in the categorization elaboration model—can benefit from empathy. It is certainly not the rule to have empathy enforcing instructions, regulations or task settings in jobs involving these kinds of tasks. Nonetheless, we believe that an organizational requirement in the form of task settings that emphasize the importance of empathy for the performance of the group can help to realize the unique potential of diverse groups.

Proposition 3: Empathy enhancing task requirements moderate the relationship between diversity and (individual- or group-level) empathy. If the importance and usefulness of empathy is highlighted through these requirements, diversity will be more positively related to empathy.

5.2 Motivation to relate to different others

The categorization elaboration model includes two more factors moderating diversity's positive or negative effects on group functioning: the members' motivation to fulfill their task and their ability to do so (Propositions 3 & 4, van Knippenberg et al. 2004). Van Knippenberg et al. pointed out that both factors have been largely neglected in diversity research. However, they argue that both motivation and ability were shown to lead to deeper processing of information (cf. Chaiken and Trope 1999). As information elaboration is the central mediating process in the categorization elaboration model, proposing motivation and ability as moderators of the diversity-information elaboration-performance relationship makes perfect sense. However, the central mediator in the present model is empathy, rather than information elaboration.

Nonetheless, group members' motivation is likely to play an important role. In the case of empathy, however, it is group members' motivation to relate to different others, rather than their motivation to do the task at hand, that is more likely to influence the relationship between diversity and empathy—except maybe for those cases in which the task itself requires empathy.

Indirect evidence for the role of motivation in this respect comes from two experimental studies that assessed the joint effect of cognitive fatigue and interpersonal dissimilarity on empathy (Nelson et al. 2003). In these studies, fatigue lead to increased need for cognitive closure—i.e. a desire for cognitive clarity or certainty. This need for cognitive closure can be interpreted as a lack of motivation to elaborate information. Nelson et al. argue that such motivation is necessary to generate the cognitive effort that is needed to take another person's perspective and, thus, to empathize with this person. Furthermore, they argue that this effort will be greater the more dissimilar the other person is. In line with these ideas, they found that fatigue reduced empathy for another person if the other person was dissimilar. It had no effect if the other person was similar to the participant. In a second study, this effect of fatigue—and hence the lack of motivation to engage in cognitive effort—was compensated through a manipulation that increased the motivation to process information about the other person. While these results are based on motivation to engage with others in a cognitive way, they nonetheless illustrate the important influence of motivation on the emergence of empathy towards different others.

Looking at this motivation from a slightly more emotional side, it is plausible that if group members are not motivated to emotionally relate to other group members who are different from themselves, diversity will not have the above outlined empathy-stimulating effect. Moreover, a lack of motivation to empathize with different others also makes it unlikely that group members will communicate about empathic experiences within the group, thereby undermining the processes necessary to create certain forms of group-level empathy.

Proposition 4: Lack of motivation to relate emotionally to members of different subgroups is disruptive to the individual group members' experience of empathy and to the emergence of group-level empathy. Therefore, low motivation to relate emotionally to different others will lead to a negative relationship between diversity and empathy. High motivation to relate emotionally to different others will lead to a positive relationship between diversity and empathy.

5.3 Knowledge about different others

With regard to group members' abilities, a similar argument can be made. Again, group members' ability to accomplish the tasks given is probably only indirectly related to the emergence of empathy—for instance, in those cases where the tasks require empathy. However, the ability to relate to different others is likely to have a more direct influence. This is fairly intuitive, if one considers the case of very homogeneous teams. In such teams, the congruence between the team members in values, norms, goals and other cognitive contents makes it easier for group members to comprehend and apprehend each other's emotional states, simply because they know exactly from their own experience "how it must feel". This way the shared cognitive content provides knowledge about other group members, on the basis of which empathy will be easier to experience.

The conditions for developing empathy are considerably different in diverse groups. The existence of subgroups increases the likelihood of differences in relevant norms, values, goals and other cognitive content between the group members—that is, group members are not familiar with different others' experiences. If one particular group member is experiencing a certain emotional state as a result of any kind of event, it is relatively unlikely that a different other member will experience this event in the same way. This difference in cognitive content also heightens the risk that group members are not able to develop adequate empathy, since they are not able to fully comprehend the experience of the other person. For example, the more a particular fellow group member differs from oneself in norms, values, or goals, the more difficult it will be to understand why a particular event made this group member angry, anxious, curious, or ashamed. Therefore, the knowledge about different others is likely to affect whether diversity will indeed have the proposed empathy-stimulating effect.

Proposition 5: Lack of knowledge about members of different subgroups hinders the experience of individual empathy in diverse groups. With a lack of such knowledge, diversity will be negatively related to empathy. Where such knowledge is available, diversity will be positively related to empathy.

While task requirements, motivation, and ability are promising contingency factors of the relationship between diversity and empathy, the remaining contingency mechanism from the categorization elaboration model received superior attention in diversity research. The basic idea behind this mechanism is that, under certain conditions, diversity can lead to social categorization—i.e. the formation of subgroups within the diverse group—and that this can entail negative affective and evaluative reactions, such as, conflict or a decrease in identification. These negative affective and evaluative reactions are proposed to moderate the relationship between diversity and information elaboration. Although relatively intuitive at first glance, the processes at work behind this mechanism are not trivial. Therefore, it is advisable to look at these social categorization processes in diverse groups in more detail.

6 Diversity and social categorization

The very nature of diversity makes it intuitively plausible that diversity should be negatively related to empathy. It just seems so much easier to relate emotionally to people who are similar and share the same experiences. Furthermore, it is often assumed that diversity leads to misunderstandings, conflicts, hostility, ingroup-favoritism, etc. Both these assumptions are in line with the traditional social categorization perspective on diversity.

Contrary to this traditional perspective, we propose that social categorization is not necessarily detrimental to group functioning. Rather, based on self-categorization theory (Turner et al. 1987), we propose that social categorization has to be conceived as the essence of diversity. This is because diversity is basically defined as the fact that there are differences between members of a social unit. According to self-categorization theory, perceiving subjectively meaningful differences between oneself and other members of a group necessarily implies categorizing oneself and these others into different social categories. This principle is valid on all levels of abstraction. Even if there are only two members in a group, they can each belong to a different sub-category. In fact, the process of perceiving diversity is one of social categorization, or, more precisely, self-categorization.

Nonetheless, social categorization is included in the categorization elaboration model as a distinct construct which is separate from diversity itself (van Knippenberg et al. 2004). In fact, the model can be interpreted such that diversity can have effects without social categorization taking place. This is very much in line with the classic social categorization perspective from general diversity research. Contrary to this approach, we propose that social categorization is the very process through which group members come to realize that other group members are different from themselves.

Proposition 6: The perception of diversity occurs through perceiving social categories or subgroups within the overall group.

It is important to emphasize that the social categories in question are in fact self-categories, that is, they form part of group members' self-concepts. As such they provide a basis on which group members form their knowledge about who they are and, maybe even more important, provide a framework of social comparison to evaluate oneself against the norms and standards of the group and to compare their own group with others (Tajfel and Turner 1979; Turner et al. 1987). Therefore, the more these group memberships are valued parts of the self, the more it becomes obvious that these self-categorizations bear a large potential to elicit a range of emotional processes.

In principle, each subgroup in a diverse group can consist of any number of members and there can be any number of such subgroups. However, with any constellation of subgroups being perceived, there will be two possible self-categorizations for each group member: (a) as a member of the overall group or (b) as a member of a particular subgroup. According to self-categorization theory, these different levels of self-categorization are mutually exclusive. The more salient the subgroups, the more the self-categorization as a member of the overall group fades and vice versa ("functional antagonism", Turner et al. 1987).

Self-categorization theory posits that self-categories tend to be positively valued and that other people are evaluated against the prototype of such positively valued self-categories. The process of categorizing oneself and other members into the same social category entails perceiving them as more similar to the prototype of the valued self-category. In consequence, they will be liked more and cooperation with them will be fostered.

Combining this with the principle of functional antagonism, the benefits stemming from sharing the same group membership shift accordingly from all (larger group's) members to those of one's own subgroup if subgroups are salient. This preference of ingroup members over outgroup members—often termed ingroup or intergroup bias—is likely to bear consequences for cross-subgroup cooperation within the group as a whole. The traditional social categorization perspective holds such intergroup bias accountable for all sorts of negative subgroup relationships in diverse groups such as conflicts, prejudice, stereotyping, or misunderstandings.

Therefore, given that most members of diverse groups will be aware of that diversity, the traditional social categorization perspective offers only dismal prospects for diverse groups. However, the accumulated empirical evidence does not support such a pessimistic view (Jackson and Joshi 2011; van Knippenberg and Schippers 2007). Although it has often been claimed, especially in diversity research, it seems that mere social categorization is *not* a sufficient precondition for negative intergroup phenomena to occur (Park and Judd 2005). Social identity theory (Tajfel and Turner 1986) is based on the minimal group experiments (Tajfel et al. 1971) which are often used to argue for the negative effects of mere categorization. However, the theory is far more complex and never included such a minimalistic assumption (McGarty 2001). Livingstone and Haslam (2008), for example, found that negative intergroup relations are contingent on the *content* of the categories in question. In a similar vein, Wolsko et al. (2000) found that acknowledging social categories did not entail negative sentiments towards outgroups.

From a social identity point of view, this is not astonishing. According to social identity theory, negative intergroup relationships do occur only if groups are compared against each other on status relevant dimensions. Following this line of thought, the categorization elaboration model includes the assumption that only when the subgroup-identities implied by diversity are threatening each other—in the sense that the value of one's own subgroup is somehow challenged by the existence of the other subgroups—will this impede the realization of the informational potential of diverse groups through information elaboration (Propositions 6 & 7, van Knippenberg et al. 2004). Similarly, we propose that intergroup bias, stemming from threatening subgroup identity relationships, will hinder group members in experiencing empathy towards one another and in communicating this understanding in any way, which is necessary for many forms of group-level empathy.

Proposition 7: Intergroup biases elicited by threatening relationships between salient subgroup identities are disruptive to the individual group members' experience of empathy and to the emergence of group-level empathy. With threatening or challenging relationships between subgroups in place, diversity will be negatively related to empathy.

7 The role of diversity beliefs and diversity climates as second order contingency factors

So far, we proposed that diversity will be negatively related to empathy when the task requirements fail to make the benefits of empathy apparent, when work group members lack the motivation or the knowledge necessary to emotionally relate to different group members, or under conditions of threatened identities. In the absence of these adverse conditions, diversity is proposed to stimulate the experience of empathy. However, if group members are motivated to relate to different others, if they command a pool of knowledge about different others, or if task requirements make the benefits of empathy apparent, this empathy-stimulating effect of diversity can even be intensified.

We propose that diversity beliefs and diversity climates can play an important role in bringing about these favorable conditions. Diversity beliefs can be defined as individual-level associations between a mental representation of a social entity's diversity and an assessment of this diversity's value for producing certain outcomes—i.e. individual beliefs whether a particular form of diversity is "good" or "bad" for a group. Diversity climates depict such valuing of diversity on a group-level—i.e. whether the group as a whole "thinks" that diversity is good or bad (Stegmann 2011). Theoretically, diversity beliefs and climates have the potential to relate the very core of a group's common identity—for instance, its task in the wider organization—to its diversity (Haslam 2004; van Knippenberg and Haslam 2003). Meta-analytically, diversity beliefs and climates have been shown to affect diverse workgroups positively—across a large variety of different conceptualizations of such beliefs/climates and all sorts of beneficial and detrimental group- and individual-level outcomes (Stegmann 2011). Important for our present argument, it is likely that, once diversity is valued as an asset of the work group, people have a strong rationale for why relating to each other emotionally might be useful. In terms of the model, motivation to relate to different others is fostered and perceptions of threat are reduced.

This effect can be derived from self-categorization theory, because to the degree that diversity is a valued aspect of the overall group, differences between members will not be seen as problematic and threatening. Rather, if diversity is deemed necessary for the group, this makes the different group members mutually dependent on each other through exactly the differences between them. In terms of the self-categorization theory, as the overall group prototype becomes more diverse, dissimilar group members can become more prototypical to this overall group prototype *because* they are dissimilar. As this group prototype is likely to be positively valued, dissimilar group members will like each other more, cohesion will be stronger, and cooperation will increased. In consequence, perceptions of threatening or challenging subgroup relationships will be reduced.

Proposition 8: Diversity beliefs and climates that stress the positive value of diversity will be negatively related to the perception of threatening or challenging relationships between subgroups in diverse groups.

In a similar vein, if diversity is seen as a valuable and integral part of the group's identity, this will foster group members' motivation to engage with different others—also in an emotional way.

Proposition 9: Diversity beliefs and climates that stress the positive value of diversity will be positively related to group members' motivation to relate emotionally to members of different subgroups.

Diversity beliefs and diversity climates can vary in their specificity. For example, they can be more or less specific with regard to the particular kind of diversity in question. If diversity beliefs or climates are specific in this way, they could include knowledge about different others that might help relating to diverse others emotionally. Diversity beliefs and climates can also be specific with regard to the outcomes diversity is supposed to be leading to. If such a detailed description of the instrumental roles of a certain kind of diversity includes detailed task knowledge, it is likely that diversity beliefs and climates could influence the way in which task or organizational requirements are conceived. However, most of the studies that addressed diversity beliefs/climates so far did not address such specific diversity beliefs or climates, but rather conceptualized these constructs in a very general way (Stegmann 2011). Therefore, the relationship between diversity beliefs/climates and task/organizational requirements as well as the relationship between diversity beliefs/climates and knowledge about different others are not likely to be found with the existing measures and manipulations of diversity beliefs/climates. These relationships might become valid, though, as more fine-grained conceptualizations of diversity beliefs/climates are applied.

The final way in which diversity beliefs and climates influence the proposed relationships in the present model is also pointed out by van Knippenberg et al. (2004) alongside their categorization elaboration model. They argue that whether diversity is believed to be beneficial or detrimental for fulfilling the task at hand is likely to influence the "normative fit" (Turner et al. 1987) of the social categories this diversity is based on. That is, the more a particular kind of diversity is perceived as meaningful with regard to the present task context, the more it makes sense to categorize people along the lines of this kind of diversity. Furthermore, valuing diversity will make diversity more accessible to the perceiver across a variety of contexts (Stegmann 2011)—through increasing the "accessibility" (Turner et al. 1987) of the entailed social categories. Thus, if people value diversity, they will be more likely to perceive it in a given situation and to actively seek out new forms of diversity in their groups. Unfortunately, a similar case can be made with regard to diversity beliefs/climates that express a strong negative value for diversity. If diversity is loathed by individuals or groups, group members might also be sensitized to the perception of diversity through the same processes as above. Therefore, diversity beliefs will influence whether objectively present group diversity will be perceived by the group members as salient social categories.

Proposition 10: Diversity beliefs and climates will moderate the relationship between objectively present differences between group members and the perception of these differences in the form of social categories or subgroups within the overall group. In conditions of strong pro- or contra-diversity beliefs/climates, this relationship will be more positive than under less pronounced beliefs/climates.

8 Discussion

The aim of the present paper was to contribute to the understanding of the mediating processes and moderating factors that shape the effects of diversity on individual- and group-level performance in organizations. Much of the research surrounding this topic has focused on the cognitive processes elicited by diversity. The present model complements this cognitive perspective by illuminating the emotional processes in diverse groups. We propose that diverse groups do not merely provide stimulating cognitive resources, but are also rich in emotional content. This emotional potential of diverse groups is proposed to be an additional resource that can be used to improve individual and group performance. Furthermore, we propose that diversity can stimulate group members, as human beings, to engage with the cognitive and emotional potential of diverse groups in both ways, cognitively and emotionally. We propose that empathy is one such way of emotional engagement. Empathy, in turn, is likely to have a range of positive effects within and between group members, ultimately enabling the individual member and the group to better performance.

However, the empathy-stimulating effect of diversity does not occur automatically and in every situation. We propose that it can be fostered to some degree through organizational requirements. Furthermore, we argue that it depends on group members' motivation to engage emotionally with different others and on their knowledge about these others. In line with previous research on the role of social categorization in diverse work groups, we propose that the relationship also depends on group members' perception that social identities triggered by the differences within the group challenge or threaten each other.

However, deviating from traditional conceptualizations of social categorization processes in diverse groups, we place social categorization at the very core of the model.

Social categorization is considered to be the very process through which group members subjectively experience their diverse environment. It is *not* in itself a negative side effect that needs to be overcome in order to avoid the negative effects of diversity.

Finally, we propose diversity beliefs and climates as second-order contingency factors of the relationship between diversity and performance. These beliefs and climates have been shown to moderate the effects of diversity on a variety of different outcomes, including performance, in a recent meta-analysis (Stegmann 2011). However, the meta-analysis also revealed that these effects do not occur all the time. Hence, more needs to be learned about how the effects of diversity beliefs and climates come about. The present theoretical model describes three different ways in which diversity beliefs and climates can influence the effects of diversity. First, diversity beliefs/climates will make it more likely that objectively present diversity will be perceived by the group members. Second, pro-diversity beliefs/climates will make relationships between subgroups in a diverse group less threatening and challenging. Third, they also will contribute to group members' motivation to relate to different others. In sum, therefore, the present model does not only include diversity beliefs and climates as additional contingency factors of the diversity-performance relationship, but also provides a more detailed description of *why* diversity beliefs and climates can have this moderating effect. In previous work on diversity beliefs and climates, their influence has been predominantly examined with regard to their effects on information elaboration. The present model complements this view by pointing out their influence on empathy in diverse groups.

8.1 Theoretical implications and directions for further research

Our model advances current theory on diversity in work groups by focusing on an emotional pathway between work group diversity and performance. To make this possible it is necessary to focus on empathy as a state rather than a personal disposition, which has been the focus in previous applications of the empathy construct within the organizational behavior literature (e.g., Kamdar et al. 2006; Settoon and Mossholder 2002). Empathy as a construct is relatively new to the organizational behavior literature and has only rarely been discussed in relation to work group diversity (Ensari and Miller 2006; Roberge 2009; Roberge and van Dick 2010).

Another distinctive feature of the present model is the conceptualization of empathy both on an individual- and on a group-level. Most often, so far, empathy has been assessed as an individual-level construct and related to other individual-level constructs, such as the willingness to help different others, and to attitudes toward outgroup members. In contrast, group-level empathy and the importance of sharing mutual empathy in diverse group settings has only rarely been discussed before (Ensari and Miller 2006; Roberge and van Dick 2010). Following from this, theorizing regarding the inter-relationships between both levels of empathy is still in its infancy. Whether individual-level empathy and group-level empathy have any interactive effects and how they might affect each other are questions for future research to answer. Furthermore, in the present model, we assumed group- and individual-level empathy to have similar relationships with regard to many of the proposed relationships. However, future research might reveal that there are other processes which are distinct to each level.

By shedding light on the emotional processes that can explain how diversity may increase group performance, the present model helps to broaden the theoretical understanding of the relationship between work group diversity and group performance. It is designed to complement other more cognitively focused models on the effects of work group diversity. However, the proposed emotional processes cannot strictly be separated from the cognitive realm. Rather, it is plausible that the emotional and cognitive processes in diverse work groups are highly interlinked, just as in general there are many intercepts between cognition and emotion in human beings. More specifically, future research might explore the interplay of the two core processes of the informational and the emotional pathways behind the diversity-performance link, to wit, information elaboration and empathy.

Focusing again on the emotional pathway, another avenue for future research might be to explore the different nature of the emotions at a group-level in diverse versus homogeneous groups. As we pointed out above, the emotional relationships in groups can take the form of members experiencing the same emotions ("feeling as") or members experiencing emotions in reaction to what emotions they perceive in others ("feeling for"). With regard to the differences between the members of groups, it is quite plausible to assume that group emotion in homogeneous groups is likely to come in the form of "feeling as". The more diversity exists and, hence, group members are different from each other, the more group emotion will have to take the form of empathy or "feeling for". We have mentioned above that both forms of emotionally relating to others have been shown to have different effects. Therefore, it appears sensible for further research to follow this distinction and explore its implications for diverse organizations.

Our model focuses on work group performance as the main outcome variable. Performance has also been the focus of much of the general research on work group diversity. However, other more proximal constructs are also likely to be affected through empathy. For example, we have mentioned above that prosocial behavior or social support in general might result from members experiencing empathy for each other. This availability of social support, or the perception that it might be available when needed, is likely to influence primary and secondary stress appraisals (Lazarus and Folkman 1984) and, hence, influence group members' well-being and health (Haslam and van Dick 2011). Our argument has been that these and other outcomes ultimately lead to better individual and group performance. However, further research is needed in this respect to elaborate the exact nature of these relationships.

Another restriction of the current model is that we focused exclusively on effects of diversity which manifest themselves through the conscious perception of differences within a group. On the one hand, this is in line with much of the previous diversity literature. On the other hand—considering that we suggest an alternative, emotional pathway for diversity's effects instead of an exclusively cognitive pathway—it is worthwhile thinking also of more covert, indirect, or less conscious processes mediating the effects of diversity. Specifically, the insights gained from research on self-fulfilling prophecies and automatic stereotyping (Bargh et al. 1999) or implicit attitudes (Jost et al. 2009) could potentially be applied to processes in diverse organizational units and provide alternative explanations for diversity's effects on performance.

8.2 Practical implications and suggestions for diversity management

Based on our model and past research, a few promising starting points for enhancing performance within diverse organizations can be identified. For example, there is evidence that empathy can be enhanced through training and that induced empathy may indeed take precedence over potential negative effects resulting from social categorization issues (Batson and Ahmad 2001; Batson and Moran 1999). Thus, diverse organizations could stress the importance of empathy by implementing training programs which focus on inducing affective empathy among employees (Stephan and Finlay 1999). A number of studies have shown that it is possible to increase levels of empathy through a variety of training programs (Crabb et al. 1983; Erera 1997; Goldstein and Michaels 1985; Pacala et al. 1995). The effects of such training programs may significantly improve interpersonal relations between diverse people and thus foster performance. According to our model this will be particularly needed in conditions that suggest a negative relationship between diversity and empathy—i.e. threatening subgroup relationships, lack of motivation to engage with different others, lack of knowledge about different others, or unfavorable task requirements. In fact, the training programs might be developed such as to alter exactly these disadvantageous conditions. This way, potential negative effects of diversity might be counterbalanced and the conditions set to use the full informational and emotional potential of diverse groups.

Another starting point to foster performance within diverse organizations would be the development of pro-diversity beliefs and pro-diversity climates. According to the proposed model, these beliefs and climates are likely to foster the motivation to relate to diverse others and to lessen the perceptions of sub-group threat. Moreover, they are likely to draw attention to diversity in the first place, which is a necessary precondition for the use of its potentials and for avoiding possible negative effects. Probably the most well-known diversity management instruments that could be used to foster pro-diversity beliefs and climates are diversity trainings (e.g., Pendry et al. 2007) and the enacting of diversity-affirming organizational policies (e.g., Kalev et al. 2006). These trainings and policies are often focused on inspiring fair, ethically correct and non-prejudiced behavior. An additional focus for these trainings and policies could be to draw attention to the informational and emotional potential of diversity that we described at the beginning of this article. Indeed, experimental studies clearly show that pointing out the value of diversity for the task at hand is a powerful way to induce pro- or contra-diversity beliefs (e.g., van Knippenberg et al. 2007). In this way, diversity trainings and policies could not only serve to advocate valuing diversity as the morally right thing to do, but could also stress the importance of diversity as a valuable asset of the organization.

9 Conclusion

Despite the restrictions outlined above, we believe that the proposed emotional pathway to the effects of work group diversity is a timely and inspiring perspective. It complements other more cognitively oriented approaches and helps exploring so far neglected potentials of diversity in organizations. The model opens up an emotional perspective on work group diversity that has the potential to stimulate a variety of interesting lines of research. We hope that the proposed model will spark further research that ultimately will help to understand the mechanisms behind the effects of work group diversity and, in this way, will contribute to the development of methods for managing diversity in organizations effectively.

Acknowledgement: We are grateful to Denise M. Rousseau, Daniel Batson and Rachel P. Kreiter for their comments on previous drafts of this paper. We also thank the editor and three anonymous reviewers for their detailed suggestions.

Endnote

1   Throughout the text we refer to group and individual level constructs for the ease of reading. The model is not necessarily restricted to these particular levels, though.

References

Anderson NR, West MA (1998) Measuring climate for work group innovation: development and validation of the team climate inventory. J Organ Beha 19(3):235–258

Anderson C, Keltner D, John OP (2003) Emotional convergence between people over time. J Pers Soc Psychol 84(5):1054–1068

Bargh JA, Chaiken S, Trope Y (1999) The cognitive monster: the case against the controllability of automatic stereotype effects. Guilford Press, New York

Barsade SG (2002) The ripple effects: emotional contagion and its influence on group behavior. Adm Sci Q 47(4):644–675

Batson CD (1991) The altruism question: toward a social-psychological answer. Erlbaum, Hillsdale

Batson CD (2010) Empathy-induced altruistic motivation. In: Mikulincer M, Shaver PR (eds) Prosocial motives, emotions, and behavior: the better angels of our nature. American Psychological Association, Washington, pp 15–53

Batson CD, Ahmad N (2001) Empathy-induced altruism in a prisoner's dilemma ii: what if the target of empathy has defected? Eur J Soc Psychol 31(1):25–36

Batson CD, Ahmad NY (2009) Using empathy to improve intergroup attitudes and relations. Soc Issues Policy Rev 3(1):141–177

Batson CD, Moran T (1999) Empathy-induced altruism in a prisoner's dilemma. Eur J Soc Psychol 29(7):909–924

Batson CD, Early S, Salvarani G (1997a) Perspective taking: imagining how another feels versus imagining how you would feel. Pers Soc Psychol Bull 23(7):751–758. doi:10.1177/0146167297237008

Batson CD, Polycarpou MP, Harmon-Jones E, Imhoff HJ, Mitchener EC, Bednar LL, Klein TR, Highberger L (1997b) Empathy and attitudes: can feeling for a member of a stigmatized group improve feeling toward the group? J Pers Soc Psychol 72(1):105–118. doi:10.1037/0022-3514.72.1.105

Batson CD, Chang J, Orr R, Rowland J (2002) Empathy, attitudes, and action: can feeling for a member of a stigmatized group motivate one to help the group? Pers Soc Psychol Bull 28(12):1656–1666. doi:10.1177/014616702237647

Bohner G, Apostolidou W (1994) Mood and persuasion: independent effects of affect before and after message processing. J Soc Psychol 134(5):707–709

Bohner G, Chaiken S, Hunyadi P (1994) The role of mood and message ambiguity in the interplay of heuristic and systematic processing. Eur J Soc Psychol 24(1):207–221

Brodbeck FC, Kerschreiter R, Mojzisch A, Schulz-Hardt S (2007) Group decision making under conditions of distributed knowledge: the information asymmetries model. Acad Manag Rev 32(2):459–479

Chaiken S, Trope Y (1999) Dual-process theories in social psychology. Guilford Press, New York

Chan D (1998) Functional relations among constructs in the same content domain at different levels of analysis: a typology of composition models. J Appl Psychol 83(2):234–246

Crabb WT, Moracco JC, Bender RC (1983) A comparative study of empathy training with programmed instruction for lay helpers. J Couns Psychol 30(2):221–226. doi:10.1037/0022-0167.30.2.221

Davis MH (1994) Empathy: a social psychological approach. Westview Press, Boulder

De Dreu CKW (2011) Conflict at work: basic principles and applied issues. In: Zedeck S (ed) Handbook of industrial and organizational psychology, vol 3. APA Press, Washington, pp 461–493. (Maintaining, expanding, and contracting the organization)

DeChurch LA, Mesmer-Magnus JR (2010) The cognitive underpinnings of effective teamwork: a meta-analysis. J Appl Psychol 95(1):32–53

Druskat VU, Wolff SB (2001a) Building the emotional intelligence of groups. Harvard Bus Rev 79(3):80–90

Druskat VU, Wolff SB (2001b) Group emotional intelligence and its influence on group effectiveness. In: Cherniss C, Goleman D (eds) The emotionally intelligent workplace. Jossey-Bess, San Francisco, pp 132–155

Edmondson AC (1999) Psychological safety and learning behavior in work teams. Adm Sci Q 44(2):350–383

Ensari NK, Miller N (2006) The application of the personalization model in diversity management. Group Process Intergroup Relat 9(4):589–607

Ensher EA, Grant-Vallone EJ, Donaldson SI (2001) Effects of perceived discrimination on job satisfaction, organizational commitment, organizational citizenship behavior, and grievances. Hum Resour Devel Quart 12(1):53–72

Erera PI (1997) Empathy training for helping professionals: model and evaluation. J Soc Work Educ 33(2):245–260

Forgas JP (1995) Mood and judgment: the affect infusion model (aim). Psychol Bull 117(1):39–66

George JM (1990) Personality, affect, and behavior in groups. J Appl Psychol 75(2):107–116

George JM, King EB (2007) Potential pitfalls of affect convergence in teams: functions and dysfunctions of group affective tone. In Mannix EA, Neale MA (eds) Research on managing groups and teams, vol 10. Elsevier, Oxford, pp 97–123

Gibbs JC (2003) Moral development and reality: beyond the theory of kohlberg and hoffman. Sage, Thousand Oaks

Gibson C, Vermeulen F (2003) A healthy divide: subgroups as a stimulus for team learning behavior. Adm Sci Q 48(2):202–239

Goldstein AP, Michaels GY (1985) Empathy: development, training, and consequences. Erlbaum, Hilldsale

Harrison DA, Kravitz DA, Mayer DM, Leslie LM, Lev-Arey D (2006) Understanding attitudes toward affirmative action programs in employment: summary and meta-analysis of 35 years of research. J Appl Psychol 91(5):1013–1036

Harrison DA, Sin H-P (2006) What is diversity and how should it be measured? In: Konrad AM, Prasad P, Pringle JK (eds) Handbook of workplace diversity. Sage, Thousand Oaks, Inc., pp 191–216

Haslam SA (2004) Psychology in organizations—the social identity approach, 2 edn. Sage, London

Haslam SA, O'Brien A, Jetten J, Vormedal K, Penna S (2005) Taking the strain: social identity, social support, and the experience of stress. Br J Soc Psychol 44(3):355–370. doi:10.1348/014466605X37468

Haslam SA, van Dick R (2011) A social identity analysis of organizational well-being. In: Cremer DD, van Dick R, Murnighan JK (eds) Social psychology and organizations. Taylor & Francis, New York, pp 325–352

Hochschild AR (1983) The managed heart: commercialization of human feeling. University of California Press, Berkeley

Hoffman ML (2000) Empathy and moral development: implications for caring and justice. Cambridge University Press, New York

Homan AC, Hollenbeck JR, Humphrey SE, Van Knippenberg D, Ilgen DR, Van Kleef GA (2008) Facing differences with an open mind: openness to experience, salience of intragroup differences, and performance of diverse work groups. Acad Manag J 51(6):1204–1222

Jackson SE, Joshi A (2011) Work team diversity. In: Zedeck S (ed) Apa handbook of industrial and organizational psychology, vol 1. American Psychological Association, Washington, pp 651–686. (Building and developing the organization)

Joshi A, Roh H (2009) The role of context in work team diversity research: a meta-analytic review. Acad Manag J 52(3):599–627

Jost JT, Rudman LA, Blair IV, Carney DR, Dasgupta N, Glaser J, Hardin CD (2009) The existence of implicit bias is beyond reasonable doubt: a refutation of ideological and methodological objections and executive summary of ten studies that no manager should ignore. Res Organ Behav 29:39–69

Judge TA, Thoresen CJ, Bono JE, Patton GK (2001) The job satisfaction-job performance relationship: a qualitative and quantitative review. Psychol Bull 127(3):376–407

Kalev A, Dobbin F, Kelly E (2006) Best practices or best guesses? Assessing the efficacy of corporate affirmative action and diversity policies. Am Soc Rev 71(4):589–617

Kamdar D, McAllister DJ, Turban DB (2006) "All in a day's work": how follower individual differences and justice perceptions predict ocb role definitions and behavior. J Appl Psychol 91(4):841–855

Kearney E, Gebert D (2009) Managing diversity and enhancing team outcomes: the promise of transformational leadership. J Appl Psychol 94(1):77–89

Kearney E, Gebert D, Voelpel S (2008) When and how diversity benefits teams: the importance of team member's need for cognition. Acad Manag J 52:452–445

Kochan T, Bezrukova K, Ely R, Jackson S, Joshi A, Jehn K, Leonard J, Levine D, Thomas D (2003) The effects of diversity on business performance: report of the diversity research network. Hum Resour Manag 42(1):3–21

Kozlowski SWJ, Klein KJ (2000) A multilevel approach to theory and research in organizations: contextual, temporal, and emergent processes. In: Klein KJ, Kozlowski SWJ (eds) Multilevel theory, research, and methods in organizations: foundations, extensions, and new directions. Jossey-Bass, San Francisco, pp 3–90

Lazarus RS, Folkman S (1984) Stress, appraisal, and coping. Springer, New York

Livingstone A, Haslam S (2008) The importance of social identity content in a setting of chronic social conflict: understanding intergroup relations in northern ireland. Br J Soc Psychol 47(1):1–21

Losoya SH, Eisenberg N (2001) Affective empathy. In: Hall JA, Bernieri FJ (eds) Theory and measurement. Lawrence Erlbaum Associates Publishers, Mahwah, pp 21–43

Marci CD, Ham J, Moran E, Orr SP (2007) Physiologic correlates of perceived therapist empathy and social-emotional process during psychotherapy. J Nerv Ment Dis 195(2):103–111

McDougall W (1908) An introduction to social psychology. Methuen, London

McGarty C (2001) Social identity theory does not maintain that identification produces bias, and self-categorization theory does not maintain that salience is identification: two comments on mummendey, klink and brown. Br J Soc Psychol 40:173–176

Mesmer-Magnus JR, DeChurch LA (2009) Information sharing and team performance: a meta-analysis. J Appl Psychol 94(2):535–546

Milton LP, Westphal JD (2005) Identity confirmation networks and cooperation in groups. Acad Manag J 48(2):191–212

Motowidlo SJ (2003) Job performance. In: Borman WC, Ilgen DR, Klimoski RJ (eds) Handbook of psychology: industrial and organizational psychology, vol 12. Wiley, Hoboken, pp 39–53

Nelson DW, Klein CT, Irvin JE (2003) Motivational antecedents of empathy: inhibiting effects of fatigue. Basic Appl Soc Psychol 25(1):37–50

Pacala JT, Boult C, Bland C, O'Brien J (1995) Aging game improves medical students caring for elders. Gerontol Geriatr Educ 15(4):45–57

Park B, Judd CM (2005) Rethinking the link between categorization and prejudice within the social cognition perspective. Pers Soc Psychol Rev 9(2):108–130

Pendry LF, Driscoll DM, Field SCT (2007) Diversity training: putting theory into practice. J Occup Organ Psychol 80(1):27–50

Pettigrew TF, Tropp LR (2008) How does intergroup contact reduce prejudice? Meta-analytic tests of three mediators. Eur J Soc Psychol 38(6):922–934. doi:10.1002/ejsp.504

Phillips KW, Lount RB (2007) The affective consequences of diversity and homogeneity in groups. In: Mannix EA, Neale MA, Anderson CP (eds) Research on managing groups and teams: affect and groups, vol 10. Elsevier, Oxford, pp 1–20

Phillips KW, Rothbard NP, Dumas TL (2009) To disclose or not to disclose? Status distance and self-disclosure in diverse environments. Acad Manag Rev 34(4):710–732

Podsakoff NP, Whiting SW, Podsakoff PM, Blume BD (2009) Individual- and organizational-level consequences of organizational citizenship behaviors: a meta-analysis. J Appl Psychol 94(1):122–141

Reiter-Palmon R, Wiener RL, Ashley G, Winter RJ, Smith RM, Richter EM, Voss-Humke A (2008) The effects of empathy on judgments of sexual harassment complaints. In: Ashkanasy NM, Zerbe WJ, Härtel CEJ (eds) Emotions, ethics and decision-making, vol 4. Emerald Group Publishing Limited, Bingley, pp 285–310. (Research on Emotion in Organizations)

Roberge M-É (2009) When and how does diversity increase group performance? A theoretical model followed by an experimental study. VCM

Roberge M-É, van Dick R (2010). Recognizing the benefits of diversity: when and how does diversity increase group performance? Hum Resour Manag Rev 20(4):295–308

Schur L, Kruse D, Blanck P (2005) Corporate culture and the employment of persons with disabilities. Behav Sci Law 23(1):3–20

Settoon RP, Mossholder KW (2002). Relationship quality and relationship context as antecedents of person- and task-focused interpersonal citizenship behavior. J Appl Psychol 87(2):255–267

Shemla M, Wegge J, Kearney E, Schraub E-M (2010) Does perceiving differences in teams make us feel less alike? The moderating role of diversity and identification on affective linkages in work teams. Unpublished Manuscript, Technische Universität Dresden. Dresden, Germany

Stahl GK, Maznevski ML, Voigt A, Jonsen K (2010) Unraveling the effects of cultural diversity in teams: a meta-analysis of research on multicultural work groups. J Int Bus Stud 41:690–709. doi:10.1057/jibs.2009.85

Stegmann S (2011) Engaging with diversity of social units—a social identity perspective on diversity in organizations (Dissertation). Goethe University, Frankfurt a. M., Germany

Stephan WG, Finlay K (1999) The role of empathy in improving intergroup relations. J Soc Issues 55(4):729–743

Tajfel H, Billig MG, Bundy RP, Flament C (1971) Social categorization and intergroup behaviour. Eur J Soc Psychol 1(2):149–178

Tajfel H, Turner JC (1979) An integrative theory of intergroup conflict. In: Austin WG, Worchel S (eds) The social psychology of intergroup relations. Brooks, Monterey, pp 33–47

Tajfel H, Turner JC (1986) The social identity theory of intergroup behavior. In: Worchel S, Austin WG (eds) Psychology of intergroup relations, 2 edn. Nelson-Hall, Chicago, pp 7–24

Todd AR, Hanko K, Galinsky AD, Mussweiler T (2011) When focusing on differences leads to similar perspectives. Psychol Sci 22(1):134–141. doi:10.1177/0956797610392929

Turner JC, Hogg MA, Oakes PJ, Reicher SD, Wetherell MS (1987) Rediscovering the social group: a self-categorization theory. Basil Blackwell, Inc., Cambridge

van der Vegt GS, Bunderson JS (2005) Learning and performance in multidisciplinary teams: the importance of collective team identification. Acad Manag J 48(3):532–547

van Knippenberg D, Haslam SA (2003) Realizing the diversity dividend: exploring the subtle interplay between identity, ideology, and reality. In: Haslam SA, van Knippenberg D, Platow MJ, Ellemers N (eds) Social identity at work: developing theory for organizational practice. Psychology Press, New York, pp 61–77

van Knippenberg D, Schippers M (2007) Work group diversity. Annu Rev Psychol 58:515–541

van Knippenberg D, De Dreu CKW, Homan AC (2004) Work group diversity and group performance: an integrative model and research agenda. J Appl Psychol 89(6):1008–1022

van Knippenberg D, Haslam SA, Platow MJ (2007) Unity through diversity: value-in-diversity beliefs, work group diversity, and group identification. Group Dyn: Theory Res Pract 11(3): 207–222

Williams KY, O'Reilly CA III (1998). Demography and diversity in organizations: a review of 40 years of research. In Staw B, Sutton R (eds) Research in organizational behavior: an annual series of analytical essays and critical reviews, vol 20. JAI Press, Greenwich, pp 77–140

Wolsko C, Park B, Judd CM, Wittenbrink B (2000) Framing interethnic ideology: effects of multicultural and color-blind perspectives on judgments of groups and individuals. J Pers Soc Psychol 78(4):635–654

ZfB-SPECIAL ISSUE 2/2012

Managing demographic change and diversity in organizations: how feedback from coworkers moderates the relationship between age and innovative work behavior

Stefan Schaffer · Eric Kearney · Sven C. Voelpel · Ralf Koester

Abstract: In a field study of 211 employees of a midsized German high-tech company, useful feedback from coworkers was examined as a moderator of the relationship between age and supervisor ratings of radical innovative work behavior. When employees perceived higher levels of useful feedback from their coworkers, the relationship between age and radical innovative work behavior followed an inverted U-shape. This inverted U-shaped relationship was decreasingly manifested as the level of perceived useful feedback from coworkers dropped. Given demographic change and the aging of the workforce of many organizations, this finding broadens the still fragmentary knowledge of the conditions under which aging is likely to have more or less positive effects on innovative work behavior. The authors discuss the theoretical and practical implications of these results on both the individual and the team level of analysis.

© Gabler-Verlag 2011

Dipl.-Kfm. S. Schaffer (✉) · Prof. Dr. S. C. Voelpel
Jacobs University Bremen, Campus Ring 1,
28759 Bremen, Germany
e-mail: s.schaffer@jacobs-university.de

Prof. Dr. S. C. Voelpel
e-mail: s.voelpel@jacobs-university.de

Prof. Dr. E. Kearney
Organizational Behavior & Human Resource Management,
GISMA Business School/Leibniz Universität Hannover,
Goethestraße 18, 30169 Hannover, Germany
e-mail: ekearney@gisma.com

Dr. R. Koester
GISMA Business School, Goethestraße 18, 30169 Hannover, Germany
e-mail: rkoester@gisma.com

Keywords: Age · Innovative work behavior · Demography · Diversity · Feedback

JEL Classification: M10 · M12

The globalization of the world's economies challenges organizations with an increasingly competitive, complex, and turbulent environment (Bigoness and Perreault 1981; Howell and Higgins 1990; Mumford 2000). In such times of change, the ability to innovate is seen as a crucial determinant of organizational performance in terms of growth, competitiveness, and even survival (Cooper 1990; Janssen et al. 2004; Amabile 1988; Kanter 1988). Because of this importance of organizational innovativeness for both firms and economies, research on the facilitators of innovation has flourished over the last decades (see Anderson et al. 2004 for a major review). So far, however, this strand of research has paid very little attention to one of the major phenomena currently taking place in Western countries: demographic change. Indeed, very little is known about the effects of an aging workforce on organizational innovativeness (Lawrence 1996; Moody 2006).

In times of demographic change, the proportions of the different age cohorts within a society shift (Leibold and Voelpel 2006). More precisely, declining birthrates, increasing life-expectancy, as well as the aging of the baby-boom generation lead to an aging society in most Western countries (Kanfer and Ackerman 2004). In the German case, for example, the shifts of the different age cohorts are massive: While the group of 60-years-and-older will represent 40% of the population in the year 2050 (compared to 24% in the year 2000), the proportion of the 19-years-and-younger group will drop from 21% to 16% (Leibold and Voelpel 2006; Voelpel et al. 2007). By 2050, half of the population will be older than 50 years. This also affects the workforce of most organizations: In Germany, the group of employees below 30 will decrease by 40%, the group of employees between 35 and 44 will decrease by 27%, and the group of employees above 45 will increase by 25% (Voelpel et al. 2007).

Why then is it important to study demographic change and age within research on organizational innovativeness? Findings from life span psychology show that aging entails a plethora of age-related changes and developments that are likely to affect work processes and outcomes (Kanfer and Ackerman 2004). For example, aging may be related to changes in cognitive abilities, experience, interests, values, and motivation (Kanfer and Ackerman 2004), which may influence the way innovative ideas are developed, promoted, discussed, modified, and/or implemented within organizations (Anderson et al. 2004). However, very little is known about the details of this age-innovation relationship. Does—according to widespread belief—aging really result in declining innovativeness? How are innovation processes of organizations affected by age-related demographic changes? Should an aging workforce be understood as an opportunity or a threat to innovation? Answering these hitherto unexplored questions will help organizations better understand how an aging workforce affects their innovative outcomes and what can be done to maintain and improve innovative performance in times of demographic change.

Studying demographic change and age also marks an important step towards a better understanding within the diversity research context. When societies and workforces undergo demographic change, their compositions change with respect to certain attributes, such as age. For example, shortages on the labor market may force a company that has previously hired only young employees—because they are stereotyped as more technologically savvy and willing to adapt (Ng and Feldman 2008; Posthuma and Campion 2009)—to employ older workers as well. In another example, a company with a lot of employees from the aging baby-boom generation might decide to recruit very young workers to counterbalance an aging of its workforce. In either case, as the age distribution within these companies' workforces changes, so does the level of their organizational age diversity (Harrison and Klein 2007). Demographic change and an aging society may therefore be understood as a cause of shifting diversity levels within organizations and, ultimately, of the positive and negative effects on work processes and outcomes as discussed in the diversity literature (Williams and O'Reilly 1998; Van Knippenberg et al. 2004; Van Knippenberg and Schippers 2007). In essence, then, insights on the age-innovation relationship may help organizations to identify the innovation specific chances/risks of age diverse workforces and to unlock the innovation potential inherent in such workforces.

The aim of this study is to expand knowledge on the age-innovation relationship and to give practical advice for the management of an aging workforce. As we will show in the course of this paper, extant research on creativity and innovation suggests that innovative work behavior simultaneously requires different components, such as knowledge and motivation (Amabile 1983a, 1983b, 1988). According to studies from life span research, these components may vary with age (Kanfer and Ackerman 2004). Combining these two strands of research and acknowledging the fact that innovative work behavior also depends on contextual factors (Zhou 2003; Shalley et al. 2004), we propose that the relationship between age and radical innovative work behavior follows an inverted U-shape under certain conditions. Based in this premise, we introduce useful feedback from coworkers as an important contextual characteristic and explain how it may lead to a curvilinear age-innovation relationship. We then propose that the inverted U-shaped relationship between age and radical innovative work behavior will be decreasingly manifested as the level of perceived useful feedback from coworkers drops and that employees who perceive lower levels of useful feedback from their coworkers will display lower levels of radical innovative work behavior at intermediate age than employees perceiving higher levels of useful feedback from coworkers.

1 Theoretical background and hypotheses

1.1 Innovative work behavior

In times of rapid change and heightened competition, organizational innovativeness is one of the major drivers of organizational performance (Davenport et al. 2006). Accordingly, research on innovation and its facilitators has developed considerably over the past decades. For example, Scott and Bruce (1994) show how leadership, individual problem solving style, and support for innovation are related to innovative work behavior; Spreitzer (1995) points out the role of psychological empowerment. In a more general review of the literature, Anderson et al. (2004) summarize the major facilitators of innovative work behavior at the individual and at the team level of analysis. These include, for example (Anderson et al. 2004): personality (e.g., tolerance of ambiguity, openness to experience), motivation (e.g., intrinsic, determination to succeed), cognitive ability (e.g., divergent thinking style, ideational fluency), job characteristics (e.g., autonomy, job demands), team structure (e.g., cohesiveness, longevity), team climate (e.g., conflict, constructive controversy), team member characteristics (e.g., heterogeneity, educational level), team processes (e.g., reflexivity, integration skills), and leadership (e.g., democratic style, participative style).

In line with previous studies, we define innovative work behavior as the intentional generation, promotion, and implementation of new ideas within a work role, work group or organization, in order to benefit role performance, the group or the organization (West and Farr 1990; Kanter 1988; West and Farr 1989; Janssen and Van Yperen 2004; Scott and Bruce 1994). Since it is individuals or teams who ultimately generate, promote, and/or implement innovative ideas (Van de Ven 1986, Scott and Bruce 1994), we follow extant organizational behavior research in adapting an understanding of innovation that focuses on the behavioral activities of the innovation process instead of on the innovation itself. Innovation differs from creativity in a way that it includes an idea's *implementation* into new products, processes or services over and above the sole *generation* of a novel, potentially useful idea (Shalley et al. 2004). In this study, we especially focus on work behavior related to radical innovations—major, dramatic improvements characterized by high degrees of novelty in contrast to modest, more evolutionary changes (Gemünden et al. 2007; Rice et al. 2001; Mumford and Gustafson 1988; Sheremata 2000). By doing so, we do not make an assumption about the value of incremental or radical innovations, but rather take into account the fact that the same causal factors might not operate in a similar manner regardless of the type of innovation (George 2007). Clearly, extant research suggests that radical innovative work behavior may require different conditions and processes than incremental innovative work behavior (Sheremata 2000). For example, in the research context of this study, the willingness to engage in work behavior characterized by doubtful and risky outcomes (e.g., radical innovative work behavior) might develop differently with age than the willingness to engage in work behavior with more predictable consequences (e.g., incremental innovative work behavior). In line with extant research, our definition finally assumes that employees in any job and at any level of the organization may engage in innovative job behavior (Shalley et al. 2004).

1.2 Age and its relation with radical innovative work behavior

1.2.1 Defining age

Given the demographic change in Western countries, aging workforces and older employees are becoming an increasingly important concern for many organizations (Ng and Feldman 2008). But what exactly is meant by "age" and who is a "younger/middle-aged/older worker"? In our study, we measure and analyze age as a continuous variable. Specifically, we focus on chronological age as opposed to subjective age or social age (Cleveland and Shore 1992). The question of who a "younger", "middle-aged" or "older worker" is has been debated in the literature for quite some time (Ng and Feldman 2008). In line with extant research, we will use the age of 40 as a cutoff value in our discussion (e.g., Thornton and Dumke 2005; Ng and Feldman 2008). This is due to two major reasons: First, active workforces are usually between 16 and 65 years old and, therefore, 40 years seems to be an appropriate choice for a dichotomous split (Ng and Feldman 2008). Second, career researchers have found that the chronological age of 40 commonly marks a major transition in work lives (Super 1980). In summary, then, we refer to 40 as "middle-age"/"intermediate age" and to the age groups <40 years of age and >40 of age as "younger" and "older", respectively. Please note, however, that our statistical analyses use a continuous measure of age.

Studies on innovative work behavior including chronological age (typically as a control variable) mostly show no effect of age on innovative work behavior (e.g., Janssen 2000, 2001; Miron et al. 2004). Similarly, a meta-analysis by Ng and Feldman (2008) finds no significant relationship between age and creativity, an important precursor of innovation. We propose that such inconsistent findings are due to three major reasons: (1) Previous research finds cumulative support for the notion that chronological age is merely a proxy or "muddied" indicator for a large number of age-related developments and processes that exert diverse, indirect, and sometimes even opposing effects on work outcomes (Kanfer and Ackerman 2004; Hambrick and Mason 1984; Davies et al. 1991; Hansson et al. 1997; Sterns and Miklos 1995; Warr 2001). When studying age and its effect on work outcomes, one should therefore carefully consider age-related changes in relevant domains such as cognitive abilities, work motivation, and knowledge level to better understand, predict, and test the proposed age effects (Kanfer and Ackerman 2004). (2) Since innovative work behavior simultaneously requires different components (Amabile 1983a, 1983b, 1988) and since these components follow different trajectories with age (Kanfer and Ackerman 2004), one should also consider the relationship between age and innovation to be curvilinear in nature rather than linear. (3) Existing studies that include both age and innovative work behavior in their research design actually focus on non-demographic predictors of innovative work behavior (e.g., Janssen 2000, 2001; Miron et al. 2004). Because age is included as a control variable, these studies do not explicitly hypothesize or test moderators of the age-innovation relationship. Specific theory and testing are therefore needed to examine the conditions under which aging either benefits or impedes innovative work behavior.

Our study addresses these shortcomings of extant research: We explicitly consider life span findings on age-related changes and developments to hypothesize a moderated, curvilinear age-innovation relationship. In doing so, we will first identify the relevant drivers for innovative work behavior on the basis of Amabile's (1983a, 1983b, 1988) componential model. We will then use findings from life span research to show how these different components may relate to age and how contextual moderators might affect this relationship.

1.2.2 A componential model for innovative work behavior

In her work on creativity and innovation, Amabile (e.g., 1983a, 1983b, 1988) defines three components necessary for creative and innovative work behavior: creativity-relevant skills, intrinsic motivation, and domain-relevant skills. The first component, determining how flexibly people approach problems, depends on an individual's personality and on how someone thinks and works (Amabile 1998). Since we examine radical innovative work behavior in this study, we will focus on cognitive skills and abilities within the component of creativity-relevant skills. Such cognitive skills and abilities include, for example, understanding and processing complexities/novelties, abstract thinking, search memory, and the ability to break one's set during problem solving (e.g., Lubart 1999). We believe that—in comparison to other subfactors of the creativity-relevant skills component like tolerance for ambiguity or feeling comfortable disagreeing with others—an individual's cognitive "capacity" (Amabile 1998) is an especially hard requirement for major, dramatic, and complex improvements. The second component refers to intrinsic motivation—an inner passion to solve the problem at hand (Amabile 1998). Such a person's internal desire to do something has been found to be more conducive to creative and innovative work behavior than extrinsic motivation coming from outside a person (e.g., monetary rewards) (Amabile 1983a, 1983b, 1988, 1998). The last component, domain-relevant skills, encompasses individual expertise, experience, technical skills, knowledge relevant to the task domain (e.g., Lubart 1999). In Amabile's (e.g., 1983a, 1983b, 1988) model, all components are likewise necessary for creative work behavior and highest levels of creativity are expected when the three components overlap (Amabile 1998).

As explained previously, innovative work behavior is the extension of creative work behavior as it refers to an idea's generation ("creativity"), promotion, and implementation. In other words, innovative work behavior comprises creative work behavior. Therefore and because past studies have shown that the theoretical subdimensions of innovative work behavior intercorrelate very highly (Janssen 2001; Janssen and Van Yperen 2004), we assume that Amabile's componential model (1983a, 1983b, 1988) also applies to innovative work behavior: Successfully generating, promoting, and implementing innovative ideas requires creativity-relevant skills, motivation, and domain-relevant skills. Mathematically speaking, we assume that the different components necessary for innovative work behavior are multiplicatively linked. We expect high levels of innovative work behavior when employees simultaneously possess creativity-relevant skills, motivation, and domain-relevant skills. In contrast, we expect lower levels of innovative work behavior when at least one component is low in value.

1.2.3 Age-related changes in the components necessary for innovative work behavior

A linear relation between age and innovative work behavior would be very likely if all processes and developments associated with aging were influencing the three components in the same direction—either positively or negatively. While extant research shows that older employees do in fact differ from younger employees in a number of ways that could potentially influence their innovative work behavior, the effects are by no means unidirectional (Kanfer and Ackerman 2004).

Our understanding of Amabile's first component as cognitive abilities for (radical) innovative work behavior is very similar to a certain kind of intellectual abilities studied by life span researchers: fluid mechanics (Cattell 1971; Cattell 1987; Baltes et al. 2006). Fluid mechanics are associated with working memory, abstract reasoning, attention, and processing of novel information (Kanfer and Ackerman 2004) and are closely linked to neurobiological brain conditions (Baltes et al. 2006). According to life span research, these fluid mechanics decline over the life span after having reached a maximum somewhere in the (early) twenties (Cattell 1987; Wechsler 1944; Schaie 1996; Baltes et al. 2006; Kanfer and Ackerman 2004). Transferring these findings to the creativity and innovation context, life span research suggests that the creativity-relevant skills component of the componential model may decline over an employee's working life. Such a decline in fluid mechanics/creativity-relevant skills will most likely impede radical innovative work behavior as aging employees will find it increasingly difficult to understand, process, and combine thus far unrelated concepts into new and abstract ideas. We expect that a decline in fluid mechanics will particularly affect radical innovative work behavior because radical innovations are characterized by especially high demands on flexibility and adaptability (Sheremata 2000).

According to the second component of Amabile's (1983a, 1983b, 1988) model, successfully generating, promoting, discussing, modifying, and implementing creative ideas also encompasses a number of cognitive and social activities requiring an employee's intrinsic motivation to innovate (Kanter 1988; Amabile 1983a, 1983b, 1988). Specifically, employees must be willing to direct their resources and efforts towards innovating, which is often associated with uncertain results and the risk of failure (George 2007). West and Farr (1989) therefore speak of "high growth needs" for innovative work behavior. Like in the case of the first component, results from life span research help to understand the influence of age on the motivational component of innovative work behavior. Kanfer and Ackerman (2004) suggest that certain dynamics of aging and adult development—such as changes in personality, values, motives, and interests—influence work motivation. Openness to experience, for example, shows a mean decline with age and older adults appear, on average, less change oriented (Kanfer and Ackerman 2004; Warr et al. 2001). Achievement motives also show mean declines with age; vocational interests and values may shift from a preference for job variety towards an increased preference for job security and a "world at peace" (Kanfer and Ackerman 2004; Warr 1997; Warr 2001). Additionally, Ebner et al. (2006) were able to empirically track developmental changes in personal goal orientation: Younger adults reported a primary orientation towards growth and older adults reported a stronger orientation toward maintenance and loss prevention. These goal orientations, in return, are associated with creative and innovative work behavior such that individuals with an orientation towards growth are more innovative than those with an orientation towards prevention (Friedman and Förster 2001). Hence, we argue that age-related changes in personality, values, motives, interests, and goals may—at a sooner or later point in time—begin to lower the motivational drive of aging employees when it comes to radical innovative work behavior.

It is important to note that we don't posit an overall motivational decline with age; instead, we acknowledge the fact that the level of intrinsic motivation for innovation may very well depend on the level of innovativeness (i.e., radical vs. incremental). For instance, an aging employee with increasing amounts of accumulated assets (e.g., reputation, position within the organizational hierarchy) and/or higher amounts of social commitments (e.g., marriage, parenthood) might be in search of predictability and control in the workplace. Because levels of uncertainty as well as risks of failure increase with rising levels of innovativeness (similar Sheremata 2000), this employee may be less motivated to engage in *radical* innovative work behavior. However, to the extent that this employee has gained knowledge and practice with age, he/she may be increasingly successful and experienced with modest, evolutionary improvements. This, in return, may lead to higher levels of self-efficacy and to higher levels of intrinsic motivation for incremental innovative work behavior.

We also acknowledge the fact that the assumed decline of intrinsic motivation for radical innovative work behavior does not necessarily begin as early as the decline of fluid mechanics. Depending on individual differences and contextual factors, the motivation for radical innovative work behavior can also be stable or even increase in earlier stages of a working life. We will pick up this thought in the next section when we introduce a potential contextual moderator of the age-innovation relationship.

According to Amabile's componential model (1983a, 1983b, 1988), domain-relevant skills make up the third necessary component for innovative work behavior. Like in the case of creativity-relevant skills, the definition of this component is closely related to a certain type of intellectual abilities studied in life span research: crystallized pragmatics (Cattell 1971, 1987; Baltes et al. 2006). Crystallized pragmatics represent broad aspects of educational or experiential knowledge—specifically including occupational (job) knowledge (Kanfer and Ackerman 2004; Ackerman 1996; Cattell 1987; Baltes et al. 2006). In contrast to fluid mechanics, measures of crystallized pragmatics increase well over the life span and researchers have found a strong positive association between adult age and knowledge level, the third component necessary for innovative work behavior (Kanfer and Ackerman 2004; Cattell 1987; Ackerman 1996, 2000; Baltes et al. 2006). Accordingly, Jones (2005) finds that the age at which innovators produce noted innovations has increased significantly over the past century. The author argues that this is caused by the accumulation of knowledge in our societies and the necessity of innovators to seek more education over time before they can successfully innovate. Radical innovations, in particular, are characterized by an increased need for learning (Sheremata 2000). From this perspective, then, accumulated experience and knowledge of older employees facilitate radical innovative work behavior, because a good grasp of a field's understanding helps to identify and solve significant problems (Mumford and Gustafson 1988). Having said this, life span research suggests that the third component necessary for innovative work behavior, domain-relevant skills, may develop positively with age.

This latter finding is not only important because it clearly refutes the notion of universal decline with age, but also because it shows that the components necessary for radical innovative work behavior may develop differently over the life span. In summary, we posit that the creativity-relevant skills component for radical innovative work behavior will decline with age. While the development of the intrinsic motivation component will depend on individual differences and contextual factors, we expect declines of the motivation for radical innovative work behavior from a sooner or later point in time on. In contrast, we expect the domain-relevant skills component (represented by accumulated experience, job knowledge, etc.) to increase with age. Picking up what we have said earlier about the multiplicative link between the three components, we therefore expect high levels of radical innovative work behavior from middle-aged employees who are likely to possess fair values of all three components necessary for innovative work behavior. In contrast, the average younger worker will probably lack the necessary domain-relevant skills for such high levels of (successful) radical innovative work behavior. Arguably, young employees' high level of intrinsic motivation for innovation may compensate for lower levels of domain-relevant skills to a certain extent (through more work input, for example). However, we follow Amabile's argument that all components of her componential model are necessary for creative and innovative work behavior (1983a, 1983b, 1988) and assume that the abundance of one or two components cannot fully compensate the lack of another. We therefore also expect lower levels of radical innovative work behavior from older workers as compared to middle-aged employees: Despite rather high levels of domain-relevant skills, the average older will probably be affected by declining levels of both the creativity-relevant skills component and the motivational component.

Under the condition that the three components necessary for innovative work behavior follow the indicated loss and growth trajectories, we expect a curvilinear relationship between age and radical innovative work behavior (inverted U-shape). However, as implied by the phrase "under the condition", the age-related changes in the components necessary for innovation are not fully predefined. Before stating our final hypotheses, we therefore need to consider the possibility that the age-related trajectories also depend on external influences. For example, an aging employee might accumulate less domain-relevant skills as expected because of low interest in/attention towards the task, which may result in less learning and less domain-specific development. In such a case, the loss trajectories are not accompanied by rising levels of domain-relevant skills. In a second example, an employee might find himself/herself in a context that boosts the motivation for radical innovative work behavior, resulting in a faster acquisition of domain-relevant knowledge and an extended retention of motivation for innovation. We therefore expect changes in the form of the age-innovation relationship to the extent that contextual variables influence the age-related developments of the components necessary for radical innovative work behavior. In the following section we specifically introduce useful feedback from coworkers as a moderator of the age-innovation relationship before stating our final hypotheses.

1.3 Useful feedback from coworkers as a moderator of the relationship between age and radical innovative work behavior

Extant research suggests that while certain personal characteristics are predictive of creative and innovative work behavior (Shalley et al. 2004), it is also important to look at contextual factors that interact with these personal characteristics (Oldham and Cummings 1996; Amabile 1988; Woodman et al. 1993; Shalley et al. 2004). For example, Oldham and Cummings (1996) point out the importance of job complexity and supervisory style; Zhou (2003) suggests creative role models as a contextual factor. Shalley et al. (2004) additionally mention relationships with coworkers, rewards, evaluation, time deadlines and goals, as well as spatial configurations of work settings as important contextual characteristics that might affect innovative work behavior. We want to tie in with this line of research by introducing useful feedback as a moderator of the relationship between age and radical innovative work behavior. We believe that feedback is an important context variable when researching the age-innovation relationship because it carries the potential to influence two of the components necessary for radical innovative work behavior: the acquisition of domain-relevant skills as well as the motivation to engage in innovative work behavior. In the first instance and according to the feedback and creativity literatures, useful feedback promotes an employee's attention towards/interest in a task and fosters an orientation towards learning and development, which may lead to the acquisition of domain related knowledge (Zhou and George 2001; Kluger and DeNisi 1996; Zhou 1998; Utman 1997). Such orientation towards learning and the development of competence is especially important for radical innovative work behavior, for which the requisite knowledge and strategies might have yet to be learned (Janssen and Van Yperen 2004; Sheremata 2000). In the second instance, useful feedback may signal interest in improvements and change to the feedback receiving employee, who then feels supported and motivated to generate and implement creative ideas (Zhou and George 2001; Farr and Ford 1990; Zhou 2003). More precisely, useful feedback may cause an employee to perceive innovative work behavior as more effective than in a situation without feedback, thereby positively influencing the perceived effort-utility and performance-utility functions and, ultimately, increasing the employee's willingness to engage in work behaviors that involve substantial levels of effort (Zhou and George 2001; Kanfer and Ackerman 2004). Since feedback is primarily a way of supplying employees with information about his/her performance on the job (Zhou and George 2001), feedback may also increase the feedback receiving employee's perceived psychological empowerment. This is important because empowered employees have been found to display higher levels of (motivation for) innovative work behavior (Spreitzer 1995). Specifically, empowered individuals feel less constrained and more efficacious and autonomous, which may lead to higher levels of (motivation for) innovative work behavior in return (Spreitzer 1995; Amabile 1988; Redmond et al. 1993). Similarly, the informational part of useful feedback may positively influence an employee's perceived ability to perform a task—either by reinforcing a sense of competence or by showing what decisions need to be made (and what behavioral actions need to be taken) in order to improve performance (Spreitzer 1995; Zhou 2003). According to Vroom's (1964) expectancy theory, this may augment an employees' motivation via the confidence that employees have in themselves. In summary, useful feedback is likely to boost intrinsic motivation (Zhou 2003; Deci and Ryan 1985).

Within the innovation context, coworkers are a good source for useful and informational feedback (Zhou and George 2001). Coworkers working within the same group or team spend working time together and probably have a good understanding of the different tasks within the team. Chances are high that their language is well understood by their colleagues and that the feedback they provide is relevant, at the appropriate level of abstraction, and comprehensible. Because coworkers often work within the same hierarchical level, employees can pose follow-up questions and engage in a real feedback-exchange without having to fear sanctions from his/her boss. Of course, supervisor feedback can be equally as useful and informational as coworker feedback (Zhou 2003). However, such cross-hierarchical feedback can also create problems. For instance, followers might not dare to critically analyze or even challenge their supervisors' words. Supervisor feedback that is meant as an input for further thoughts may be understood as an order; employees are reluctant to pose follow-up questions because they are afraid to "lose face" and, ultimately, their job. In essence, supervisor feedback runs the risk of being interpreted as supervisor close monitoring. This refers to supervisors keeping a close check on their employees and making sure that they do exactly what they are told (Zhou 2003). As a consequence of supervisor close monitoring, employees feel constantly watched, evaluated, and controlled, which may undermine their intrinsic motivation for innovative work behavior and the motivation to acquire domain-specific knowledge (Zhou 2003; Zhou and George 2001; Deci and Ryan 1985). In the current study, we therefore focus on feedback from coworkers.

In line with extant research, we define useful feedback from coworkers as helpful or valuable information provided by coworkers that enables an employee to make improvements on the job (Zhou and George 2001). As put forth earlier, high levels of useful feedback have a twofold positive effect on the components necessary for radical innovative work behavior: Useful feedback promotes the acquisition of domain-relevant knowledge and also supports an employee's motivation to innovate. Therefore, under the condition of high levels of useful feedback from coworkers, the age-related loss of creativity-relevant skills is complemented by a strong age-related growth in domain-relevant skills. Also, high levels of useful feedback from coworkers may stabilize the potentially negative development of the motivational component with age. In such a situation, we expect high levels of radical innovative work behavior at middle age, when employees possess fair levels of all three components necessary for innovative work behavior. At younger age, lower levels of radical innovative work behavior are expected because employees are likely to lack the necessary domain-relevant skills. As employees age under the condition of high levels of useful feedback from coworkers, they develop considerable levels of domain-relevant skills while retaining rather high levels of intrinsic motivation for innovation. This leads to rising levels of radical innovative work behavior up to a point where declining levels of creativity-relevant skills begin to kick in. This effect of declining levels of creativity-relevant skills begins to override the other two components and the overall level of radical innovative work behavior declines. We therefore posit:

Hypothesis 1: Under the condition of high levels of useful feedback from coworkers, the relationship between age and radical innovative work behavior is curvilinear (inverted U-shape).

Arguably, increasing levels of domain-relevant skills may compensate for losses in creativity-relevant skills (similar Kanfer and Ackerman 2004). However, we do not believe that such a compensation mechanism changes the shape of the proposed inverted U-shaped relationship. This is due to the fact that—at very high levels of domain-relevant skills—employees will probably reach a point where prior knowledge and experience no longer act as enablers of radical innovative work behavior but rather as blinders. In such a case, familiar theories and practices might cause employees to remain on the track of established reasoning when solving problems, finding it increasingly difficult to look at things in a new and innovative way (Mumford and Gustafson 1988; Lehman 2006). Similarly, Wu et al. (2005) argue that past experience may lead to functional fixedness, in which problems are no longer solved in unusual and creative ways. In essence, then, the relationship between age and radical innovative work behavior will still follow the proposed U-shape when the described compensation mechanism is at work.

Similarly, one could argue that high levels of intrinsic motivation—evoked through high levels of useful feedback, for example—are able to compensate for declines in fluid mechanics/creativity-relevant skills through increased effort. Even though we acknowledge this possibility, we do not believe that it changes the proposed U-shaped relationship. First, more effort will probably not be able to fully compensate declining abilities. Second, declining performance in the face of increased effort is likely to undermine self-efficacy and self-concept, eventually leading to reduced work motivation (Kanfer and Ackerman 2004).

Hypothesis 1 made an assumption about the curvilinear shape of the age-innovation relationship at a fixed—high—value of the moderator. We now turn to lower levels of useful feedback from coworkers. A work context with lower levels of useful feedback from coworkers will most likely reduce an employee's attention towards as well as interest in a task; the orientation towards learning and development is likely to suffer and less or no domain-related skills are acquired (Zhou and George 2001; Kluger and DeNisi 1996; Zhou 1998; Utman 1997). In other words, a decreasing level of useful feedback from coworkers will probably impede the acquisition of domain-related skills, causing this component for radical innovative work behavior to be less associated with age-related growth than before. Also, with lower levels of useful feedback from coworkers, an employee's motivational component will probably suffer. Similar to our earlier argument, we assume that less useful feedback from coworkers negatively influences an employee's motivation to engage in innovative work behavior via changes in the perceived effort-utility/performance-utility functions, lower levels of perceived psychological empowerment as well as through lower levels of perceived ability to perform a task (Kanfer and Ackerman 2004; Vroom 1964; Spreitzer 1995; Zhou and George 2001; Zhou 2003). We therefore assume that decreasing levels of useful feedback from coworkers change the form of the relationship between age and radical innovative work behavior. More specifically: As employees age under the condition of lower levels of useful feedback, they probably acquire less domain relevant-skills as compared to a situation of higher levels of feedback. This special component that carries the potential to increase levels of radical innovative work behavior becomes less effective. In addition, the motivational component's potential age-related decline is not buffered by coworker feedback. Hence, under the condition of lower levels of useful feedback, the age-related losses in creativity-relevant skills and motivation gain influence in determining the overall level of radical innovative work behavior. The age-related growth of domain-relevant skills, on the other hand, loses influence. Graphically speaking, the inverted U-shaped relationship between age and radical innovative work behavior is expected to flatten with decreasing levels of perceived useful feedback from coworkers. This leads to the following hypotheses:

Hypothesis 2: Useful feedback from coworkers moderates the inverted U-shaped relationship between age and radical innovative work behavior such that this curvilinear relationship is decreasingly manifested as the level of perceived useful feedback from coworkers drops.

Hypothesis 3: Useful feedback from coworkers moderates the inverted U-shaped relationship between age and radical innovative work behavior such that employees who perceive lower levels of useful feedback from their coworkers will display lower levels of radical innovative work behavior at middle age than employees perceiving higher levels of useful feedback from coworkers.

2 Method

2.1 Sample

We collected data in a German mid-sized high-tech company as part of a broader study on employee innovative work behavior. The company is considered a world market leader in its field and has won numerous rewards for its breakthrough innovations, which relate to both products/services and processes. For example, the company was officially decorated as a "TOP 100 Innovator" and "Hidden Champion". Because innovative products, services, and processes are the foundation of the company's success, innovative work behavior is expected from *all* employees. Correspondingly, past innovations have come from many different departments (e.g., innovative products from R&D, breakthrough service models from Sales and Product Management, innovative production methods from Manufacturing). We therefore invited all 256 employees of the company's biggest site to participate in our study. Service providers whose job did not relate to the business purpose of the company were excluded (e.g., cleaning staff).

Of the 256 employees, 211 filled in a paper-pencil survey that included the independent and the control variables of the study. The resulting response rate was 82%. After 6 months, the dependent variable—radical innovative work behavior—was rated by 37 direct supervisors of the respective employees. Based on Brislin's (1980) translation-back-translation procedure, surveys for employees as well as for supervisors included all items in German translations. The mean age of the sample was 39.83 years (SD = 11.69) ranging from 16 to 61 years. The share of workers in the different age groups were: < 20 (3.8%), 20–29 (16.5%), 30–39 (25.9%), 40–49 (27.4%), > 50 (26.4%). The organizational tenure of the participants ranged from less than 1 year to 33 years averaging 11.70 years (SD = 9.18). 34% of the participants were women. Most participants (74.1%) had a dual education system degree (combination of in-firm training and vocational education).

2.2 Measures

Useful feedback from coworkers was measured with Zhou and George's (2001) three useful feedback from coworkers items: "I find the feedback I receive from my coworkers very useful", "My coworkers provide me with valuable information about how to improve my job performance", "The feedback I receive from my coworkers helps me improve my job performance". We used a response format ranging from 1 (strongly disagree) to 5 (strongly agree). The three items were averaged for an overall score ($\alpha = 0.90$). Data on *age* were measured in years.

Six months after the collection of the other data, *radical innovative work behavior* was measured with supervisor ratings concerning the criteria used in previous research (Janssen 2000, 2001): Idea generation (three items), idea promotion (three items), and idea implementation (three items). Supervisors were specifically instructed to rate the employees regarding their *radical* innovative work behavior. A "radical" innovation was defined as an innovation that is completely new and differs fundamentally from existing ideas, products, processes and/or methods. The items included, for example, "Generating original solutions to problems", "Mobilizing support for innovative ideas", and "Transforming innovative ideas into useful applications". The response format ranged from 1 ("never") to 5 ("always"). In line with previous research, a high reliability was reached for the innovative work behavior scale and the nine items were averaged for an overall score ($\alpha = 0.96$).

Control variables. We included four control variables that could conceivably influence the relationships we examined. Above all, we included *Tenure* because there is the possibility that tenure is confounded with age. Tenure was measured in years. *Gender* was measured dichotomously (1 = female; 2 = male) and *Educational Level* was measured on an eight-point scale ranging from 1 (secondary school) to 8 (PhD). Finally, we included *Hierarchical Position* within the organization as measured on a scale ranging from 1 (lowest level) to 5 (highest level).

2.3 Results

Table 1 presents the means, standard deviations, and correlations among all study variables. While age and useful feedback from coworkers are not linearly related to our measure of radical innovative work behavior, educational level (r=0.41, p<0.01), position in the organizational hierarchy (r=0.55, p<0.01), and gender (r=0.16, p<0.05) are positively related to the outcome scale. The negative correlation between age and useful feedback from coworkers (r=−0.28, p<0.01) is consistent with previous research stating that, over time, employees may place reduced importance on feedback (Warr 1997) and/or are offered less feedback (Greller and Simpson 1999)—an important finding which we will pick up in our discussion of the results.

In our sample, 37 supervisors provided performance ratings for the 211 employees. In other words, the 211 employees were nested in organizational units led by those 37 supervisors, creating a situation in which our observations were not independent of each other. Since this is a major assumption of the ordinary least squares (OLS) approach, we used clustered regression analysis (clustered robust standard errors method) to test our hypotheses. This method corrects the standard errors to account for the intraclass correlation (correlation between observations) as in our case of nested data. Without such a correction of standard errors, the significance tests would not be valid. To facilitate testing of quadratic and interaction effects, we used normalized independent variables throughout the analyses (Aiken and West 1991).

The procedure to test our hypotheses consists of the following three steps. We will first perform a clustered regression analysis of the independent and control variables on radical innovative work behavior. Since our hypotheses involve an interaction term (useful feedback from coworkers as a *moderator* of the age-innovation relationship) and the nature of such an interaction effect is by no means self-explanatory, we will then complement the clustered regression with a simple slope analysis. To better understand and interpret our findings, we will conclude with a figure that graphically illustrates the relationship

Table 1: Means, standard deviations, and correlations[a]

Variables	Mean	s.d.	1	2	3	4	5	6	7
1. Tenure	11.70	9.18							
2. Gender	1.66	0.48	−0.05						
3. Educational Level	3.97	1.30	−0.08	0.39**					
4. Position in Hierarchy	3.67	1.20	−0.06	0.27**	0.55**				
5. Age	39.83	11.69	0.64**	0.06	−0.09	0.03			
6. Feedback from Coworkers	3.82	0.92	−0.28**	0.09	0.03	0.13	−0.23**	(0.90)	
7. Radical Innovative Work Behavior	1.99	0.98	−0.13	0.16*	0.41**	0.55**	−0.10	0.08	(0.96)

*p<0.05; **p<0.01
[a] n=211. Coefficient alpha reliabilities are in parentheses along the diagonal

between age and radical innovative work behavior at different levels of useful feedback from coworkers.

In the theory section of our paper, we hypothesized a curvilinear relationship between age and radical innovative work behavior contingent upon the level of useful feedback from coworkers. Since our hypotheses posit non-linearity, we need to add specific higher order terms to the regression equation (Aiken and West 1991). In our specific case, we assume a quadratic-by-linear interaction (the *quadratic* relationship between age and radical innovative work behavior is *moderated* by useful feedback from coworkers). Following Aiken and West (1991), the following equation should be used to test the hypothesized quadratic-by-linear interaction between age (X) and useful feedback from coworkers (Z): $Y = b_1 X + b_2 X^2 + b_3 Z + b_4 XZ + b_5 X^2 Z + c_0$. This equation includes the different components of the age effect (X and X^2), the linear term for the useful feedback from coworkers effect (Z) as well as the linear-by-linear (XZ) and the quadratic-by-linear ($X^2 Z$) interaction terms. All of these terms must be included into the equation to correctly test our quadratic-by-linear interaction hypothesis (Aiken and West 1991).

In line with previous research (Janssen 2001), the predictors were entered into the regression equation in the following six successive steps: (1) Tenure, gender, educational level, and position in the organizational hierarchy to control for confounding effects, (2 & 3) linear (X) and quadratic (X^2) terms of age to detect linear and quadratic main effects, (4) feedback from coworkers as a linear moderator (Z), (5) the linear interaction between age and feedback from coworkers (XZ), and (6) the quadratic-by-linear $X^2 Z$ term to test the hypothesis that the curvilinear relationship of age with radical innovative job behavior varies as a function of useful feedback from coworkers.

Table 2 presents the standardized regression coefficients of stepwise clustered regression analysis on radical innovative work behavior.[1] Entering tenure, gender, educational level, and position in the organizational hierarchy into the regression as control variables

Table 2: Results of clustered regression analysis on radical innovative work behavior[a]

Variables	Radical Innovative Work Behavior					
	Step 1	Step 2	Step 3	Step 4	Step 5	Step 6
Tenure	−0.09	−0.05	−0.05	−0.05	−0.05	−0.04
Gender	−0.07	−0.05	−0.04	−0.03	−0.03	−0.05
Educational Level	0.15†	0.14†	0.14†	0.13†	0.13†	0.15†
Position in Hierarchy	0.46**	0.47**	0.45**	0.45**	0.45**	0.43**
Age		−0.07	−0.08	−0.08	−0.08	−0.12
Age squared			−0.08	−0.08	−0.09	−0.09
Feedback from Coworkers				−0.01	−0.01	0.10
Age x Feedback from Coworkers					0.00	0.01
Age squared x Feedback from Coworkers						−0.12**
R^2	0.32	0.33	0.33	0.33	0.33	0.35
ΔR^2	0.32**	0.00	0.00	0.00	0.00	0.02**

†p<0.10; *p<0.05; **p<0.01
[a] n=211. F (full model) = 12.07***

yielded a significant equation ($\Delta R^2 = 0.32$, $p < 0.01$). Educational level (b = 0.15, $p < 0.10$) and position in the organizational hierarchy (b = 0.46, $p < 0.01$) were both positively related to radical innovative work behavior. Neither the main effect of age (step 2), the quadratic term of age (step 3), feedback from coworkers (step 4) nor the age-feedback from coworkers interaction (step 5) were predictive for radical innovative work behavior as can be seen in Table 2. The quadratic-by-linear-interaction of age and useful feedback from coworkers (step 6) in the last column of Table 2, however, was negatively related to radical innovative work behavior (b = − 0.12, $p < 0.01$) and yielded a significant change in the amount of variance explained ($\Delta R^2 = 0.02$, $p < 0.01$).

To further reveal the nature of this quadratic-by-linear interaction effect, we conducted simple slope analyses at low (1 SD below the mean), medium (mean), and high (1 SD above the mean) levels of age with both low and high levels of useful feedback from coworkers (Aiken and West 1991). A slope that changes from positive to negative values with increasing levels of X would be indicative of a U-shaped curvilinear relationship between X and Y. To obtain the simple slopes, we started out by taking the first partial derivative of our regression equation $Y = b_1 X + b_2 X^2 + b_3 Z + b_4 X Z + b_5 X^2 Z + c_0$ with respect to X. Together with the previously obtained regression coefficients, the resulting derivative can be used to indicate the slope of the regression of Y (radical innovative work behavior) on X (age) at particular values of Z (useful feedback from coworkers) and X (Aiken and West 1991). For example, the simple slope of the regression of radical innovative work behavior on age at low age and high levels of useful feedback from coworkers (1 SD below and 1 SD above the mean, respectively) is $dY/dX = b_1 + 2b_2 X + b_4 Z + 2b_5 XZ = (-0.12) + 2*(-0.09)*(-1) + (0.01)*(+1) + 2*(-0.12)*(-1)*(1) = 0.31$. The results for all possible combinations of low, mean, and high age with low and high levels of feedback from coworkers are displayed in Table 3.

To test whether the obtained simple slopes at different levels of age and useful feedback from coworkers differed significantly from zero, we calculated standard errors of the simple slopes. In our case of a curvilinear X by linear Z relationship, the standard error of the simple slope ($b_1 + 2b_2 X + b_4 Z + 2b_5 XZ$) is $SQRT(s_{11} + 4X^2 s_{22} + Z^2 s_{44} + 4X^2 Z^2 s_{55} + 4X s_{12} + 2Z s_{14} + 4XZ s_{24} + 4XZ s_{15} + 8X^2 Z s_{25} + 4XZ^2 s_{45})$ with s_{11}, s_{22}, s_{44}, s_{55}, s_{12}, s_{14}, s_{24}, s_{15},

Table 3: Probing simple slopes

		Low feedback level (1 SD below mean)	High feedback level (1 SD above mean)
Low age (1 SD below mean)	Simple slope	− 0.19	0.31
	SE	0.18	0.18
	t	− 1.06	1.72†
Mean age (mean)	Simple slope	− 0.13	− 0.11
	SE	0.11	0.10
	t	− 1.18	− 1.10
High age (1 SD above mean)	Simple slope	− 0.07	− 0.53
	SE	0.15	0.23
	t	− 0.47	− 2.30*

†$p < 0.10$; *$p < 0.05$

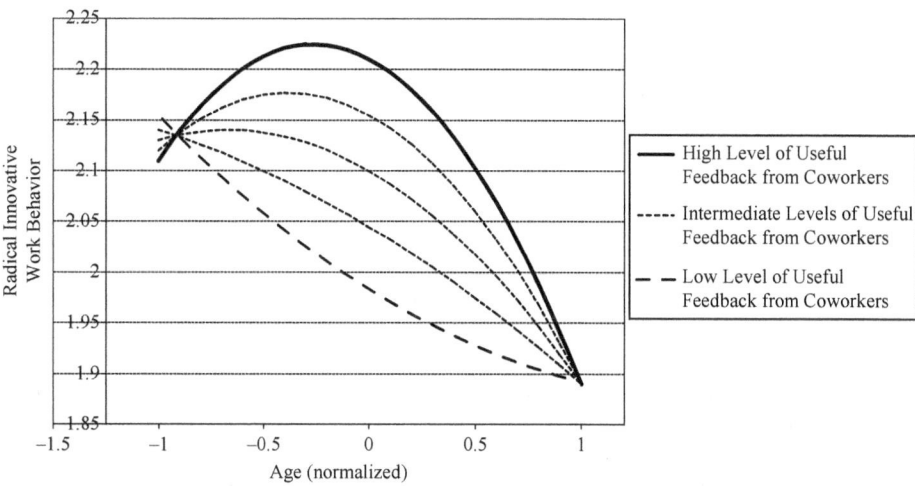

Fig. 1: Results of clustered regression analyses of radical innovative work behavior on age at high, intermediate and low levels of useful feedback from coworkers. (Low values were set at one standard deviation below the mean, high values were set at one standard deviation above the mean. Intermediate levels of Useful Feedback from Coworkers were set at 0,5 SD above the mean, the mean, and 0,5 SD below the mean)

s_{25}, s_{45} taken from the variance-covariance matrix of the regression coefficients (Aiken and West 1991). The standard errors as well as the results of the t-tests for the simple slopes are displayed in Table 3.

Table 3 shows that—at high levels of useful feedback from coworkers—the simple slope of the regression curve was positive for young age (b = 0.31, t = 1.72, p < 0.10)[2], did not differ significantly from zero at mean age (b = − 0.11, t = − 1.10, n.s.), and was negative for older age (b = − 0.53, t = − 2.30, p < 0.05). For low levels of feedback, the slope of the regression curve did not differ significantly from zero for young (b = − 0.19, t = − 1.06, n.s.), mean (b = − 0.13, t = − 1.18, n.s.), or high age (b = − 0.07, t = − 0.47, n.s.). To better understand and interpret this quadratic-by-linear interaction effect, Fig. 1 illustrates the relationship between age and radical innovative work behavior at both low and high levels of useful feedback from coworkers.

As depicted in Fig. 1, the relationship between age and radical innovative work behavior does follow an inverted U-shaped function under the condition of high levels of useful feedback from coworkers. This in combination with the result of the simple slopes test (right column of Table 3) lends support to our hypothesis 1. Hypothesis 2 posited that this curvilinear relationship is decreasingly manifested as the level of perceived useful feedback from coworkers drops. Figure 1 shows how the relationship between age and radical innovative work behavior no longer follows an inverted U-shape relationship under the condition of low coworker feedback, which is also confirmed by the simple slopes test (middle column) of Table 3. To better demonstrate the gradual change in the form of the relationship between age and radical innovative work as the level of useful feedback drops, we added three extra curves (the gray dotted lines) representing three intermediate levels of coworker feedback (mean + 0,5SD, mean, mean − 0,5 SD) to Fig. 1. As hypothesized, the inverted U-shaped relationship between age and radical innovative work behavior flattens with decreasing levels of useful feedback from coworkers. Lastly, we hypothesized that employees who perceive lower levels of useful feedback from their coworkers will display lower levels of radical innovative work behavior at intermediate age than employees perceiving higher levels of useful feedback from coworkers. Again, the results depicted in Fig. 1 confirm our hypothesis.

3 Discussion

This study aimed at researching the relationship between age and innovative work behavior and how this relationship depends on contextual factors. Specifically, we examined the hypothesis of a curvilinear-by-linear interaction with useful feedback from coworkers. Empirical results confirm that the relationship between age and radical innovative work behavior follows an inverted U-shape under the condition of high levels of useful feedback from coworkers and that this inverted U-shaped relationship is decreasingly manifested as the level of perceived useful feedback from coworkers drops. Employees who perceive lower levels of useful feedback from their coworkers display lower levels of radical innovative work behavior at middle age than employees perceiving higher levels of useful feedback from coworkers.

Even though there is a large body of literature examining the influence of personal characteristics on creative and innovative work behavior (see Shalley et al. 2004 for an overview), attention has focused mainly on differences in personality and cognitive styles and less on demographic variables (Shalley et al. 2004). In face of the major demographic shifts currently taking place in many Western countries, the lack of research in this area represents a serious gap in our knowledge (Kanfer and Ackerman 2004). For example, from a practical perspective, organizations know too little about how demographic change really affects their innovation processes and what appropriate management responses might look like. Additionally, such a knowledge gap might foster a false understanding of aging as universally declining innovativeness, which may lead to negative age stereotypes, and, ultimately, to negative consequences for organizational processes and outcomes (Posthuma and Campion 2009).

Of the few past studies that investigated the relationship between age and creative and innovative work behavior, no clear picture seems to emerge (see Ng and Feldman 2008 for a review). This might be due to the fact that age is commonly treated as a linear predictor while there are actually more complex relationships at work. As argued in this paper, recent findings from life span research indeed suggest that aging is associated with multidirectional developments that may lead to curvilinear relationships with work outcomes (Ng and Feldman 2008; Kanfer and Ackerman 2004). When researching age, it is therefore imperative to identify the specific pathways through which aging influences work outcomes and to consider curvilinear relationships. Specifically, our study suggests that the association between age and radical innovative work behavior results from the joint impact of three components (creativity-relevant skills, motivation, and domain relevant skills) and also depends on contextual factors.

This finding has important implications for both scholars and practitioners. Past studies have shown that motivation is an important driver for innovative work behavior (for an overview see Anderson et al. 2004). Accordingly, a lot of research has investigated contextual characteristics that may positively influence employees' intrinsic motivation (for an overview see Shalley et al. 2004). These studies, however, have not yet taken into account the role of aging and—more precisely—of aging-related developments in determining work motivation and innovative work behavior. This is a noteworthy limitation, especially in times of demographic change. Therefore, it becomes necessary to extend contemporary, process-oriented theories of work motivation (e.g., expectancy theories) to identify the sources of age-related differences in work motivation and outcomes (Kanfer and Ackerman 2004). Precisely because of this reason, we incorporate developmental changes in, for example, personality, values, and goals to explain age-related differences in innovation-related intrinsic work motivation.

Incorporating such knowledge is also very important to identify appropriate moderators of the age-innovation relationship, which may be recommended to organizations as management tools in times of demographic change. For example, past research has identified job complexity as a contextual characteristic to foster innovative work behavior (see Shalley et al. 2004 for an overview). It is argued that complex jobs are likely to enhance employees' excitement about their work activities, leading to higher levels of motivation and innovative work behavior (Shalley et al. 2004). However, in times of aging workforces, increasingly complex jobs might not deliver the desired results. As we have explained earlier, aging is associated with declines in fluid intellectual abilities such as working memory, attention, and processing of novel information. To the extent that more complex jobs also require higher levels of fluid intellectual abilities, we would therefore expect less positive or even negative effects of increasing levels of job complexity on motivation and work outcomes. For example, Kanfer and Ackerman (2004) propose that aging employees who try to sustain performance in jobs that require high amounts of fluid abilities will eventually suffer from negative effects of self-efficacy, self-concept, and, ultimately, from negative effects on work motivation. In other words, some common and well-intentioned management practices carry the potential to discriminate certain age groups because they don't consider what we know about age-related developments.

In essence, then, we argue that it is necessary to think well about management strategies in times of demographic change. Conditions that have been found to foster innovative work behavior in past studies might not be applicable without further thought to the context of aging workforces. Appropriate solutions to this problem must consider the mechanisms that mediate between age and work outcomes and how the contextual factors interact with these mediating mechanisms. In our study, we therefore deliberately chose useful feedback from coworkers as a moderator of the age-innovation relationship. As we have explained earlier, useful feedback gives employees helpful information about how to improve their job performance, thereby positively influencing the domain-relevant skills as well as the motivational component of innovative work behavior. These positive effects of useful feedback are not restricted to certain age groups. For example, for aging employees, useful feedback may consist of advice on how to discover age-related strengths (e.g., domain-relevant skills) and how to successfully concentrate on these strengths instead of relentlessly trying to compensate for certain losses. For young employees, useful feedback may consist of advice on how to use high levels of fluid intellectual abilities to engage in innovative work behavior. Useful feedback may therefore be considered a contextual promoter of innovative work behavior that respects age-related differences. In other words, high levels of useful feedback do not discriminate certain age-groups per se. Instead, employees of all age levels are likely to profit from high feedback levels. This makes useful feedback an appropriate management tool to maintain and improve innovative performance in times of demographic change.

Therefore, organizations and organizational leaders might use our findings to increase the innovation performance of their workforce. More specifically, if organizations want aging employees to engage in innovative work behavior, they should ensure high levels of feedback within the organization and within teams. This is an important recommendation in light of the fact that older employees may place less importance on feedback and/or may receive less feedback from their coworkers (Warr 1997; Greller and Simpson 1999). In line with these findings, we also replicate a negative correlation between age and useful feedback from coworkers in our study (see Table 1). Given the potential positive effect that feedback may have for radical innovative work behavior over the life span, this secondary finding is quite disappointing. Installing appropriate feedback structures will therefore be an important task for leaders that want to tap the innovation potential of their aging workforce.

Our findings also have practical implications on how to view age diversity (Wegge et al. 2008; Kearney and Gebert 2009; Kearney et al. 2009) in organizations. First, employees of different ages do seem to differ in terms of their radical innovative work behavior when contextual factors are considered. We argue that this is due to different levels of creativity-relevant skills, motivation, and domain-relevant skills. Such differences may enhance the innovative performance of age diverse teams as proposed by the information/decision-making perspective (Williams and O'Reilly 1998). For example, in an age diverse team, young employees might stipulate innovation through high levels of fluid intellectual abilities, whereas older employees support innovation with their extended knowledge, experience, and network (domain-relevant skills).

Second, if organizational leaders wish to increase levels of useful feedback to better tap the innovation potential of an aging workforce, they should probably consider age diverse teams over age homogenous teams. We believe that because employees of different ages work at different levels of creativity-relevant skills, motivation, and domain-relevant skills, this will most likely influence the feedback they give to others. In return, the feedback receiving employees will probably perceive a diverse, multifaceted, and non-redundant feedback from age-diverse team members as very helpful. In contrast, feedback from an age-homogenous team is more likely to be similar, overlapping, and, therefore, less useful.

3.1 Limitations, future research, and conclusion

We acknowledge limitations of our study. First, we studied only one organization and only one type of innovative work behavior. Further research is needed to investigate whether the obtained results generalize to other types of organizations and to other types of innovative work behavior (e.g., incremental). Second, we relied on subjective ratings of radical innovative work behavior rather than on objective performance indicators. Third, we did not measure age-related differences in creativity-relevant skills, motivation, and domain-relevant skills, which we assume to mediate between age and radical innovative work behavior. Although we base our premises on empirical findings from the life span literature, further research is needed to examine whether this assumption is valid. Also, further research should consider other moderators of the age-innovation relationship to increase the amount of explained variance in radical innovative work behavior. Following up on what has been said in the discussion about previous findings and how they might or might not apply to aging workforces, future research could revisit these findings to test their stability in times of demographic change. Possible moderators of the age-innovation relationship include, for example, leadership styles, rewards, demand-ability fit, organizational culture or psychological safety. Fourth, despite the fact that we collected data from different sources—thereby circumventing the problem of common-method bias—and used a partly longitudinal design, our study relied on correlational data. Hence, other factors not considered here may have influenced our findings too. Fifth, we argue that age-related differences in creativity-relevant skills, motivation, and domain-relevant skills are the result of individual development over time. Because, however, tracking an individual's development over an entire working-life is extremely hard to handle, we based our empirical analyses on a comparison between differently aged employees at a certain point in time. It is therefore possible that our results are a confounding of aging differences and cohort effects (similar Kanfer and Ackerman 2004). Lastly, in our discussion, we considered the implications that our findings have for the management of diverse workforces. For example, we proposed that the feedback of age-diverse teams may be perceived as especially useful, thereby positively influencing innovative work behavior of employees working in diverse teams. Further research on the team level of analysis is needed to examine whether our predictions are valid.

In conclusion, our study shows how useful feedback from coworkers can help to foster an aging workforce's innovative work behavior. More specifically, high levels of useful feedback from coworkers that support motivation and the accumulation of domain-relevant skills can turn an aging workforce into an opportunity for rather than a threat to innovation. Since the form of the relationship between age and innovative work behavior seems to depend very much on contextual factors, we hope that our results will stimulate further research in this field to better understand the conditions and mechanisms that help make the most out of an aging workforce.

Acknowledgement: We would like to thank Editor Barbara Beham and two anonymous reviewers for their insightful comments and suggestions that greatly improved the quality of this article. We would also like to thank the Volkswagen Foundation for generously supporting our research.

Endnotes

1. Since the option for standardized beta coefficients may not be combined with clustered regression analysis in STATA, we normalized all independent variables before analysis to obtain standardized beta coefficients.
2. Because this slope was only marginally significant, we also tested the slope at younger age (1.5 SD below the age mean, which corresponds to 22.3 years). At -1.5 SD, the slope is significantly positive ($p < 0.05$).

References

Ackerman PL (1996) A theory of adult intellectual development: process, personality, interests, and knowledge. Intelligence 22:229–259

Ackerman PL (2000) Domain-specific knowledge as the "dark matter" of adult intelligence: gf/fc, personality and interest correlates. J Gerontolo Psycholo Sci 55B(2):69–84

Aiken LS, West SG (1991) Multiple regression: testing and interpreting interactions. Sage, Newbury Park

Amabile TM (1983a) The social psychology of creativity. Springer, New York

Amabile TM (1983b) Social psychology of creativity: a componential conceptualization. J Pers Soc Psychol 45:357–377

Amabile TM (1988) A model of creativity and innovation in organizations. In: Staw BM, Cummings LL (eds) Research in organizational behavior. JAI Press, Greenwich, pp 187–209

Amabile TM (1998) How to kill creativity. Harvard Bus Rev 76(5):76–87

Anderson N, De Dreu CKW, Nijstad BA (2004) The routinization of innovation research: a constructively critical review of the state-of-the-science. J Organ Behav 25(2):147–173

Baltes PB, Lindenberger U, Staudinger U (2006) Life span theory in developmental psychology. In: Damon W, Lerner RM (eds) Handbook of child psychology: Vol. 1. Theoretical models of human development, 6th ed. Wiley, New York

Bigoness WJ, Perreault WD Jr (1981) A conceptual paradigm and approach for the study of innovators. Acad Manag J 24(1):68–82

Brislin RW (1980) Translation and content analysis of oral and written material. In Triandis HC, Berry JW (eds) Handbook of cross-cultural psychology, Vol. 2: Methodology. Allyn and Bacon, Boston, pp 349–444

Cattell RB (1971) Abilities: Their structure, growth and action. Houghton Mifflin, Boston

Cattell RB (1987) Intelligence: Its structure, growth, and action. North-Holland

Cleveland JN, Shore LM (1992) Self- and supervisory perspectives on age and work attitudes and performance. J Appl Psychol 77:469–484

Cooper RG (1990) Stage-gate systems: a new tool for managing new products. Bus Horiz 33(3):44

Davenport T, Leibold M, Voelpel S (2006) Strategic management in the innovation economy: strategy approaches and tools for dynamic innovation capabilities. Wiley, New York

Davies DR, Matthews G, Wong CSK (1991) Ageing and work. Int Rev Ind Organ Psycholo 6:149–211

Deci EL, Ryan RM (1985) Intrinsic motivation and self-determination in human behavior. Plenum, New York

Ebner NC, Freund AM, Baltes PB (2006) Developmental changes in personal goal orientation from young to late adulthood: from striving for gains to maintenance and prevention of losses. Psychol Aging 21(4):664–678

Farr JL, Ford CM (1990) Individual innovation. In: West MA, Farr JL (eds) Innovation and creativity at work. Wiley, New York

Friedman RS, Förster J (2001) The effects of promotion and prevention cues on creativity. J Pers Soc Psychol 81(6):1001–1013

Gemünden HG, Salomo S, Hölzle K (2007) Role models for radical innovation in times of open innovation. Creat Innov Manag 16(4):408–421

George JM (2007) Creativity in organizations. Acad Manag Ann 1(1):439–477

Greller MM, Simpson P (1999) In search of late career: a review of contemporary social science research applicable to the understanding of late career. Hum Resour Manag Rev 9:309–347

Hambrick DC, Mason PA (1984) Upper echelons: the organization as a reflection of its top managers. Acad Manag Rev 9(2):193–206

Hansson RO, DeKoekkoeck PD, Neece WM, Patterson DW (1997) Successful aging at work. Annual review, 1992–1996: The older worker and transitions to retirement. J Vocat Behav 51:202–233

Harrison DA, Klein KJ (2007) What's the difference? Diversity constructs as separation, variety, or disparity in organizations. Acad Manag Rev 32:1199–1228

Howell JM, Higgins CA (1990) Champions of Technological Innovation. Adm Sci Q 35(2):317–330

Janssen O (2000) Job demands, perceptions of effort-reward fairness and innovative work behaviour. J Occup Organ Psychol 73(3):287–302

Janssen O (2001) Fairness perceptions as a moderator in the curvilinear relationships between job demands, and job performance and job satisfaction. Acad Manag J 44:1039–1050

Janssen O, Van Yperen NW (2004) Employees' goal orientations, the quality of leader-member exchange, and the outcomes of job performance and job satisfaction. Acad Manag J 47(3):368–384

Janssen O, van de Vliert E, West M (2004) The bright and dark sides of individual and group innovation: a Special Issue introduction. J Organ Behav 25(2):129–145

Jones BF (2005) Age and great invention. Paper presented at NBER working paper series. Cambridge

Kanfer R, Ackerman PL (2004) Aging, adult development, and work motivation. Acad Manag Rev 29(3):440–458

Kanter RM (1988) When a 1000 flowers bloom—structural, collective, and social conditions for innovation in organization. Res Organ Behav 10(1):169–211

Kearney E, Gebert D (2009) Managing diversity and enhancing team outcomes: the promise of transformational leadership. J Appl Psychol 94(1):77–89

Kearney E, Gebert D, Voelpel SC (2009) When and how diversity benefits teams: the importance of team members' need for cognition. Acad Manag J 52(3):581–598

Kluger AN, DeNisi A (1996) The effects of feedback interventions on performance: historical review, a meta-analysis and a preliminary feedback intervention theory. Psychol Bull 119:254–284

Lawrence BS (1996) Interest in indifference: the role of age in the organizational sciences. Res Pers Hum Resour Manag 14:1–59

Lehman HC (2006) Age and achievement. In: Moody HR (ed) Aging: concepts and controversies, 5th ed. Pine Forge Press, Thousand Oaks

Leibold M, Voelpel S (2006) Managing the aging workforce: challenges and solutions. Wiley, New York

Lubart TI (1999) Componential models. In: Runco MA, Pritsker SR (eds) Encyclopedia of creativity. Academic, New York, pp 295–300

Miron E, Erez M, Naveh E (2004) Do personal characteristics and cultural values that promote innovation, quality, and efficiency compete or complement each other? J Organ Behav 25(2):175–199

Moody HR (2006) Aging: concepts and controversies, 5th ed. Pine Forge Press, Thousand Oaks

Mumford MD (2000) Managing creative people: strategies and tactics for innovation. Hum Resour Manag Rev 10(3):313

Mumford MD, Gustafson SB (1988) Creativity syndrome: integration, application, and innovation. Psychol Bull 103(1):27–43

Ng TWH, Feldman DC (2008) The relationship of age to ten dimensions of job performance. J Appl Psychol 93(2):392–423

Oldham GR, Cummings A (1996) Employee creativity: personal and contextual factors at work. Acad Manag J 39(3):607–634

Posthuma RA, Campion MA (2009) Age stereotypes in the workplace: common stereotypes, moderators, and future research directions. J Manag 35(1):158–188

Redmond MR, Mumford MD, Teach R (1993) Putting creativity to work: effects of leader behavior on subordinate creativity. Organ Behav Hum Decis Process 55:120–151

Rice MP, Kelley D, Peters L, O'Connor GC (2001) Radical innovation: triggering initiation of opportunity recognition and evaluation. R&D Manag 31(4):409

Schaie KW (1996) Intellectual development in adulthood: the Seattle longitudinal study. Cambridge University Press, New York

Scott SG, Bruce RA (1994) Determinants of innovative behavior: a path model of individual innovation in the workplace. Acad Manag J 37(3):580–607

Shalley CE, Zhou J, Oldham GR (2004) The effects of personal and contextual characteristics on creativity: where should we go from here? J Manag 30(6):933–958

Sheremata WA (2000) Centrifugal and centripetal forces in radical new product development under time pressure. Acad Manag Rev 25(2):389–408

Spreitzer GM (1995) Psychological empowerment in the workplace: dimensions, measurement, and validation. Acad Manag J 38(5):1442–1465

Sterns HL, Miklos SM (1995) The aging worker in a changing environment: organizational and individual issues. J Vocat Behav 47:248–268

Super DE (1980) A life-span, life-space approach to career development. J Vocat Behav 16:282–298

Thornton WJL, Dumke HA (2005) Age differences in everyday problem-solving and decision-making effectiveness: a meta-analytic review. Psychol Aging 20:85–99

Utman CH (1997) Performance effects of motivational state: a meta-analysis. Personal Soc Psychol Rev 1:170–182

Van de Ven AH (1986) Central problems in the management of innovation. Manag Sci 32(5):590–607

Van Knippenberg D, De Dreu CKW, Homan AC (2004) Work group diversity and group performance: an integrative model and research agenda. J Appl Psychol 89:1008–1022

Van Knippenberg D, Schippers MC (2007) Work group diversity. Annu Rev Psychol 58:515–541

Voelpel S, Leibold M, Früchtenicht J-D (2007) Herausforderung 50 plus: Konzepte zum Management der Aging Workforce: Die Antwort auf das demographische Dilemma. Wiley, Erlangen

Vroom VH (1964) Work and motivation. Wiley, New York

Warr P (1997) Age, work, and mental health, the impact of work on older adults. Springer, New York

Warr P (2001) Age and work behaviour: physical attributes, cognitive abilities, knowledge, personality traits, and motives. Int Rev Ind Organ Psychol 74:165–199

Warr P, Miles A, Platts C (2001) Age and personality in the British population between 16 and 64 years. J Occup Organ Psychol 74:165–199

Wechsler D (1944) The measurement of intelligence. Williams & Wilkins, Baltimore

Wegge J, Roth C, Neubach B, Schmidt KH, Kanfer R (2008) Age and gender diversity as determinants of performance and health in a public organization: the role of task complexity and group size. J Appl Psychol 93:1301–1313

West MA, Farr JL (1989) Innovation at work: psychological perspectives. Soc Behav 4(1):15–30

West MA, Farr JL (1990) Innovation at work. In: West MA, Farr JL (eds) Innovation and creativity at work: psychological and organizational strategies. Wiley, Chichester

Williams KY, O'Reilly CA (1998) Demography and diversity in organizations: a review of 40 years o research. In: Staw BM, Cummings LL (eds) Research in organizational behavior. JAI Press, Greenwich, pp 77–140

Woodman RW, Sawyer JE, Griffin RW (1993) Toward a theory of organizational creativity. Acad Manag Rev 18:293–321

Wu CH, Cheng Y, Ip HM, McBridge-Chang C (2005) Age differences in creativity: task structure and knowledge base. Creat Res J 17(4), 321–326

Zhou J (1998) Feedback valence, feedback style, task autonomy, and achievement orientation: interactive effects on creative performance. J Appl Psychol 83:261–276

Zhou J (2003) When the presence of creative coworkers is related to creativity: role of supervisor close monitoring, developmental feedback, and creative personality. J Appl Psychol 88(3):413–422

Zhou J, George JM (2001) When job dissatisfaction leads to creativity: encouraging the expression of voice. Acad Manag J 44(4):682–696

Gender and nationality pay gaps in light of organisational theories
A large-scale analysis within German establishments

Elke Wolf · Miriam Beblo · Clemens Ohlert

Abstract: This paper analyses wage inequality with respect to gender and nationality within German establishments. It is a large-scale analysis based on linked employer-employee data from the Institute for Employment Research (LIAB). Wage inequality is measured as the intra-establishment pay gap by gender and nationality, taking into account that human capital may not be equally distributed across the different groups of employees. Consistent with economic theories of discrimination we find significant pay gaps by gender and nationality, even taking into consideration employees' qualifications. We can show that pay differentials between men and women are much larger on average than those between Germans and non-Germans, and that both pay gaps exhibit a tremendous variation across establishments. Drawing on organisational theories we inquire as to how selected firm characteristics are related to the variation of these intra-firm pay gaps and derive hypotheses about which establishments have a greater incentive and/or are more able to pursue wage equality in their

© Gabler-Verlag 2011

Prof. Dr. E. Wolf (✉)
Hochschule München – University of Applied Sciences München,
Lothstr. 64, 80335 Munich, Germany
e-mail: elke.wolf@hm.edu

Dr. M. Beblo
Hochschule für Wirtschaft und Recht Berlin,
Badensche Straße 52, 10825 Berlin, Germany
e-mail: beblo@hwr-berlin.de

Dipl. Sozialwirt C. Ohlert
Welckerstraße 8, 20354 Hamburg, Germany
e-mail: clemens.ohlert@wiso.uni-hamburg.de

workforces. By use of regression analysis we then investigate whether variables that reflect the firms' social, institutional and cultural environment and their resource requirements are empirically related to the sizes of the pay gaps. The results are rather ambiguous, suggesting larger, innovating and foreign-owned establishments with a larger share of non-German employees and with a collective bargaining agreement to have smaller gaps, particularly with respect to gender.

Keywords: Diversity · Pay gap · Discrimination

JEL Classification: M52 · J31 · J71

1 Introduction

There are several aspects, in which women and non-German workers are faced with disadvantages in the (German) labour market. In terms of earnings, women receive about 23% lower wage rates than men on average (Destatis 2010; Heinze and Wolf 2010) and immigrants receive about 15% less than German natives (Beblo et al. 2011a; Granato and Kalter 2001; Constant and Massey 2003). The possible causes for these pay gaps are manifold and differ between female and non-German employees, but differences in education and work experience are the most prominent explanatory factors. It is argued that employment breaks and time invested in household production reduce future earnings, particularly for women (see e.g. Beblo and Wolf 2003, 2002; Beblo et al. 2008). For immigrants, non-transferability of skills acquired in their home country or language difficulties may be responsible for an (initial) disadvantage in the labour market (Chiswick 1978).

While there exist a variety of theories and empirical studies investigating the average wage cut for female and non-German employees, knowledge on the intra-firm wage distributions is much more fragmentary. Also, the intersection of the wage cuts for different disadvantaged groups has only begun to be analysed (exemptions are McCall 2005 or Longhi and Platt 2008). And finally, even if the idea that organisations play an important role in creating and maintaining unequal pay has become more and more popular during the past decades, very few studies analyse the link between management strategies and the resulting wage distribution. Recent use of linked employer-employee data provided first insight into the wage structure within firms and establishments and reveals serious heterogeneity across units as well as systematic links to specific firm characteristics (see e.g. Abowd et al. 1999; Addison et al. 2006; Heinze and Wolf 2010; Beblo et al. 2011a, b). The fact that some firms do exhibit more egalitarian wage distributions and the observation of small or even positive wage gaps for women leads one to suppose that wage equality may be a targeted management strategy in some organisations. Firms offering equal opportunities to all employees may, for example, attract more productive workers or are less likely to suffer from labour turnover or skill shortage. Using a large employer-employee data set, we therefore estimate within-establishment pay differentials between female and male, non-German and German employees respectively and investigate their links with organisational theories, in particular the resource dependence and the neoinstitutional theory.

Our paper is structured as follows: Sect. 2 recalls briefly how economic theories of discrimination set off to explain the existence of wage gaps in the labour market in general. Section 3 draws on organisational theories and empirical evidence based on the business cases literature explaining why firms may want to foster wage equality. Whereupon, we derive hypotheses on the distribution of intra-firm pay gaps depending on the firms' characteristics. In Sect. 4, the data set and descriptive statistics are presented. Section 5 expounds our methodological approach: using matched employer-employee data for Germany, we calculate establishment-specific measures of observed as well as residual pay gaps, i.e. the gaps that would remain even if male and female employees or Germans and non-Germans respectively had the same education, work experience and job tenure. By regression analyses of (1) the residual intra-establishment pay gap of female employees, (2) the residual intra-establishment pay gap of non-German employees and (3) the probability of an extraordinarily large pay gap (largest 25%) for both groups within an establishment, we show which establishment environments promote a high or low degree of pay inequality. The empirical results of this approach are presented in Sect. 6 and Sect. 7 provides concluding remarks.

2 The rationale of pay gaps: economic theories of discrimination

In economic theory, only differences in the returns to *equal* endowments by gender or nationality/ethnicity are ascribed to discrimination (Arrow 1973). There are three theoretical approaches to explain discrimination in the labour market, which may manifest in non-employment, segregation or direct wage discrimination. These approaches assume either (i) preferences for discrimination, (ii) statistical discrimination or (iii) segmented labour markets which create monopsony power or overcrowding. According to Becker (1957), wage discrimination arises from the employers' (or employees' or customers') preferences for members of one group over those of another, regardless of their equal labour productivities. Discriminating employers act as if hiring female or foreign workers will not only impose wage costs but an additional disutility to the firm. Since discrimination should theoretically result in a suboptimal allocation of resources it has been argued that the likeliness of discrimination is reduced under strong market competition (Arrow 1973; Cain 1986). The meta-analysis by Weichselbaumer and Winter-Ebmer (2005) provides some empirical evidence for this argument with regard to the gender pay gap across countries. The statistical discrimination approach refers to the underestimation of minority workers' productivity by employers due to a lower average productivity of this group compared to native men when incomplete information is assumed (Phelps 1972; Arrow 1973). The theory of overcrowding finally explains lower wages of female or non-German employees by their excess labour supply in specific segments or occupations which they either choose themselves or are assigned to (Edgeworth 1922; Bergmann 1974). According to monopsony theory, employers with monopsony power can maximize profits by differentiating wages between groups with unequal elasticities of labour supply. Therefore, wage discrimination may arise if the labour supply of women or immigrants is less elastic at the firm level than that of native and/or male employees (Robinson 1933; Cain 1986). While for immigrants there are no obvious reasons that this should be the case, a lower labour supply elasticity could arise for women from lower mobility or higher travel costs compared to men, e.g. based on the assumption of higher domestic responsibilities. The empirical results from Ransom and Oaxaca (2005) and Hirsch et al. (2010) support that female labour supply at the firm level is less elastic than male labour supply and imply that a substantial part of the gender pay gap may in fact be explained by monopsony discrimination.

Whether residual wage inequality (after controlling for differences in human capital endowments), may be adequately interpreted as the result of discrimination depends obviously on the respective variables chosen to capture the employees' productivity. The more sketchy the information on productivity-relevant skills, the less precise the estimated unexplained pay gap will be and hence the measure of discrimination is reduced.[1] The widespread use of school and professional education as well as former work experience as productivity measures neglect the attribution and appreciation of potential gender- or ethnicity-specific skills. In fact, female and immigrant employees may hold—or at least be attributed—qualities, skills and potentials (such as parental skills, potential language skills, caring skills and further cultural capital) that are of particular interest to employers. Cox and Blake (1991) expounded areas where diversity management can reveal its productivity enhancing effects and generate competitive advantages. These advantages are improved resource acquisition, cost savings and "added value" through improved creativity, problem solving and flexibility. If these management goals are not equally important across firms, diversity management will differ between firms as well—and so will the pay gaps.

3 Which establishments seek to reduce pay inequality?

Companies are adopting equality and diversity policies not only for legal and moral reasons, but also for economic reasons. In Germany, the General Equal Treatment Law (Allgemeines Gleichbehandlungsgesetz (AGG) from 2006) describes the anti-discrimination rules which are relevant in all organisations. Even if pay discrimination as well as employment discrimination of various groups of potentially discriminated employees are prohibited by this law, the notion that equal opportunities now actually exist is a myth (see e.g. the BMFSFJ 2011). Apart from legislation, the enforcement of equal opportunities is supported by voluntary corporate agreements to promote equality, the German Genderdax, the audit "Beruf und Familie" as well as the Total E-Quality-Certificate which is conferred to firms with successful and sustainable concepts of equal opportunities. Comprehensive equality, however, can only be achieved if theses values are part of the business culture. In order to overcome the most common obstacle, that is opposition against change amongst employees, good practice companies approach equality and diversity issues through a culture change process.

While moral and social justice arguments dominated the discussions in the 1980s, business arguments became more popular in the early 1990s—not at least because of government funded research about the firm-specific benefits of equal opportunity programs and diversity management (see e.g. 'The Business Case for Diversity—good practices in the workplace', a study carried out for the European Commission 2005). In the meanwhile there exist many empirical studies pointing at specific benefits of equal opportunity programs and diversity strategies (see e.g. Thomas and Ely 1996; Richard 2000; Amstrong et al. 2010), albeit most findings are rather context specific and difficult to generalize. Despite this evidence, only 5% of all German establishments adopted a voluntary agreement of equal opportunities in 2008 (Kohaut and Möller 2009).

3.1 Theoretical frameworks

In the following, we will expound upon different theoretical approaches and some empirical evidence elaborating why establishments might be interested in adopting management strategies fostering wage equality within plants. Along these lines of arguments, we argue that pay equality among employees can be part of a comprehensive corporate strategy[2], independent of the prior driving force: moral and institutional motives or economic reasons.

Economic reasons to assure equal opportunities for all employees are provided by the resource dependence theory and the business case analysis of equal opportunity programs and diversity management. The core argument of the resource dependence theory by Pfeffer and Salancik (1978) is that organisations depend on decision makers in their external environment (e.g. potential employees, business partners, investors) because they are in need of resources such as capital, specific knowledge or technology. Hence, organisational strategies aim at securing the accrual of critical resources and limiting the dependency of external actors.

Different strategies can help in avoiding or manipulating resource dependence on the environment. While Pfeffer and Salancik (1978) focus mainly on the horizontal and vertical boundaries of the establishment, Ortlieb and Sieben (2008) apply the dependency idea to the recruitment of a diverse workforce. Since an organisation needs resources (e.g. knowledge about markets and institutions in other countries) which are often in the hand of other organisations, they suppose that the recruitment of immigrant employees may be an effective strategy to acquire relevant resources, one would otherwise not obtain. Based on this rationale, we will derive several hypotheses about which establishments are more likely to face binding resource dependencies and hence adopt human resource measures aiming to overcome existing labour shortages.

Empirical evidence about the economic benefits of equal opportunity programs or diversity management is provided by several business cases. A business case describes a planned proposal for business change based on terms of costs and benefits. Business Cases for Diversity (European Commission 2005) illustrates that effective, efficient diversity and equality management strategies can open up new and various opportunities, such as strengthening corporate values, tackling manpower shortages, generating more creativeness and innovation, increasing motivation and with it, efficiency among their employees, and broadening the customer base. Furthermore, the business case literature provides an important contribution to the question of which firms are most likely to benefit from the variety of equal opportunity policies and practices (see e.g. Riley et al. 2008). Based on this evidence, we can derive hypothesis about the adoption of these policies and the resulting wage gaps within heterogeneous establishments.

Neoinstitutional theory provides a framework to explain why moral-based arguments may induce establishments to reduce pay gaps across employees. The core argument of this approach is that, apart from technical requirements and boundaries, the social, institutional and cultural environment of an organisation shape their corporate governance and decision making rules. In contrast to the classical technocratic view that successful organisational structures solely rely on the efficient coordination of internal processes, Meyer and Rowan (1977) argue that in order to survive, organisations must conform with the rules, expectations and beliefs prevailing in their environment. Common expectations towards successful firms are, for instance, that they use modern information technology, quality management, modern recruiting procedures, innovative human resource practices (i.e. team work, employee involvement or empowerment), respect sustainability and last but not least that they provide equal opportunities or even actively manage diversity. Institutional theory argues that organisations actually adopt these practices, not necessarily because they believe or know that these practices improve the efficiency of their work processes[3], but rather because they rely on internal and external patronisation. Hence, organisations accommodating prevalent social norms and rules in their formal structures maximize their legitimacy[4] and have a higher chance of survival. As a result, the adaptation to institutionalized expectations is not irrational, because legitimacy generates competitive advantages and may improve the accrual of important resources (see e.g. Zuckermann 1999 or Singh et al. 1986)

DiMaggio and Powell (1983) used these arguments to rationalise the homogeneity and persistence of organisational structures and management practices. Establishments within a specific organisational field—embedded in a common set of social, moral and institutional norms—interact in the same environment and hence adopt similar organisational structures and management practices. Organisational fields generally include more than the firms within industrial sectors, and are defined as the whole of actors (such as customers), institutions (such as the antitrust agency or unions) and regulations (such as disclosure requirements) influencing the structure, behaviour and survival of the establishments. Based on this approach, we can derive specific hypothesis about which firms are more likely to integrate equality in their business strategy and adopt organisational structures and human resource practices aiming at wage equality within the establishment.

3.2 Study hypotheses

In the following, we expound our hypotheses about the link between firm characteristics and the gender or the nationality pay gap respectively and discuss how they can be derived from the theoretical approaches and the evidence from business cases presented above.

H1: Establishments with a large number of employees exhibit smaller wage gaps with respect to gender and nationality.

Since larger establishments are in need of more employees (due to natural fluctuation), resource dependence theory would suggest that these firms will adopt management practices to enlarge their pool of potential employees. Obvious wage discrimination would presumably banish potential job candidates and hence shrink the pool of potential applicants (Riley et al. 2008). Neoinstitutional theory also predicts smaller wage gaps with respect to gender and nationality in larger establishments because inequality is more visible and hence more prone to the pressure of social norms (Edelman 1990; Ingram and

Simons 1995; Walgenbach and Meyer 2008; Süß and Kleiner 2008). Finally, business case analysis suggests that larger firms are more likely to enhance their productivity by equal opportunities measures (Riley et al. 2008). As a result, we should observe lower unexplained pay gaps both between men and women as well as between German and non-German employees.

Furthermore, one may argue that the quality of employee selection is better in larger establishments. First, the benefit from formalised and effective selection processes increases with the variance of job applicants, which is higher amongst highly qualified employees (Nerdinger et al. 2008, p. 268). As large firms employ a larger share of educated employees, they presumably attach more importance to the recruiting process. Second, the validation and subsequent improvement of an internal selection mechanism is only reliable with a certain number of observations and hence only feasible for larger firms (Nerdinger et al. 2008, p. 261). Following these arguments, we expect that larger firms have better means to assess the actual productivity of newcomers and overcome asymmetric information—a major source of statistical discrimination against job candidates. As a result, residual wage gaps with respect to gender and nationality should be smaller.

H2: Establishments that are in need of (highly) qualified employees exhibit smaller wage gaps with respect to gender and nationality.

A key element to detect the establishment-specific costs and benefits of equal opportunity agendas within the business case analysis is the recognition of global trends. Concerning labour markets, increased skill shortage due to demographic change as well as skill biased technological change are well known and ongoing trends. In general, those sectors facing serious skill shortages (such as engineering or information technology) have especially low numbers of women and ethnic minority employees. Cassell (1997) hence argues that the loss or lack of recognition of skills and potentials of women can be very costly to companies. Furthermore, considering the unbroken trend of globalisation suggests an increasing need for internationally diverse workforces. As a result, wage cuts for female or non-German employees should be small in establishments that are in need of (highly) qualified employees and/or face staffing problems.

Resource dependence theory also implies that firms relying on a (highly) qualified workforce are more likely to pursue wage equality for all groups of employees in order to enlarge the pool of job applicants in times of severe skill shortages.

H3: Innovative establishments exhibit smaller wage gaps with respect to gender and nationality.

Establishments that are involved in process and product innovations require (highly) qualified employees with new and diverse ideas, perspectives and approaches to work. We therefore expect that these establishments actively recruit a diverse workforce—especially at the management level and among highly qualified employees—in order to exploit the mixture of perspectives and approaches. In this setting, the integration of female and immigrant candidates in higher positions seems crucial to exploit the creative potentials in the workforce. According to resource dependence theory, we therefore suppose that innovative establishments use diversity strategies, promote the various abilities of women and non-German employees and hence exhibit more wage equality. Apart from that, they might improve their recruitment outcome if they adopt an equal opportunity policy.

H4: Establishments which are subject to collective bargaining exhibit smaller wage gaps with respect to gender and nationality.

H5: Establishments with work councils exhibit smaller wage gaps with respect to gender and nationality.

If establishments strongly rely on social acceptance in order to secure their moral legitimacy, and hence their access to specific resources, neoinstitutional theory predicts that they are more likely to accommodate social values, such as the conception of emancipated labour relations by approving corporative agreements and implementing work councils.

In theory, the adoption of co-determination (via work councils) as well as collective bargaining agreements help to restrain managers' discretionary power and thereby conform to the strategy of anti-discrimination.

Collective bargaining models provide further arguments for why collective agreements tend to reduce wage inequality within establishments. First of all, it is argued that unions generally reduce the wage dispersion among employees covered by the same collective bargaining agreement, especially those working in the same occupation (Freeman and Medoff 1984; Fitzenberger and Kohn 2005). As a consequence, unionization should reduce the wage discount for female and non-German employees performing the same activity as male and German employees within the same establishment. Elvira and Saporta (2001) apply the same logic to the wage setting process. They argue that collective wage agreements reduce the arbitrariness in wage rates and therefore tend to reduce wage discrimination.

Work councils are also known to have an impact on the wage distribution within an establishment (Hübler and Jirjahn 2003; Addison et al. 2006). Even if work councils cannot directly engage in wage bargaining, they may influence the firm's wage structure by their right of co-determination in placing workers in different wage groups. They are also involved in the decision-making for pay systems, such as performance-related pay schemes, and the setting of wages above the agreed upon tariff and bonus rates. According to Baron (1984), work councils often act as equalizing agents by monitoring compliance with corporate or legal principals aimed at achieving equal opportunities and avoiding discrimination. As a result, the existence of a work council should counteract any policies within the establishment that are suspected to enhance wage inequality.

H6: Establishments that offer measures to foster gender equality exhibit smaller gender wage gaps.

As discussed above, a firm's corporate governance is shaped by its social, institutional and cultural environment. Measures to foster gender equality may be seen as one part of innovative human resource practices, just as a human resource management that produces lower pay gaps between female and male employees. But there may also exist a reversed causality, which is consistent with signalling theory (Spence 1973). One may argue that gender equality measures are less costly to implement for firms accommodating prevalent norms and rules in their formal structures already, and thereby exhibiting smaller pay gaps. Albeit differing motives, effective programs ease the reconciliation of work and family, improve the career opportunities of women and may further reduce the pay gap between men and women.

H7: Foreign-owned establishments exhibit smaller wage gaps with respect to gender and nationality.

It is a well established fact that foreign owned firms hold a significant and persistent productivity advantage (Bellmann et al. 2002; Jungnickel and Keller 2003; Criscuolo and Martin 2009; Mattes 2010). There exist two ways to interpret this finding. First, multinationals transfer superior technology and organisational practices to their foreign subsidiaries (see the survey of empirical evidence in Stiebale and Reize 2011). Second, multinational firms only annex the most productive and innovative domestic firms. Therefore, the selection of higher-performing domestic firms is part of the explanation (see e.g. Guadalupe et al. 2010). Either way, highly qualified and internationally experienced employees represent a key resource to foreign-owned establishment in order to master new technological challenges.

Furthermore, ownership changes generally evoke fundamental reorganisations with substantial changes in the composition of the workforce. The empirical evidence suggests that the significant wage premiums paid by foreign-owned establishments can be explained by differences in the qualification of employees, for the most part (Andrews et al. 2009; Hijzen et al. 2010). These results hint at a selection effect towards (highly) qualified workers (see also Jungnickel and Keller 2003). In order to attract adequate job applicants and limit worker turnover during the turbulent times of an organisational change, firms may try to improve working conditions and staff satisfaction by adopting equal opportunity policies.[5]

Apart from these internal adjustments due to foreign ownership, we expect establishments owned by multinational firms to operate on international markets and hence to require specific skills typically held by non-German employees (e.g. language or cultural skills). Attractive wage offers may help to attract qualified non-German employees and hence moderate the resource dependency.

H8: Establishments with a larger share of non-German or female employees exhibit smaller nationality or gender wage gaps, respectively.

Pressure to adopt equal opportunity policies may not only appear from the outside environment of an establishment, but also from the inside, that is, from their own employees (Oliver 1991). For instance, an organisation's female employees/managers have been identified as important in fostering responsiveness to work-family-issues (Goodstein 1994; Ingram and Simons 1995). Hence, women represent constitutes within establishments who claim organisational change in terms of a family friendly working arrangement. Applying this argument to wage equality within establishments implies that the higher the share of non-German or female employees, the stronger the internal pressure to implement a productivity-based pay scheme.

H9a: Establishments operating in different organisational fields exhibit different pay gaps with respect to gender and nationality.

Institutional theory suggests that organisations react to social and cultural demands in their environment in order to improve legitimacy or survival capabilities. DiMaggio and Powell (1983) hence argue that members of any sort of group—a so-called organisational field—behave in a very similar way, first because they are exposed to the same external expectations, second because interactions, competition and dependencies within a field increase the homogeneity of organisational structures, norms and strategies. Using the industrial sector as a proxy for an organisational field, we expect significant differences between industrial sectors with respect to human resource strategies and hence wage structures.

H9b: Establishments operating in markets where the share of female customers is higher, and/or where customers may have a preference for female employees, exhibit smaller gender wage gaps.

According to the resource dependence theory, hiring female employees may be particularly observed in sectors where the market has become more attractive for female customers, which would explain higher pay for women (see also Thomas and Ely 1996). Ingram and Simons (1995) subsume this interaction under countervailing power. As long as organisations have no countervailing sources of power to respond to the demands of constituents, in our case female employees, the likelihood of resistance to pressures for institutional conformity is rather low.

4 Data

The impact of diversity strategies on wage inequality within firms can only be evaluated with data including both information on employers and employees. For this reason we use the linked employer-employee panel (LIAB) from the Institute for Employment Research (IAB Nuremberg), which is constructed by merging the IAB-establishment panel and the IAB employment statistic of the German Federal Services based on a unique establishment identification number.

The IAB-establishment panel is an annual survey of German establishments, which started in West-Germany in 1993 and was extended to East Germany in 1996 (Kölling 2000). The sample of selected establishments is random and stratified by industries, firm size classes and regions. The sample unit is the establishment which is officially defined as the establishment's head office or a local branch office of a firm with several headquarters.[6] The surveyed establishments are selected from the register of all German establishments that employ at least one employee covered by social security. The LIAB-data set is thus a representative sample of German establishments employing at least one employee liable to social security. The establishments covered by the survey are interviewed annually on employment trends, business strategies, investments, wage policies, industrial relations and varying special topics such as perceived personnel problems, hours of work and vocational training.

The IAB employment statistic of the German Federal Services, the so-called Employment Statistics Register, is an administrative panel data set of all employees in Germany paying social security contributions (see Bender et al. 2000). This data covers all the people who were employed for at least one day since 1975. Social security contributions are mandatory for all employees who earn more than a lower earnings limit. Civil servants, self employed and people with marginal jobs, that is, employees whose earnings are below the lower earnings limit or temporary jobs which last 50 working days at most, are not covered by this sample. Altogether, the Employment Statistics Register comprises about 80% of all West German employees. According to the statutory provisions, employers have to report information for all employed contributors at the beginning and at the end of their employment spells. In addition an annual report for every employee is compulsory at the end of each year. This report contains information on the employee's occupation, the occupational status, qualification, sex, age, nationality, industry and the size of the establishment. Also, the available information on daily gross earnings refers to employment periods that employers report to the Federal Employment Service. If the wage rate exceeds the upper earnings limit ("Beitragsbemessungsgrenze"), the daily social security threshold is reported instead. Note that the daily wage rate is therefore censored from above and truncated from below.

Both data sets contain a unique firm identifier which is used to match information on all employees paying social security contributions with their respective establishment in the IAB-establishment panel. Due to the lack of explicit information on working hours we consider only full-time employees. We also exclude employees under the age of 20 and over the age of 60 in order to eliminate the particularities of early retirement and transition from school to work. Since migration background is not captured in the data, German and non-German employees are distinguished by their nationality.

For the purpose of our analysis, we only include establishments with a minimum number of ten full-time employees in each category; men, women, German or non-German employees, because the calculation of a firm-specific wage gap would not yield very robust results in all other cases. Second, considering that non-German employees usually make up only a small fraction of the workforce, only establishments with at least 200 employees in total are selected for the sample. Moreover, we restricted our sample to West German establishments of the private sector. Eastern German establishments are not considered because both the wage levels as well as the wage setting processes are still very different in this part of the country. Unfortunately, a separate analysis for East Germany is not possible, either, because the number of firms in the data set which meet the required minimum number of employees is too small to derive reliable results. Third, in contrast to the private industry, pay systems in the public sector are highly centralized and regulated by the Federal Act on the Remuneration of Civil Servants (Bundesbesoldungsgesetz). This bill requires equal pay for all individuals with the same seniority and qualification who work in a specific job. As a result, wage gaps in the public sector are significantly lower (though not negligible) than in private firms (see e.g. Melly 2005). We therefore focus on the private sector only. Finally we chose the cross section 2004 for our analysis, because for that year the IAB-establishment panel questionnaire included specific questions on personnel problems anticipated by the firm and questions about measures taken to foster equal opportunities for women and men. We end up with a sample of 654 establishments.

Table 1 summarizes the employees' education, work experience, age and sector attachment in our sample. Except for the group of non-German employees, the majority of all employees have completed at least one professional education degree (apprenticeship or professional school). Among the non-Germans, 44% do not have any professional education and only 8% have completed a university degree, which is the lowest percentage of all groups. The share of university graduates is highest among German men. With respect to the sector attachment, we observe significant differences between men and women, but

Table 1: Average human capital endowment and sector attachment by gender and nationality. (Source: LIAB 2004, own calculations)

2004	German employees	Non-German employees	Female employees	Male employees
No professional education (in %)	11.67	44.14	18.77	13.73
Completed professional education (in %)	64.69	43.53	57.14	64.12
High school graduation (German Abitur) (in %)	7.50	4.10	12.88	5.67
University degree (in %)	16.13	8.23	11.20	16.48
Age	41.04	40.44	39.35	41.41
Tenure in firm (in years)	12.37	12.06	10.58	12.81
Sector (in %):				
Agriculture	1.45	0.97	0.54	1.63
Manufacturing	72.38	80.58	52.58	78.63
Construction	0.34	0.28	0.19	0.38
Trade	2.65	2.00	5.08	1.93
Finance	6.45	1.74	11.82	4.46
Gastronomy	0.02	0.13	0.04	0.03
Health care	7.08	4.30	20.47	3.19
Other services	9.62	10.00	9.28	9.76
Number of employees	693,292	73,471	160,296	606,467

less variation by nationality. Women are much more likely to work in the health care, trade and finance sector, whereas men are very much concentrated in manufacturing. Compared to non-German employees, Germans are more often in the health care and finance sector. The vast majority of all groups, but particularly the non-Germans are employed in manufacturing, the traditional guest-worker sector.

Among the non-German employees, Turks represent the largest group (36.8%) (see Table 3 in the Appendix). Guest workers originally from Italy, former Yugoslavia and Greece form the other large groups. Somewhat surprising is the relatively large share of French employees (7.1%). Despite the free mobility of labour within the European Community, the percentage of employees from other European countries is much smaller.

5 Measuring and analyzing pay gaps at the establishment level

In analogy to Heinze and Wolf (2010) and Beblo et al. (2011a, 2011b), we apply the seminal Oaxaca-Blinder wage decomposition at the firm level and decompose the observed wage differentials by gender and nationality, within each firm, into an endowment and a remuneration effect. The observed wage gap is given by:

$$Gap_j^{obs} = \overline{\ln w_{ij}^1} - \overline{\ln w_{ij}^2} \qquad (1)$$

where w_{ij} denotes the earnings for individual i at firm j; superscripts 1 and 2 refer to observations of male and female, German and non-German employees respectively. Since the wage information in our data set is right-censored (see Sect. 4 for more details), the observed wage gap defined in Eq. 1 underestimates the actual raw wage differential. In order to determine the actual observed wage gap we apply a simple Tobit model. By estimating the following equation for each firm, we can directly derive the wage differential between different groups of employees:

$$\ln w_{ij} = \alpha_j + \gamma_j D_{ij}^2 + \mu_{ij} \qquad (2)$$

where α is an absolute term measuring the average wage rate in firm j, D_{ij}^2 is a dummy variable indicating that individual i is female or non-German, respectively, and μ_{ij} denotes the error term. The estimated coefficient $\hat{\gamma}_j$ represents the raw wage gap in firm j (Gap_j^{obs}) taking into account that w_{ij} is censored from above.

Secondly, we calculate the wage differential that remains even after accounting for differences in the human capital endowment between the respective groups, i. e. the residual or unexplained wage gap. For that purpose we determine the firm-specific remunerations to selected human capital variables ($\hat{\beta}_j^1$), by estimating wage equations for male and German employees, respectively, within each firm:

$$\ln w_{ij}^1 = \beta_j^1 X_{ij}^1 + \varepsilon_{ij}^1 \qquad (3)$$

The dependent variable describes the daily log wage rate of individual i in firm j belonging to group 1. We use a standard Mincer wage equation aiming to adjust the observed wage gap by differences in the human capital endowment (measured by education, potential work experience and firm tenure) between male and female, German and non-German employees respectively. Since wages vary by both gender and nationality and we are interested in isolating the respective effects, we also control for the endowment effects of the "secondary" diversity feature. I.e. we control for the different shares of non-Germans among male and female employees when calculating the gender wage gap and vice versa. Other possible wage determinants, such as the occupational status and the occupational group, may be predetermined by basic human capital variables themselves. Because of its nature of labour market outcome, we do not consider information on occupations as an explanatory variable in our wage equation. It has to be stressed, however, that the residual pay gap may also be fed by unobserved individual characteristics that are related to productivity, e.g. language skills and the degree of integration of non-German employees. The right-censoring of the dependent variable again requires the estimation of a Tobit model. Given the firm specific observed wage gaps (Gap_j^{obs}) and the results from Eq. 3, we can calculate $Gap_j^{un\,exp}$:

$$Gap_j^{unexp} = Gap_j^{obs} - \left(\hat{\beta}_j^1 \overline{X_{ij}^1} - \hat{\beta}_j^1 \overline{X_{ij}^2}\right) \qquad (4)$$

Where $\bar{X}_{ij}$ includes mean characteristics of the individuals i at firm j and $\hat{\beta}_j^1$ is a vector of estimated coefficients—derived from wage regressions—of the individual characteristics X_{ij} of male respective German employees in firm j. Hence, Gap_j^{unexp} reflects the difference in the rewards for individual human capital characteristics and unobserved wage effects between the respective groups of individuals within each firm j.

Using the residual firm-specific wage differentials by gender and nationality as dependent variables allows us to analyse the relationship between our indicator variables for diversity strategies and intra-firm wage inequality.

$$Gap_j^{un\,exp} = \delta Z_j + \varepsilon_j \qquad (5)$$

The wage gaps, which are adjusted for the difference in human capital characteristics ($Gap_j^{un\,exp}$), are assumed to depend on the vector Z_j, including selected firm characteristics, or indicator variables, that reflect the importance of different types of resources and management strategies dealing with diversity. δ captures the connection of these variables with the residual wage gaps. Supposing that firms' resource requirements are linked to different equality strategies, as expounded in Sect. 3, our analysis allows new insights into the nature and sources of gender and nationality wage gaps within establishments.

6 Estimation results

In our sample of establishments, the average within-firm wage differential observed between German and non-German employees amounts to 12% (measured by Gap_j^{obs} in Eq. 1). As such, it is about 5 percentage points smaller than the overall wage gap between these groups in the labour market as a whole (see Beblo et al. 2011a). The smaller average wage gap within establishments points to a selection of non-German employees in low-paying firms. The within-firm wage cut for non-German employees is for the most part explained by differences in education and work experience. Nonetheless, confirming the classical economic arguments for discrimination, there remains an "unexplained" wage differential of 3.1% on average (measured by $Gap_j^{un\,exp}$ in Eq. 4). Furthermore, there is a substantial variance in wage inequality across firms. Figure 1 illustrates the distribution of observed and residual wage gaps with respect to gender and nationality. Positive values imply corresponding wage cuts for women and non-German employees respectively. The right tail

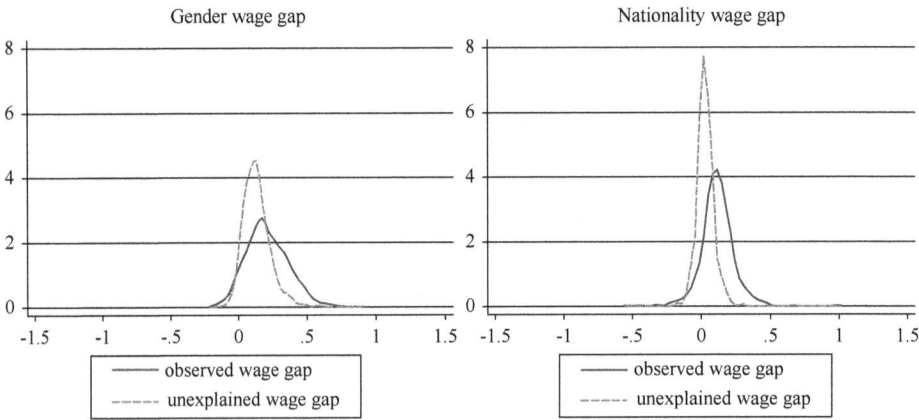

Fig. 1: Distribution of gender and nationality pay gaps within establishments. (Source: LIAB 2004, own calculations)

of the distribution shows that the quarter of firms with the largest residual nationality wage gap pays about 6–21% lower wages to non-German than to German employees. Note, however, that more than a quarter of all establishments remunerate their non-German employees at a higher rate than their German colleagues, at a given level of education and work experience. These pay schemes become plausible, if the expected benefits from equal treatment outweigh the saved labour costs due to discrimination.

The average observed within-firm wage gap between female and male employees amounts to 21%.[7] Again, the observed gender wage gaps within establishments are much larger than the residual ones, which take 13% on average. However, the fraction of the observed wage gap which can be ascribed to differences in measured human capital endowments is much smaller compared to the explained part of the nationality wage gaps. Conditional on the level of education and work experience, less than 5% of the establishments remunerate female employees better than male employees (compared to a quarter with regard to non-German versus German employees). The firms in the highest quartile of the residual gender wage gap pay women between 18 and 43% less than men with comparable human capital endowments.

In the following, we will analyse empirically whether the variations in the residual wage inequality by gender and nationality go along with our hypothesis about the in-plant benefits and hence the adoption of equal opportunity policies. To do so, we run linear regressions with the establishments' residual gender and nationality wage gaps as dependent variables according to Eq. 5. We use the residual wage gaps as the dependent variables, as they best reflect intra-firm wage structures going beyond qualification differentials. All explanatory variables Z_j should be interpreted as proxy variables aiming to capture the establishments' resource requirements or pressure due to expectations in the organisational field or they refer to the empirical results on business cases for equality. The descriptive statistics and definitions of all explanatory variables are presented in Table 4 in the appendix. Comparing the results from the separate analyses of the nationality and gender pay gaps will help to detect similarities and discrepancies in the relative remunerations of these two groups. Additionally, we want to analyse the intersection of gender and nationality pay differences.

At first glace, the data reveal a rather weak correlation between the observed intra-firm pay gaps by gender and nationality of 0.10 which is statistically significant at the 10%-level only. The correlation between the residual pay gaps amounts to slightly larger 0.11 and is statistically significant at the 1%-level. Hence, there seems to be some statistical congruency across firms in the valuation and disesteem of employees from "minority" groups. Therefore, we also estimate the determinants of a firm's probability to exhibit extraordinary large wage cuts for both groups, female and non-German employees. In the underlying probit model, establishments with a gender pay gap in the highest quartile (among the 25% highest gender pay gaps) as well as a nationality pay gap in the highest quartile (among the 25% highest nationality wage gaps) are coded 1. Based on the probit estimation results, we will characterise those establishments with the highest potential to pay lower wages to female and non-German employees.

All estimation results are presented in Table 2. Please note that, since we have no direct information about the reasons why establishments discriminate less against female and non-German employees, we can only derive indirect evidence on the motives and use of equal opportunity policies. Of course, there may always exist alternative and economically consistent interpretations of the coefficient estimates.

Table 2: Determinants of the gender and nationality pay gaps within establishments. (Source: LIAB 2004, own calculations)

	Variables	Residual gender pay gap		Residual nationality pay gap		Probit: high pay gaps for both groups[a]	
		Coeff.	Standard Errors	Coeff.	Standard Errors	Coeff.	Standard Errors
H1	Number of employees/1000	−0.004*	0.0022	0.0013	0.0017	−0.1326*	0.0805
H1	(Number of employees/1000)^2	0.0001	0.0001	−0.0000	0.0000	0.0026	0.002
H2	Share of qualified employees	−0.0096	0.0167	0.00433	0.013	0.1554	0.4050
H2	Shortage of employees (yes = 1/no = 0)	0.0016	0.0168	−0.0198	0.0131	−0.4045	0.4454
H2	Problems due to quitting of qualified employees (1/0)	−0.0178	0.0117	0.014	0.0091	0.1971	0.2735
H2	Problems with recruitment of qualified employees (1/0)	0.0241***	0.0074	−0.0073	0.0058	0.1018	0.1779
H3	Innovative Firm (1/0)	−0.0271**	0.0092	−0.0073	0.0072	−0.5216**	0.2096
H3	Research and Development (1/0)	0.0038	0.0085	−0.0004	0.0066	−0.0260	0.2087
H4	Collective bargaining agreement (1/0)	−0.0429***	0.0126	−0.0092	0.0098	0.0655	0.2751
H5	Works council (1/0)	−0.0237	0.0170	0.0169	0.0132	−0.2091	0.3536
H6	Measures to enhance gender equality (1/0)	−0.0094	0.0073	0.0028	0.0057	−0.1140	0.1763
H7	Foreign ownership (1/0)	−0.0162*	0.0086	−0.0042	0.0067	−0.1272	0.2112
H8	Share of non-German employees	−0.0933**	0.0446	0.0534	0.0347	−1.162	1.1150
H8	Share of female employees	0.1532***	0.0263	0.0949***	0.0205	1.569***	0.5812
H9	Sector: trade (1/0)	−0.0285	0.0163	0.0222*	0.0127	−0.0797	0.3244
H9	Sector: gastronomy (1/0)	−0.0847	0.0881	0.1173*	0.0686	–	–
H9	Sector: health care (1/0)	−0.1358***	0.0175	−0.0515***	0.0137	−1.4377***	0.4477
H9	Sector: other services (1/0)	−0.0345***	0.0126	−0.0115	0.0098	−0.3450	0.2939
	Observations	654		654		646	
	R^2	0.2592		0.1453		0.1454 (Pseudo R2)	

Dummy variables for regions are also included in the estimation. Further control variables include the remaining sector dummies and shares of atypical employment. The results are available on request
***indicates statistical significance at the 1%-level, **at the 5%-level and *at the 10%-level
[a]Only establishments with both wage gaps in the upper quartile of the distribution of gender respective nationality wage gaps are coded 1

Our results show that both, the gender pay gap as well as the probability of belonging to the groups of establishments with large wage inequality are negatively related to the number of employees (H1).[8] With respect to the nationality pay gap, there is no statistically significant effect. We hence conclude that the impact of the firm size on the residual pay gap is weakly consistent with the implications derived from resource dependence theory, neoinstitutional theory and the business case analysis. Apart from this interpretation there may of course exist other channels for how firm size may affect the wage distribution within establishments.

For the empirical test of hypothesis H2 we assume that the need for (highly) qualified employees correlates positively with the share of qualified employees in the establishment. Furthermore, we use reported staffing problems, namely difficulties in recruiting qualified employees, general shortage of employees and quitting of qualified employees as signals of the establishment's dependency on specific human resources. As presented in Table 2, only some of the coefficients of the relevant explanatory variables are negative, and even if so, they are not statistically significant. That is, our auxiliary variables capturing the need for (highly) qualified employees are not systematically related to more wage equality for women and non-German employees. Establishments reporting problems with the recruitment of qualified employees even show significantly larger gender pay gaps. This result seems surprising at first glance, but may suggest that the pay gaps in turn are causing recruitment problems and therefore constitute incentives for a reduction of the gender pay gap in the future. Also firms struggling with quitting qualified employees tend to have larger nationality wage gaps, albeit not statistically significant. When estimating the probability of establishments to exhibit both at the same time, wage inequality against women and wage inequality against non-German employees, none of the estimated coefficients of the indicator variables for recruitment problems can be rejected to be different from zero (see probit model in Table 2). Hence, there is no empirical evidence for the argument that establishments with a need for (highly) skilled employees care more about wage equality.

In contrast to this, we do find supportive evidence for the hypothesis that innovating firms—also relying on a highly-qualified and creative workforce—attract people by offering equal opportunities (H3). Innovative establishments, that is, establishments that declare having implemented innovations within the past two years, show significantly lower differences in the remuneration of women and men as well as a lower probability of exhibiting high pay gaps for both groups at the same time. This finding is consistent with the implications of the learning strategy in the sense of Ortlieb and Sieben (2008). The authors argue that establishments that rely on their innovative capacities are in need of new perspectives and approaches to work and hence employ a more diverse workforce. In order to attract the required staff, one could argue that establishments following this strategy offer more wage equality. Activities in research and development, however, have no statistically relevant effect on the wage distribution within establishments. To summarize, the overall hypothesis that establishments concerned about the innovative potential of their employees exhibiting greater wage equality is at least partly supported by our indicator variables.

According to the estimations results in Table 2, the institutional embedding of social norms with respect to labour relations is only partly correlated with wage equality (see H4 and H5). Our results show that collective bargaining agreements go along with significantly lower pay gaps for female employees. This finding is in line with previous evidence from Stephan and Gerlach (2003) as well as Heinze and Wolf (2010). However, Antonczyk et al. (2010) discovered that the recent drop in collective bargaining coverage led to rising wage inequality in the labour market both for male and female employees, but that the overall gender wage gap was hardly affected. The pay gap between German and non-German employees is also negatively related to agreements on collective bargaining, although the coefficient estimate is not statistically significant. In terms of the classification of diversity strategies by Ortlieb and Sieben (2008), this result could also be interpreted as a pursuit of the *anti-discrimination* strategy.

Surprisingly, an establishments' probability to exhibit notably high pay gaps with respect to both gender and nationality does not seem to be linked to the adoption of collective agreements. In contrast to our hypothesis H5, establishments with work councils do not vary significantly from those without formal co-determination with respect to unexplained wage inequality by gender or nationality. However, the signs of the point estimates are in line with the theoretical considerations.

We find only limited empirical support for the equal-opportunity-measure hypothesis H6. The regression results show that unexplained wage differentials by gender are indeed somewhat lower in firms which offer these measures. However, the estimate is not statistically significant. One way to interpret our finding is that measures fostering equal opportunities do not necessarily result in higher incomes for women, but rather facilitate the compatibility of work and family (e.g. by flexible work schedules or childcare facilities). Meyer and Rowan (1977) even argue that the adoption of management practices can not only be rationalised by their "technical efficiency", but also by their contribution to assure legitimacy. This implies that equal opportunity programs may pay off in terms of access to crucial resources, even if wage equality or the participation of women in all hierarchical levels is not effectively targeted.

As argued above, foreign ownership often goes along with a higher demand for (highly) skilled employees with international experience, that is, a scarce resource. A policy of equal opportunities may therefore help to limit labour shortage by drawing on a larger pool of candidates (see H7). In fact, our results suggest more wage equality in foreign-owned firms, albeit the coefficient is not significant in the nationality pay gap regression and the probit model.[9]

As regards the proportion of female and non-German employees (H8), the empirical analysis yielded mixed results. A larger share of non-Germans is negatively related to the gender pay gap, whereas the proportion of female employees in an establishment is significantly, positively related to wage disadvantages for both groups. This finding may indicate labour market segmentation where some low-paying establishments have a large proportion of female employees. In these establishments, diversity could be enhanced by hiring more male employees (hence, the coefficient estimate is positive). Another explanation is that these establishments employ more women because of their lower wages. According to Ortlieb and Sieben (2008), they apply a strategy of *adding value through mere labour*.

In the last set of hypotheses (H9a and H9b), we analyse the relationship between an establishment's sector attachment and the residual pay gaps. Using the industrial sector as a proxy for an establishment's organisational field, we expect the coefficient estimates of the sector dummies to be statistically significant, indicating systematic differences in their human resource strategies and hence wage structures (H9a). The estimation results suggest heterogeneity across industries, though sometimes only for one dimension of the pay gap. We further use the sector attachment to detect markets where the share of female customers is higher or customers may have a preference for female employees (H9b). Our findings on the wage inequality by sector illustrate significant differences between industries that are dominated by female, male, German or non-German employees. Compared to the manufacturing sector, where women are underrepresented (see Table 1) and wage differentials are relatively large, unexplained gender pay gaps are significantly lower in the health care sector, where the share of female employees is high and customers may have a preference for female service providers. Other sectors with a relatively larger proportion of women (i.e. trade and finance) also exhibit lower gender pay gaps. This last interpretation is based on the point estimates, though, the coefficients do not prove significant. Establishments operating in the male dominated construction sector, both with respect to employees and customers, pay even larger wage differences between men and women. Being aware that the sector attachment provides only a very rough indicator of the specific skill requirements of an establishment, we conclude that our results are in line with hypothesis H9b.

7 Conclusion and discussion

To date, the coincidence of the well-known gender and nationality pay gaps has not been analysed in depth and neither have the respective wage distributions within establishments. Comparing within-firm wage inequality by gender and nationality can help to detect similarities and discrepancies in the relative disadvantages of these two groups. Even though the idea that organisations play an important part in creating, maintaining and even resolving wage inequality has become more popular during the past decades, very few studies have analysed the link between management strategies and the resulting pay gaps, particularly by gender and nationality.

Based on the linked employer-employee dataset LIAB for the year 2004, we therefore estimated the within-establishment wage differentials between female and male, non-German and German employees respectively. We focussed on the so-called "unexplained" pay gaps which capture wage differentials due to unequal rewards for basic human capital characteristics and could be attributed to unobserved individual characteristics and/or discriminatory behaviour according to economic theory. Unique information on the wage distribution within each establishment allowed us to analyse the heterogeneity of the pay gaps in light of organisational theories and empirical business cases. Based on neoinstitutional and resource dependence theory as well as the business cases literature, we tested hypotheses on how the (de)valuation of work performed by "fringe" groups in the labour market may be linked to a firms' social, institutional and cultural environment and their resource requirements. Our main contribution to the existing literature is that we look at the internal wage structure of establishments with respect to organisational theories. While there exist some studies using neoinstitutional and resource dependence theory to explain the disseminations of diversity management or equal opportunity policies (see e.g. Süß and Kleiner 2008 or Ingram and Simons 1995), we are the first to derive theory-based hypotheses of these theories with respect to the pay gaps between men and women as well as between Germans and non-German employees.

Our estimation results show that the residual pay gaps by gender are on average much higher than those between German and non-German employees, while both measures vary substantially across establishments. Despite the overall variance, there seems to be a systematic intersection of gender and nationality pay gaps at the establishment level. The statistically highly significant correlation between the residual pay gaps amounts to 0.11.

A subsequent analysis of variation in estimated residual pay gaps exposes those firm characteristics related to an establishment's wage distribution. All firm characteristics used as explanatory variables are derived from economic and organisational theory. Consistent with neoinstitutional theory, pay gaps are smaller in larger establishments and those with collective bargaining agreements and they differ significantly between industrial sectors. In support of resource dependence theory, pay gaps are smaller in larger, innovating and foreign-owned establishments with a larger share of non-German employees. On the contrary, greater pay gaps in establishments with a high share of female employees are not consistent with either theory. Finally, we can replicate some predictions from the business case literature: Larger establishments and those in need of (highly) qualified employees and/or those who face staffing problems are more likely to benefit from equal opportunity policies and hence exhibit more wage equality.

Even though our results yield some new insights, the study has some limitations: First, our results provide only indirect evidence for the pursuit of specific management strategies. When using matched employer-employee data sets, we can only conclude on the conformity of the observed outcomes with the theoretical predictions, as the personnel policy of the firms remains somewhat of a black box. Further qualitative and quantitative research is warranted to open this box and link observed outcomes to specific management strategies. A second major restriction is that only information on the nationality of the employees is available in our data. Hence, interpretation with regard to immigrant employees or second generation migrants is limited.

To conclude, the link between organisational theories and the intra-firm wage structure as well as the wage cuts for migrant and female workers should be further investigated in theory and empirical analyses.

Endnotes

1. Recent studies build on taste discrimination in equilibrium search models and were able to separate the effects of discrimination and unobserved characteristics (see Flabbi 2010, Bowlus and Eckstein 2002).
2. Also Ortlieb and Sieben (2008) argue that depending on their human resources requirements, establishments choose a specific diversity strategy and are hence more or less likely to employ immigrant employees.
3. The missing reliance on the effectiveness of managerial actions is a crucial antagonism to the resource dependence theory, supposing that the organisational practices actually help to overcome the existing dependencies.
4. Legitimacy should not be interpreted as a specific resource, such as reputation, but is rather a necessary condition to secure the accrual of specific resources. Legitimacy is supposed to

increase with the accordance between laws, regulations, normative expectations, common social values and the management principles (Walgenbach and Meyer 2008).

5   Hijzen et al. (2010) analyse whether foreign-owned firms differ in terms of working conditions from their domestic counterparts. In particular, they look at differences with respect to hours of work, worker turnover, union coverage and low pay and find no clear-cut evidence.

6   Note however that, though we try to minimize confusion, the terms firm and establishment are used as synonyms in this paper.

7   Deviations between this result and the overall gender pay gap of 23% reported by the German Federal Statistical Office (Destatis 2010) may result from our focus on large firms, as well as from the exclusion of part time employees, who earn lower hourly wage rates on average (Wolf 2010), in our sample. Furthermore, our figure refers to the average gender wage gap within establishments and not to the difference between average male and female wages in the whole labour market. Lower within-firm wage gaps may also indicate at a selection of women into low paying firms (see Heinze and Wolf 2010).

8   We used the number of employees as well as the quadratic transformation of this variable as explanatory variables to allow for a non-linear relationship between firm size and pay gap.

9   It is also argued that foreign-owned firms have better access to export markets. We hence analysed whether exporting establishments differ in terms of wage gaps. Our results show that establishments' export quotas are negatively related to both residual wage differentials, but the point estimates are not statistically significant. As this variable suffers from a large number of missing values, we decided to skip it in the final specification presented in Table 2. However, the other estimation results did not change with the exclusion of the export quota.

Appendix

Table 3: Employees by nationality (proportion in %). (Source: LIAB 2004, own calculations)

2004	Proportion of the whole sample	Proportion of the sample of all non-Germans
Germany	90.4	–
Turkey	3.53	36.8
Italy	1.12	11.7
France	0.68	7.12
Yugoslavia, Serbia and Montenegro	0.67	6.99
Greece	0.56	5.89
Austria	0.41	4.26
Croatia	0.32	3.33
Spain	0.24	2.50
Poland	0.17	1.73
Portugal	0.15	1.60
Great Britain und Northern Ireland, Ireland	–	1.58
Netherlands, Luxembourg	0.12	1.22
USA, Canada	–	1.14
Bosnia and Herzegovina	–	1.10
Asia (open)	–	1.08

Nationality groups that amount to less than 1% of all non-German employees are not presented in the table

Table 4: Description of the estimation sample

Variable	Comment	Min.	Max.	Mean	Std. Dev.
Observed gender wage gap	See Sect. 5 Eq. 1 (in %)	−0.17	0.86	0.2111	0.1543
Unexplained gender wage gap	See Sect. 5 Eq. 4 (in %)	−0.13	0.59	0.1320	0.0970
Observed nationality wage gap	See Sect. 5 Eq. 1 (in %)	−0.53	0.99	0.1165	0.1197
Unexplained nationality wage gap	See Sect. 5 Eq. 4 (in %)	−0.56	0.67	0.0310	0.0685
Number of employees/1000		0.04	49.72	1.5408	3.1984
Share of qualified employees	Qualified employees completed a vocational training or have a university degree.	0	1	0.6917	0.2331
Share of non-German employees		0.01	0.68	0.1014	0.0862
Share of female employees		0.01	0.90	0.2622	0.1965
Measures to enhance gender equality	Indicator variable: 1 = the establishment provides child care facilities, involvement of employees during parental leave, systematic endorsement of women in career programs, mentoring, quotas etc.	0	1	0.4052	0.4913
Works council	Indicator variable: 1 = the establishment has a works council	0	1	0.9495	0.2191
Collective bargaining agreement	Indicator variable: 1 = the establishment adopts collective bargaining agreements	0	1	0.9006	0.2994
Foreign ownership	I Indicator variable: 1 = majority of ownership held by Non-Germans.	0	1	0.1972	0.3982
	The following variables are based on the question: "Which personnel problems do you expect in your establishment in the next two years?"				
Shortness of employees	Indicator variable: 1 = yes	0	1	0.0459	0.2094
Problems due to quitting of qualified employees	Indicator variable: 1 = yes	0	1	0.0963	0.2951
Problems with recruitment of qualified employees	Indicator variable: 1 = yes	0	1	0.3456	0.4759

Table 4: (continued)

Variable	Comment	Min.	Max.	Mean	Std. Dev.
Innovative firms	Product or process innovations implemented in the last two years.	0	1	0.7921	0.4062
Research and development	Indicator variable: 1 = yes	0	1	0.5734	0.495
Sectors					
Manufacturing (reference)					
Agriculture				_[a]	_[a]
Construction				_[a]	_[a]
Trade		0	1	0.0627	0.2426
Finance		0	1	0.0459	0.2094
Gastronomy				_[a]	_[a]
Health care		0	1	0.1055	0.3074
Other services		0	1	0.1086	0.3113
Schleswig-Holstein		0	1	0.0321	0.1764
Hamburg		0	1	0.0367	0.1882
Lower Saxony		0	1	0.0917	0.2889
Bremen				_[a]	_[a]
North Rhine-Westphalia		0	1	0.1223	0.3279
Hesse		0	1	0.1942	0.3959
Baden-Württemberg		0	1	0.1728	0.3783
Bavaria		0	1	_[a]	_[a]
Berlin		0	1	0.0749	0.2635
Observations				654	

[a] Means and standard deviations not published due to secrecy obligations

References

Abowd J, Kramarz F, Margolis D (1999) High-wage workers and high-wage firms. Econometrica 67(2):251–333

Addison JT, Teixeira P, Zwick T (2006) Works councils and the anatomy of wages. ZEW Discussion Paper 06(086), Centre for European Economic Research (ZEW), Mannheim

Amstrong C, Flood PC, Guthrie JP, Liu W, Maccurtain S, Mkamwa T (2010) The impact of diversity and equality management on firm performance beyond high performance work systems. Hum Resour Manag 49(6):977–998

Andrews M, Bellmann L, Schank T, Upward R (2009) The takeover and selection effects of foreign ownership in Germany. Ana analysis using linked worker-firm data. Rev World Econ 142(2):293–317

Antonczyk D, Fitzenberger B, Sommerfeld K (2010) Rising wage inequality, the decline of collective bargaining, and the gender wag gap. Lab Econ 17(5):835–847

Arrow KJ (1973) The theory of discrimination. In: Ashenfelter O (ed) Discrimination in labor markets. Princeton University Press, pp 3–33

Baron JN (1984) Organizational perspectives on stratification. Ann Rev Sociol 10:37–69

Beblo M, Wolf E (2003) Sind es die Erwerbsunterbrechungen? Ein Erklärungsbeitrag zum Lohnunterschied zwischen Frauen und Männern in Deutschland. Mitteilungen Arbeitsmarkt- Berufsforschung 36(4):560–572

Beblo M, Wolf E (2002) How much does a year off cost? Estimating the wage effects of employment breaks and part-time periods. Cah Économique de Brux 45(2):191–217

Beblo M, Ohlert C, Wolf E (2011a) Intra-firm wage differentials between German and Non-German employees. Harriet Taylor Mill-Institut, Berlin

Beblo M, Ohlert C, Wolf E (2011b) Logib-D und die Entgeltunterschiede zwischen Männern und Frauen in deutschen Betrieben * eine Abschätzung des politischen Handlungsfeldes. Z ArbeitsmarktForschung 44(1/2):43–52

Beblo M, Bender S, Wolf E (2008) Establishment-level wage effects of entering motherhood. Oxford Econ Pap 61(Suppl 1):i11–i34

Becker GS (1957) The economics of discrimination. University of Chicago Press, Chicago

Bellmann L, Ellguth P, Jungnickel R (2002) Produktivität in auslandskontrollierten Betrieben Ostdeutschlands. In: Bellmann L (ed) Die ostdeutschen Betriebe in der internationalen Arbeitsteilung, Beiträge zur Arbeitsmarkt- und Berufsforschung 263. Bertelsmann, pp 85–110

Bender S, Haas A, Klose C (2000) IAB Employment Subsample 1975–1995. Opportunities for analysis provided by the anonymised subsample. IZA discussion paper 117, institute for the study of labor, Bonn

Bergmann B (1974) Occupational segregation, wages and profits when employers discriminate by race or sex. Eastern Econ J 82(2):103–110

BMFSFJ (2011) Neue Wege – Gleiche Chancen. Gleichstellung von Frauen und Männern im Lebensverlauf. Bundesministerium für Familie, Senioren, Frauen und Jugend

Bowlus AJ, Eckstein Z (2002) Discrimination and skill differences in an equilibrium search model. Int Econ Rev 43(4):1309–1345

Cain GG (1986) The economic analysis of labor market discrimination: a survey. In: Ashenfelter O, Layard R (eds) Handbook of labor economics, vol 1. North-Holland, Amsterdam, pp 693–785

Cassell C (1997) The business case for equal opportunities: implications for women in management. Women Manag Rev 12(1):11–16

Chiswick BR (1978) The effect of americanisation on the earnings of foreign born men. J Polit Economy 86:897–921

Constant A, Massey DS (2003) Labor market segmentation and the earnings of German guestworkers. IZA discussion paper 774, Institute for the Study of Labor, Bonn

Cox T, Blake S (1991) Managing cultural diversity: implications for organizational competitiveness. Acad Manag Exec 5(3):45–56
Criscuolo C, Martin R (2009) Multinationals and U.S. productivity leadership: evidence from Great Britain. Rev Econ Statist 91(2):263–281
Destatis (2010) Verdienstunterschiede zwischen Männern und Frauen, Study by Claudia Finke, commissioned by Bundesministeriums für Familie, Senioren, Frauen und Jugend, Wiesbaden
DiMaggio PJ, Powell WW (1983) The iron cage revisited: institutional isomorphism and collective rationality in organizational fields. Am Sociol Rev 48(2):147–160
Edelman LB (1990) Legal environments and organizational governance: the expansion of due process in the American workplace. Am J Sociol 95(6):1401–1441
Edgeworth FY (1922) Equal pay to men and women. Econ J 32(128):431–457
Elvira MM, Saporta I (2001) How does collective bargaining affect the gender pay gap? Work Occup 28(4):469–490
European Commission (2005) The business case for diversity. Good practices in the workplace. Directorate-general for employment, social affairs and equal opportunities unit D3. European Commission.
Fitzenberger B, Kohn K (2005) Gleicher Lohn für gleiche Arbeit? Zum Zusammenhang zwischen Gewerkschaftsmitgliedschaft und Lohnstruktur in Westdeutschland 1985–1997. Z Arbeitsmarktforschung 38(2/3):125–146
Flabbi L (2010) Gender discrimination estimation in a search model with matching and bargaining. Int Econ Rev 51(3):745–783
Freeman RB, Medoff JL (1984) What do unions do? Basic Books, New York
Gebert D (2004) Durch diversity zu mehr Teaminnovativität? Betriebswirtschaft (DBW) 64:412–430
Goodstein JD (1994) Institutional pressure and strategic responsiveness: employer-involvement in work-family issues. Acad Manag J 37:350–382
Granato N, Kalter F (2001) Die Persistenz ethnischer Ungleichheit auf dem deutschen Arbeitsmarkt. Diskriminierung oder Unterinvestition in Humankapital? Kölner Z Soziologie Sozialpsychologie 53:497–520
Guadalupe G, Kuzmina O, Thomas C (2010) Innovation and Foreign Ownership. NBER working paper no. 16573
Heinze A, Wolf E (2010) The intra-firm gender wage gap: a new view on wage differentials based on linked employer-employee data. J Population Econ 23(3):851–879
Hijzen A, Martins PS, Schank T, Upward R (2010) Do foreign-owned firms proviede better working conditions than their domestic counterparts? A comparative analysis, IZA discussion paper no. 5259, Bonn
Hirsch B, Schank T, Schnabel C (2010) Differences in labor supply to monopsonistic firms and the gender pay gap: an empirical analysis using linked employer-employee data from Germany. J Lab Econ 28(2):291–330
Hübler O, Jirjahn U (2003) Works councils and collective bargaining in Germany: the impact on productivity and wages. Scot J Polit Economy 50(4):471–491
Ingram P, Simons T (1995) Institutional and resource dependence determinants of responsiveness to work-family issues. Acad Manag J 38(5):1466–1482
Jungnickel R, Keller D (2003) Foreign-owned firms in the German labour market. HWWA discussion paper 233, Hamburg
Kölling A (2000) The IAB-establishment panel. Schmollers Jahrbuch Z Wirtsch Sozialwissen 120(2):291–300
Kohaut, S, Möller I (2009) Vereinbarungen zur Chancengleichheit. Kaum Forschritte bei der betrieblichen Förderung, IAB-Kurzbericht Nr. 26, Institute for Employment Research, Nuremberg
Longhi S, Platt L (2008) Pay gaps across equality areas. Institute for Social and Economic Research. University of Essex.

Mattes A (2010) Foreign takeovers: no negative effects on employment and productivity. Weekly Report, DIW Berlin. Ger Inst Econ Res 32:239–244

McCall L (2005) Gender, race, and the restructuring of work: Organizational and institutional perspectives. In: Tolbert P, Batt R, Ackroyd S, Thompson P (eds) The oxford handbook of work and organization. Oxford University Press, New York, pp 74–94

Melly B (2005) Public-private sector wage differentials in Germany: evidence from quantile regression. Empirical Econ 30(2):505–520

Meyer JW, Rowan B (1977) Institutionalized organizations: formal structures as myth and ceremony. Am J Sociol 83(2):340–363

Nerdinger F, Blickle G, Schaper N (2008) Arbeits- und Organisationspsychologie. Springer, Heidelberg

Oliver C (1991) Strategic response to institutional processes. Acad Manag Rev 16(1):145–179

Ortlieb R, Sieben B (2008) Diversity strategies focused on employees with a migration background: an empirical investigation based on resource dependence theory. Manag Revenue 19(1/2):70–93

Phelps ES (1972) The statistical theory of racism and sexism. Am Econ Rev 62(4):659–661

Pfeffer J, Salancik GR (1978) The external control of organizations. A resource dependence perspective. Harper & Row, New York

Ransom MR, Oaxaca RL (2005) Sex differences in pay in a new monopsony model of the labor market. IZA discussion paper no. 1870, Institute for the Study of Labor (IZA), Bonn

Richard, O (2000) Racial diversity, business strategy, and firm performance: a resource-based view. Acad Manag J 43:164–177

Riley R, Metcalf H, Forth J (2008) The business case for equal opportunities—an econometric investigation. Department for work and pensions, research report no. 483

Robinson J (1933) The economics of imperfect competition. Macmillan, London

Singh JV, Tucker DJ, House RJ (1986) Organizational legitimacy and the liability of newness. Adm Sci Q 31:171–193

Spence M (1973) Job market signaling. Quart J Econ 87(3):355–374

Stephan G, Gerlach K (2003) Firmenlohndifferenziale und Tarifverträge: Eine Mehrebenenanalyse. Mitteilungen Arbeitsmarkt- Berufsforschung 36:525–538

Stiebale J, Reize F (2011) The impact of FDI through mergers and acquisitions on innovation in target firms. Int J Ind Organ 29:155–167

Süß S, Kleiner M (2008) Dissemination of diversity management in Germany: a new institutional approach. Euro Manag J 26:35–47

Thomas DA, Ely RJ (1996) Making differences matter: a new paradigm for Managing Diversity. Harvard Bus Rev 74(6):79–90

Walgenbach P, Meyer R (2008) Neoinstitutionalistische Organisationstheorien. Kohlhammer, Stuttgart

Weichselbaumer D, Winter-Ebmer R (2005) A meta-analysis on the international gender wage gap. J Econ Surveys 19(3):479–511

Wolf E (2010) Lohndifferenziale zwischen Voll- und Teilzeitbeschäftigten in Ost- und Westdeutschland. WSI Diskussionspapier Nr. 174, Düsseldorf

Zuckermann EW (1999) The categorical imperative: securities analysts and the illegitimacy discount. Am J Sociol 104:1398–1438

ZfB-SPECIAL ISSUE 2/2012

Women on German management boards
How ownership structure affects management board diversity

Jana Oehmichen · Marc Steffen Rapp · Michael Wolff

Abstract: In this paper we want to investigate the impact of company owners on the low percentage of women on management boards and whether they are attempting to increase this percentage. After analysing whether ownership concentration influences the number of women on management boards we distinguish between different types of owners. We find that ownership concentration has no effect on the presence of women on German management boards, we show however that institutional and individual owners have a significantly positive effect. Classifying institutional owners into national and foreign owners illustrates that foreign investors are the primary driver of the positive effect within the class of institutional owners; the presence of national investors that are strongly influenced by the national banking system does not show any effect. Our analyses are based on 15,976 management board member positions from 2000 to 2007 in approximately 600 German-listed companies.

Keywords: Management board · Gender · Women · Corporate governance

JEL Classification: G30 · G34 · C23

© The Author(s) 2011. This article is published with open access at Springerlink.com

Dr. J. Oehmichen (✉) · Prof. Dr. M. Wolff
Chair of Management and Control, Georg-August-University Göttingen,
Platz der Göttinger Sieben 3, 37073 Göttingen, Germany
e-mail: jana.oehmichen@wiwi.uni-goettingen.de

Prof. Dr. M. Wolff
e-mail: michael.wolff@wiwi.uni-goettingen.de

Prof. Dr. M. S. Rapp
Institute of Management Accounting, Philipps-University Marburg,
Am Plan 1, 35032 Marburg, Germany
e-mail: msr@m-s-rapp.de

1 Introduction

Since the financial crisis began in 2008, in many countries there has been greater attention to the diversity in companies' boardrooms, even though only a modest increase in the percentage of women in these positions can be observed worldwide. After analyzing 4,200 companies around the world, GovernanceMetrics International found that the percentage of female board members increased marginally between 2009 and 2011, from 9.2 to 9.8% (GovernanceMetrics International (GMI) 2011).

The public discussion in Germany has also noted for some time that there are too few women in German top management positions. German policy has recognised this issue at least since 2001 when the German Federal Ministry for Family Affairs, Senior Citizens, Women and Youth enacted the agreement on the promotion of gender equality in the German private sector. However, the impact of this agreement has not been satisfactory (Holst and Wiemer 2010). Therefore, further possible solutions remain a topic in the public discussion. The German Corporate Governance Codex requires the consideration of an adequate level of diversity when appointing management and supervisory board members (Weber-Rey 2009). In addition, the option of a hard quota law following the example of Norway is frequently discussed. At a company level, the German Telekom was the first DAX company to introduce an internal quota law in 2010 (Holst and Wiemer 2010). Today, 20% of the companies listed in the DAX are committed to an internal quota regulation.[1]

At the same time, researchers have focused more and more on female board representation. They have found evidence that while it is important for companies to have women on management teams, they are underrepresented—especially among top managers and board members (Adams and Ferreira 2009; Daily et al. 1999; Hillman et al. 2007). The identification of the factors supporting the presence of women on boards is essential (Hillman et al. 2007). Naturally, one of the most influential institutions involved in decisions on the corporate governance structure are the companies' owners.[2] Drawing on the assumptions of the classical agency theory, they rely on finding an adequate representative of their interests as manager. This search might have interesting effects on the gender diversity among board members.

Among existing investigations of the ownership impact on board diversity the following gaps can be identified: Since different types of owners generally have different interests, a detailed distinction of the impact of different types of owners on the presence of women on the management board is indispensable. While there are some studies that focus on the impact of a specific type of owner—the institutional investors—on board diversity (Carleton et al. 1998; Farrell and Hersch 2005), no holistic examination of different owners exists. This holds first, concerning the type of owner and second, concerning the geographic origin of the owner. We close these gaps by first distinguishing between families, banks and insurance companies, strategic and institutional owners and by second separating domestic and foreign owners. From a German point of view, an additional gap is the general lack of a representative empirical analysis of corporate governance drivers for the presence of women on management boards. We close this gap by analysing 15,976 management board member positions including approximately 600 German-listed companies from 2000 to 2007.

In this paper, we focus on the following three research questions: First, does ownership concentration affect the presence of women among management board members? Owners with large shares have a stronger influence on strategic decisions in the companies they own. Large shareholders are more involved in the process of appointing management board members and therefore prevent the reproduction of the same male elite in German top management positions. Second, do specific types of owners focus more on management board diversity than others? For example, institutional investors such as investment funds and private equity investors have a higher impact on strategic decisions and changes in corporate governance patterns (Thomsen and Pedersen 2000). Third, do differences exist between the impacts of foreign and national institutional investors on the representation of women in management boards? While German institutional owners are mostly subsidiaries of German banks or insurance companies (Böhler et al. 2010; Edwards and Nibler 2000), foreign institutional investors can be considered as the classical, active owners and specialised investors whose success is measured by the success of their investments (Thomsen and Pedersen 2000). They are even more reliant on trustworthy corporate governance structures, since they are generally exposed to higher monitoring costs (Leuz et al. 2009). Hence, we expect mainly foreign institutional investors to positively affect the presence of female managers.

Our study contributes to literature in three dimensions: understanding of the *influence of ownership structure on strategic decisions*, *drivers of board diversity* and *the German corporate governance system*. The term diversity can thereby cover a multitude of dimensions. Demographic diversity attributes such as race, age, gender can be considered, as well as educational and functional background (McPherson and Smith-Lovin 1987; Pelled 1996; Simons et al. 1999). However, researchers have identified gender as the strongest driver for stereotypes and categorisation behaviour (Hollingshead and Fraidin 2003). For this reseaon, we pay special attention to this dimension and use the terms diversity and gender diversity interchangeably. We extend the existing literature on the *influence of ownership structure* on company performance and strategic decisions made in companies (Anderson and Reeb 2003a; Andres 2008; Barclay et al. 2009; Kronborg and Thomsen 2009; Renneboog 2000) by the dimension of management board diversity. We show that the influence of owners on board diversity does not depend on their concentration, but rather on the specific type of owner. We thereby extend the classical agency theory based research on the owners as principals and the managers as agents (Fama and Jensen 1983) by an additional dimension for conflicts of interest: while managers want to demographically "reproduce" themselves, owners are interested in implementing state-of-the-art corporate governance structures. Concerning *drivers of board diversity*, we provide a unique investigation of ownership microstructures, such as the impact of international institutional owners on the acceptance of women on management boards. Thereby, we clearly extend the results of Farrell and Hersch (2005) and Carleton et al. (1998), who do not distinguish between national and international owners. We also enhance the research community's *understanding of the German corporate governance system* with our unique data set. Based on 5,203 company years and a consideration of 15,976 management board member positions, our study is the first representative empirical analysis of women on German management boards and the variables associated with their presence.[3]

The paper is structured as follows. Part two gives an overview of the existing literature. Part three outlines the theoretical framework and introduces the hypotheses. Our sample and the variables used are explained in part four. In part five, we present our empirical results and the robustness checks. Finally, part six concludes our study and discusses the results.

2 Literature review

Academic research of women on corporate boards can generally be classified into two groups: the first group of papers analyses the *impact* of top female managers on companies' performance and decision quality while the second group focuses on *drivers and detractors* of women on corporate boards. To give an overview of the existing literature, we summarise the current status of research results in the first group and continue with a detailed description of the placement of our paper within the current results of the second group.

Research on the *impact* of female managers on company performance and decision quality is generally driven by two arguments. The first argument is that women represent additional human capital for top management positions that is as yet unused (Westphal and Milton 2000). By not considering one half of society for its management positions, companies generally lose a large pool of potential intelligence (Brammer et al. 2009; Oehmichen 2010). The discriminated minority therefore becomes demotivated (Brammer et al. 2009) and unlikely to invest in its human capital (Becker 1985; Coate and Loury 1993). The second argument is that diversity enhances divergent thinking and thereby improves the quality of decisions made by the management board (Aretz and Hansen 2003; Hillman et al. 2007; Lederle 2007). An increased share of women in management can increase the pool of points of view, knowledge, skills and experiences. Furthermore, via an extended intellectual spectrum, the comprehensive range of experience and creativity can be strengthened (Arfken et al. 2004). Additionally, the acceptance of the company in employee and product markets can be improved by increased legitimacy through board diversity (Daily et al. 1999; Hillman et al. 2007). However, these expected advantages of diversity are accompanied by potential costs, such as insufficient communication (Ferreira 2010; Kilduff et al. 2000) or the decrease in psychological attachment to the company (Tsui et al. 1992). The aggregate effect of diversity depends on the company's environment (Goodstein et al. 1994). Empirical studies on the impact of female board members on company performance yield ambiguous results. Cater et al. (2003) found a positive (Carter et al. 2003), whereas Adams and Ferreira (2009) found a negative effect (Adams and Ferreira 2009) on performance.

The existing literature on *drivers and detractors* of female careers and especially of women on corporate boards covers country-specific institutional (Straub 2007; Terjesen and Singh 2008) and company-specific organisational aspects (Fryxell and Lerner 2009; Harrigan 1981; Hillman et al. 2007). Research on the country level shows that the presence of women on boards strongly depends on countries' social, political, and economic patterns (Terjesen and Singh 2008). Countries that adopt the cultural norm of stay-at-home mothers, in other words women delaying their careers in order to keep their husband's options open or to educate their children, have lower percentages of women in management positions (Tharenou 2008).The possibility to deduct housekeeping expenses from income tax on the other hand is a significant country-wide incentive for women to occupy management positions (Henrekson and Stenkula 2009).

Among company-specific organisational drivers, we distinguish between industry affiliation, company characteristics and corporate governance characteristics. Two kinds of industry effects are possible: the availability of more female employees in specific industries (Hillman et al. 2007), and the social pressure of more female customers in some industries (Fryxell and Lerner 2009). Harrigan (1981), one of the first academic authors to address drivers of female directors, using an US-American sample, found certain industries such as pharmaceuticals, cosmetics and chemical processing to positively affect the likelihood of women being members of the board (Harrigan 1981). Companies affiliated with an industry with more female customers are expected to have a higher percentage of female managers in order to provide higher credibility in the product market. Having no female manager can have a destructive effect on the company's reputation among its female customers. Fryxell and Lerner (2009) identified in their US-American sample food, drug and cosmetic product groups as companies with a higher rate of acceptance of female board members because they recognise that these are industries with augmented numbers of female customers (Fryxell and Lerner 2009). Though industry affiliation is not part of our hypotheses, we control for it in our multivariate models (Farrell and Hersch 2005).

Company characteristics that might influence the presence of female managers are organisational details, such as company size, as well as concrete activities the companies undertakes to increase the percentage of women among their managers. Empirical results regarding the effect of company size on the acceptance of women on boards are mixed. Harrigan (1981) detects a negative effect between company size and women board members, whereas the more current publications of Hillman et al. (2007) and Farrell and Hersch (2005) observe a positive effect. This trend however is not surprising; female managers have gradually moved to the fore of public opinion in the last 10 years and the resulting social pressure is most relevant for large companies. Specific programs that companies can engage in to increase the percentage of female managers include the following: the introduction of diversity responsibilities such as a diversity commissioner, the elimination of distorted perceptions of female managerial abilities via trainings and workshops, programs to facilitate the integration of work and family activities, and the reduction of social isolation via mentoring programmes and networking events (Kalev et al. 2006; Krell 2008; Noe 1988; Süß 2008).

Corporate governance structures that might drive or detract female managers from top management positions are the board and ownership structure. Research results concerning the impact of the board structure include the following: In their 2SLS regression analysis, Carter et al. (2003) identified board size as a positive driver for the presence of women on boards. Conversely, the number of inside directors negatively affects the presence of female directors. Their results are based on an empirical analysis of 638 US-American companies for only one cross-section (Carter et al. 2003). Farrell and Hersch (2005) questioned which kind of director a woman is most likely to replace on the board. They discovered that a departing woman increases the likelihood of another woman being added. Furthermore, Farrell and Hersch controlled for board size. Hillman et al. (2007) extended these analyses by investigating whether there is an expected positive effect of an "outside female director link". They show that boards that network with other female board members have a positive impact on the acceptance of female board members.

The impact of owners on the presence of women on boards is mainly covered by Carleton et al. (1998) and Farrell and Hersch (2005). Carleton et al. (1998) investigated the general impact of institutional investors on corporate governance decisions. Within these analyses, they found some significant influence of institutional investors (TIAA-CREF in their case) on the gender diversity of boards (Carleton et al. 1998). Farrell and Hersch (2005) came to the same conclusion: they show that the percentage of institutional ownership has a positive impact on the appointment of women as directors (Farrell and Hersch 2005). They also showed that institutional investors seem to generate some outside pressure for more board diversity. Farrell and Hersch included banks and insurance companies in their definition of institutional owners but disregarded other types of owners, which could also influence the appointment of female directors.

This is where we fill the research gap. From an agency theoretical perspective, it is important to consider different dimensions of the major interests of different types of owners and to follow different attitudes concerning the importance of women on boards. Therefore, we extend their findings in three ways. First, in our analyses of the impact of ownership structure on the presence of women on management boards[4] we further separate the definition of institutional investors into investment funds, private equity funds and venture capitalists on the one hand, and banks and insurance companies on the other hand. Second, we add strategic and individual owners to our models, and third, we distinguish between national and international institutional investors. We thereby close an existing gap, since the current research offers little detailed guidance as to "why some companies do have female representatives on their boards and others do not" (Hillman et al. 2007).

Our research is of (Barth et al. 2005) additional relevance for research on general ownership effects. Many papers investigating the impact of shareholders focus on the effects on a company's performance (Anderson and Reeb 2003a; Himmelberg et al. 1999; Morck et al. 1988) instead of looking for concrete strategic decisions that active owners could influence. Strategic dimensions covered so far include dividend payout (Barclay et al. 2009), corporate diversification (Anderson and Reeb 2003b; Denis et al. 1997), productivity (Barth et al. 2005) or company leverage (Anderson and Reeb 2003b). By analysing shareholders' effects on the acceptance of female managers, we add a further exemplary strategic decision to this area of research.

3 The impact of the ownership structure on the presence of female managers: hypotheses

Many researchers have investigated the impact of ownership structure over time. The foundation was laid by Berle and Means (1968), who observed the following effects of the separation of ownership and control, a trend that started in the 19th century. Owners turn from active to passive agents, the spiritual value of ownership is replaced by its monetary value and the owners lose their active influence on their personal wealth (Berle and Means 1968). The resulting conflicts of interests between owners and managers, as well as possible dimensions for owners to reduce their agency costs, find consideration in many academic publications (Fama and Jensen 1983; Jensen 1986, 1993; La Porta et al. 2000; Shleifer and Vishny 1997).

Many studies on the effects of ownership characteristics focus on the influence of ownership structure on a company's performance (Anderson and Reeb 2003a; Edwards and Weichenrieder 2004; Franks and Mayer 2001; Himmelberg et al. 1999). They often presume that owners with larger shares have lower agency costs of monitoring, exert more influence over the companies' management and therefore increase their company's value (Edwards and Weichenrieder 2004; Jensen and Meckling 1976).

To examine the impact of owners on questions of board composition, we first need to understand the preferences of management board members. These (primarily male) board members stick to certain behavioural structures when deciding on a new colleague or successor. They try to reproduce themselves and thereby follow a so called homophilous behaviour. This means that an individual is acting in favour of other individuals that are similar to himself (Pearce and Xu 2010). To determine similarity, individuals revert to demographical attributes such as race, age or gender (McPherson and Smith-Lovin 1987). Given an atomistic ownership structure, managers are exposed to fewer obstacles and are enabled to continue this self-producing behaviour. Under an atomistic ownership structure, the managers' idea of future colleagues is opposed to many different interests of the many minority shareholders. From a group-theoretical perspective, the probability that they agree on the same candidate is very low. Large groups tend to get involved in more conflicts than small groups (Forbes and Milliken 1999). The managers' risk of a reclamation of the shareholders against the managers' candidate is therefore lower for the case of dispersed ownership. But a single or a few large owners are expected to have fewer conflicts in the decision process on suitable candidates and to exert their influence on the decision on management board composition. These influential owners appoint candidates that they expect to best represent their interests. Thereby it is possible that the owners' candidate does not fit the existing stereotypes. The blockholder might be an obstacle for the homophilous request of the existing management and is therefore more capable to change existing patterns such as that of male dominance on management boards. A higher ownership concentration consequently results in greater board diversity.

H1: A higher ownership concentration of a company is associated with a higher probability of having at least one woman on the management board.

One basic assumption of hypothesis 1 is that owners influence the appointment process of management board members and choose those kinds of managers that they expect to best represent their interests. However, those interests might differ among the different types of owners. In short, different types of shareholders have different agendas (Kim et al. 2008; Thomsen and Pedersen 2000). For example, the level of emphasis that an owner places on company performance depends on the ownership type (Chaganti and Damanpour 1991). We distinguish between individual owners (including families), bank and insurance companies, strategic investors such as non-financial corporations[5] and governmental organisations, and institutional investors such as investment funds, venture capitalists or private equity companies (Dharwadkar et al. 2008; Thomsen and Pedersen 2000).

Individual and family owners are mainly interested in the survival of the company (Berrone et al. 2010; Sraer and Thesmar 2007). Generally, they do not have the opportunity to invest in more than one company due to liquidity restrictions (Anderson and Reeb 2003b). Therefore, their risk aversion is assumed to be high (Andres 2008). One of the best ways to ensure their company's survival is to maintain a highly productive and stable performance (Anderson and Reeb 2003a). To enable and sustain this high performance level, family owners strongly depend on managers who represent their best interests. Hence, they often fall back on family members as their managers (Bennedsen et al. 2006; Cucculelli and Micucci 2008). Concerning the impact of family ownership on the percentage of female managers, supply arguments are the strongest drivers (Farrell and Hersch 2005). The pool of potential female managers is naturally higher, since on average, half of a family's members are women. We therefore expect the presence of women in management boards to be higher for companies with individual and family owners.

H2a: The more shares are owned by individuals and families, the higher is the probability of having at least one woman on the management board.

Banks and insurance companies, as well as strategic investors, often have objectives that go beyond the maximisation of their share value. They can optimise their own benefits by improving existing business relations with the company they have invested in. For example, banks may decide to promote their own business as viable lenders and M&A advisors (Dittmann et al. 2010). Strategic investors might be interested in joint ventures with the company they have invested in or are contractors such as customers or suppliers of their investments. To improve these forms of co-operation, they must ensure that the manager they find in these companies is someone they can work with. To understand this decision process we revert to the social network theory. Researchers found that it is a natural group-building process to pick a member of one's own social network (Jehn et al. 1999). This results in the board composition being a reflection of the deciders social network (Lynall et al. 2003). By choosing people from within their network with similar demographic attributes[6] such as race or gender (following the homophily principal of McPherson et al. 2001), they expect to maximise the probability that the manager meets their expectations. Due to their homophily-influenced thinking (McPherson et al. 2001) and their social networks as external labour pools, they do not believe in women's ability to be good managers and convenient business partners. Thus, we expect banks and insurance companies, as well as strategic investors, to have a negative impact on the acceptance of women on management boards.

H2b: The more shares are owned by banks or insurance companies, the lower is the probability of having at least one woman on the management board.

H2c: The more shares are owned by strategic investors such as non-financial companies or the government, the lower is the probability of having at least one woman on the management board.

With institutional investors, we come to a group of owners whose major interest is value maximisation. As professional investors whose only business activity is the management of investments, the success of institutional investors is solely measured by the value proposition of their investments (Thomsen and Pedersen 2000). Their own survival depends on the performance and success of their investments (Chaganti and Damanpour 1991). To achieve this objective, institutional investors exhibit a strong level of activity: they are involved in many strategic decisions related to their investments (e.g., they have a positive effect on the performance sensitivity of CEO compensation (Dharwadkar et al. 2008)). Concerning the kind of decisions institutional investors are involved in, they are usually very active in the sustainable behaviour of the companies they invest in. They divest from companies that do not fulfil their expectations in terms of sustainability. Sustainable companies are expected to be more successful und provide large profits in the long run. The Norwegian Government

Pension Fund, for example, sold its shares of Wal-Mart due to violations of labour rights. They also terminated their engagements with Boeing and EADS because of involvements in the production of nuclear weapons. The Norwegian fund excludes all companies from their portfolio that do not fulfil its social, ethical and environmental requirements (Simpson et al. 2008). This desire for sustainable change also plays a major role concerning the active involvement of institutional owners in decisions on the companies' corporate governance structure (Carleton et al. 1998). They aim to break open out-dated corporate governance patterns (such as dominantly male management board members) and thereby help to increase the diversity on management boards (Carter et al. 2003) Therefore, we expect that the investment of institutional owners has a positive effect on the presence of women among management board members.

H2d: The more shares are owned by institutional owners, the higher is the probability of having at least one woman on the management board.

Institutional owners should be investigated in particular detail when studying a German sample and we must distinguish between national and foreign institutional investors. The bank-orientation of the German corporate governance system (Conyon and Schwalbach 2000; Deeg 2005; Edwards and Nibler 2000; Franks and Mayer 2001) plays a decisive role for national institutional investors. Most of the national institutional investors do not act independently, but are bank subsidiaries (Böhler et al. 2010). As a bank subsidiary, their objectives are aligned with those of the bank. They are embedded in the same social network as banks and therefore access the same primarily male external labour pool when deciding on suitable candidates. Foreign institutional investors, on the other hand, are the genuinely active institutional investors described in the paragraph above. They pursue the objectives of sustainable and long-term oriented value proposition and maximisation. In addition, foreign investors are exposed to higher information costs (Ahearne et al. 2004) and higher monitoring costs in cases of poor governance than local investors (Leuz et al. 2009). It has been shown that the investment decisions of foreign institutional investors are driven by aspects of transparency (Aggarwal et al. 2005). Hence, once an investment has been made, for foreigner institutional owners, it is even more important to implement corporate governance patterns that they can trust. In this way, they avoid the reproduction of the established national management elite, which is primarily male, and use a more diversified external pool of candidates. This increases the probability of a woman being appointed and thereby has a positive impact on the presence of women on the management board.

H3: Only foreign active owners have a positive influence on the probability of having at least one woman on the management board.

4 Sample and data

4.1 Sample definition

Our initial sample consisted of all companies listed in the German CDAX between 2000 and 2007.[7] We removed all companies with foreign ISINs, since they have their origin in countries with different corporate governance systems (most often one-tier systems) which would complicate comparison across companies. To avoid double-counting, we also removed all companies that were listed twice with their common and their preferred stock. We ended up with 5,455 company years. All our data is hand collected from annual reports such as *Hoppensted Aktienführer* or the *Lexis-Nexis* database or by request to the investor relationship departments because no database exists that contains information on the composition of management boards and their members' gender in Germany. Extraction of the details of the corresponding 15,976 management board member positions was completed in the following way: we matched three criteria (first name, surname and residence) to check if any two list entries were for the same person. The data in *Hoppenstedt Aktienführer* were partly inconsistent and therefore had to be cleaned; for example, the names were often written in different ways due to typographical errors or inconsistent notations for double-barrelled names (e.g., "Hans-Werner", "Hans-W."). Similar inconsistencies were present within the data containing information about area of residence, since sometimes the city and sometimes the suburb was mentioned. To identify possible misleading information, we sorted the list according to first names and then compared each row with the following and previous rows. We double-checked all the cases we were unsure about by collecting information from annual reports. This was made possible since every company listed in the German CDAX must report all members of its management board in the annual report. We repeated the whole procedure for the list sorted by surnames. Following this procedure, we collected data for 5,203 company years.

Based on a list of typical male and female first names, we identified the gender of the 15,976 management board member positions. Whenever the classification was unclear, we investigated the person's gender further. This way, we obtained data for the number of women on management boards. In Table 1, we report annual statistics of the management board members. We report the number of companies whose management boards we found

Table 1: Sample description

Year	Number of firms	Management board members		Women on management boards	
		Total number	Average	Total number	Average
2000	709	2409	3.3977	44	0.0183
2001	717	2373	3.3096	49	0.0206
2002	682	2173	3.1862	44	0.0202
2003	646	1910	2.9567	43	0.0225
2004	621	1793	2.8873	38	0.0212
2005	607	1762	2.9028	44	0.0250
2006	610	1773	2.9066	43	0.0243
2007	611	1783	2.9182	44	0.0247
All	5203	15976	3.0705	349	0.0218

This table provides general information on the sample. The sample includes the number of companies based on all companies listed in the German CDAX for the specific year, excluding all double listings (common and preferred shares of a company are both listed) and foreign ISINs. We found board information for 95% of these companies (5,203 out of 5,455).

Table 2: Distribution by industry

Industry	Number of firms	Management board members		Women on management boards	
		Total number	Average	Total number	Average
Automobile	17	69	4.0588	0	0.0000
Banks	10	48	4.8000	1	0.0208
Basic resources	8	24	3.0000	0	0.0000
Chemicals	15	58	3.8667	1	0.0172
Construction	15	58	3.8667	0	0.0000
Consumer	44	121	2.7500	6	0.0496
Financial services	92	239	2.5978	7	0.0293
Food & Beverages	15	36	2.4000	0	0.0000
Industrial	121	352	2.9091	6	0.0170
Insurance	9	61	6.7778	3	0.0492
Media	40	101	2.5250	2	0.0198
Pharma & Healthcare	45	132	2.9333	9	0.0682
Retail	28	75	2.6786	1	0.0133
Software	93	221	2.3763	7	0.0317
Technology	30	86	2.8667	1	0.0116
Tel ecommunication	10	28	2.8000	0	0.0000
Transportation & Logistics	11	41	3.7273	0	0.0000
Utilities	8	33	4.1250	0	0.0000

This table presents the distribution of women on German management boards by industry

information on, the total number of managers we analysed and the absolute and average numbers of female managers. Among the 15,976 management board member positions, we found a total of 349 female management board member positions.

Tables 2 and 3 present the distribution of women on German management boards across different industries and companies of different sizes. Table 2 shows that the highest number of women on management boards were found especially in companies affiliated to the pharmaceutical industry, or in consumer goods companies. Two explanations are possible for this effect—the *supply* and the *demand* argument. According to the idea of women *supply*, one might expect more women in industries with more female employees (Hillman et al. 2007). Companies in these industries should have a higher proportion of female board members since we do not expect them to "waste the resources of female talent" by leaving them in lower hierarchy levels or even allowing them to resign from their position at this company (Broome 2008).[8] The women *demand* represents the need for women because of women-specific topics. The stakeholders of many companies, such as customers and (potential) employees, are women. To support legitimacy, the board should echo this company environment (Lynall et al. 2003).

The distribution by company size in Table 3 shows that very small companies with less than 100 employees in particular have a higher percentage of women on their management boards. A possible explanation might be that these companies are mostly family businesses which appoint family members to the management board.

Information on the ownership structure is extracted from the Thomson Financial database. This database includes every investor that owns at least 0.5% of the company's

Table 3: Distribution by company size

Number of employees	Number of firms	Management board members		Women on management boards	
		Total number	Average	Total number	Average
1–100	104	222	2.1346	11	0.0495
100–500	145	367	2.5310	9	0.0245
500–1000	65	170	2.6154	4	0.0235
1000–5000	119	371	3.1176	10	0.0270
5000–10000	37	131	3.5405	2	0.0153
10000–50000	42	200	4.7619	4	0.0200
>50000	99	322	3.2525	4	0.0124

This table presents the distribution of women on German management boards by company size. Size is measured by the number of employees

common stock. In case of obvious inconsistencies, we double-checked the data with information from the *Hoppenstedt Aktienführer* or from annual reports, and made corrections if necessary. Regarding the adjusted sample, we achieved an availability of 4,170 company years. Board characteristics such as size and tenure of the supervisory board were extracted from *Hoppenstedt Aktienführer* in the same way as the information on management board members. To measure the supervisory board members' tenure for the first years of our samples correctly, we went even further back in time and collected data starting in 1992. Company characteristics such as the number of employees, performance and information on the companies' diversification were collected from Thomson Datastream Worldscope and are available for between 4,561 and 5,267 company years.

Due to the need for simultaneous availability of all the variables used, we ended up with 3,678 company years for our multivariate regression models.

4.2 Variables

The endogenous variable in our statistical models is *female manager*. This is a dummy variable indicating if the specific company has a woman among the management board members.

The exogenous variables can be categorised as either *ownership*, *board* or *company characteristics*. The determination of the endogenous and exogenous variables is based on the recent research explaining the presence of women on boards (Gregoric et al. 2010; Harrigan 1981; Hillman et al. 2007).

Within the variables of *ownership structures*, we analysed the impact of the *freefloat* and in further models distinguish between four different types of owners as follows: *individual investors* that include individual owners or families such as the Porsche family; *banks and insurance companies*; *strategic investors* such as corporations or government agencies; and *institutional investors* such as investment funds, private equity investors, venture capitalists and hedge funds. For the active owners, we also distinguished between *institutional investors national*, indicating that the owners are based in Germany, and *institutional investors foreign*, for owners based abroad. All ownership variables are expressed in percentage and indicate which percentage of the shares is held by the specific type of owner.

In addition, we controlled for the following management and supervisory *board characteristics*: *size management board* represents the number of management board members, *size supervisory board* counts the number of shareholder representatives in the supervisory board[9] and *codet* indicates the type of codetermination. This variable can take the values zero (in the case of no codetermination), 0.5 (in the case of one-third codetermination) and one (in the case of parity codetermination). *Tenure* is the average tenure of all shareholder representatives on the supervisory board.

For *company-specific* control variables, we considered *size*, which is approximated through the natural logarithm of the number of employees; *diversification*, for which we counted the number of industries the company is conducting business with based on the four-digit SIC logic; *leverage* as the ratio of total debt to the sum of total debt and common equity; *founded age* as the companies' age; and among our robustness checks, *performance* as the ROIC (return on invested capital) of the company. In every model, we additionally controlled for *industry* affiliation based on the information provided by the German stock exchange. Table 4 summarises all used variables, their means, medians

Table 4: Data description

Variable	No. of observations	Mean	Median	VIFs 1.1	VIFs 1.2	VIFs 1.3
Ownership Structure						
Freefloat	4170	41.4305	38.0600	1.0822		
Individual investors	4170	22.5603	8.4150		1.9694	1.9695
Banks and Insurance companies	4170	0.9063	0.0000		1.1201	1.1201
Strategic investors	4170	24.7178	7.2700		2.0890	2.0915
Institutional investor	4170	10.3851	4.8650		1.5557	
Institutional investor national	4170	5.8508	1.7900			1.2910
Institutional investor foreign	4170	4.5343	0.0000			1.3376
Board Characteristics						
Female manager (0,1)	5203	0.0661	0.0000	–	–	–
Size management board	5203	3.0705	3.0000	2.0002	2.0136	2.0141
Size supervisory board	5268	4.7764	4.0000	2.2243	2.2928	2.2952
Codetermination (0,0.5,1)	5267	0.3144	0.0000	3.1730	3.2031	3.2073
Tenure	5267	3.2237	3.0000	1.4327	1.4668	1.4746
Firm Characteristics						
Size	4561	6.6048	6.4907	3.8052	3.8236	3.8242
Diversification	5240	3.7664	3.0000	1.5045	1.5139	1.5210
Performance	5267	4.8086	6.7200	–	–	–
Leverage	4672	0.2106	0.1528	1.1498	1.1535	1.1536
Founded Age	5247	48.8938	22.0000	1.6334	1.6541	1.6565

This table provides descriptive statistics for the companies in our sample. The initial sample consisted of 6,295 company years for the years 2000 to 2007, whereas the descriptive statistics for the single variables were based on individual numbers of company years, depending on the availability, range between 4,170 and 5,267 company years. Companies are included when they are listed at the CDAX of the German stock exchange for the specific year, excluding all double listings (common and preferred shares of a company are both listed) and foreign ISINs. The table represents the mean, median and the variance inflation factors of regression model 1.1–1.3

and standard deviations. A table of variable descriptions and the used sources per variable can be found in Table 6 in the appendix. Additionally, Table 4 contains the variance inflation factors (VIFs) of our regression models to challenge potential problems of multi-collinearity. A discussion of the values can be found in paragraph 5.3.

5 Empirical analyses

To test our hypotheses, we created a logistic regression model. We introduced the empirical design, discuss our empirical results and closed with robustness tests.

5.1 Empirical design

To investigate the impact of ownership characteristics on the representation of women in management boards empirically, we analysed several variants of the following multivariate model specification:

$$\textit{Female manager} = f(\text{ownership structure, board characteristics, company characteristics}) \quad (1)$$

Since the endogenous variable of our model—*female manager*—is a binary variable, we used a logistic regression (Hoetker 2007). To investigate the impact of the ownership structure, we took the following three-step approach: the control variables for board and company characteristics are included in every model. To measure the impact of the owners' model, model 1.1 only contains *freefloat*. In model 1.2, we replaced *freefloat* with the four variables indicating the type of owner: *individual investors, banks and insurance companies, strategic investors* and *institutional investors*. For model 1.3, we chose a more detailed classification of the active owners using the variables *institutional investors national* and *institutional investors foreign*.

To challenge the model quality, we also considered the possible problems of heteroscedasticity and multi-collinearity. To resolve the problem of heteroscedasticity, we used Huber/White (QML) standard errors (Freedman 2006), and to detect potential problems of multi-collinearity, we calculated the variance inflation factors (VIFs) for all models.

5.2 Empirical results

Table 5 represents the results of the estimation of our logit-model.

Model 1.1 shows that ownership concentration (defined as 1 minus *freefloat in percent divided by 100*) generally has no statistically significant effect on the likelihood of having a woman among the management board members. This means that we cannot give evidence if the existence of a dominant owner affects the probability of having at least one female manager, meaning that hypothesis 1 cannot be confirmed.

The influence of specific types of owners is investigated in models 1.2 and 1.3. Both models show that *individual investors* have a significant positive effect on the probability of having at least one woman among the management board members. Therefore, hypothesis H2a can be confirmed: private owners have more female representatives on the management boards of the companies they own. However, shares owned by *banks and insurance*

Table 5: Regression models

Dependent variable Method	Model 1.1 Female manager (0,1) Logit		Model 1.2 Female manager (0,1) Logit		Model 1.3 Female manager (0,1) Logit	
	Coefficient	z-Statistic	Coefficient	z-Statistic	Coefficient	z-Statistic
Ownership Structure						
Freefloat	−0.2312	(−0.8190)				
Individual investors			0.0062*	(1.7476)	0.0061*	(1.7171)
Banks and Insurance companies			0.0118	(0.9416)	0.0120	(0.9653)
Strategic investors			0.0000	(0.0109)	0.0000	(0.0028)
Institutional investor			0.0122***	(2.5979)		
Institutional investor national					0.0092	(1.2880)
Institutional investor foreign					0.0146***	(2.7074)
Board Characteristics						
Size management board	0.1872***	(4.2308)	0.1814***	(4.0391)	0.1817***	(4.0434)
Size supervisory board	0.0020	(0.0463)	0.0021	(0.0479)	0.0003	(0.0063)
Codetermination (0,0.5,1)	0.5603*	(1.9142)	0.6149**	(2.1315)	0.6020**	(2.0811)
Tenure	−0.1132***	(−3.2729)	−0.1074***	(−3.0646)	−0.1054***	(−2.9833)
Firm Characteristics						
Size	−0.2417***	(−4.7234)	−0.2520***	(−4.8031)	−0.2505***	(−4.8004)
Diversification	0.0379	(0.8666)	0.0344	(0.7841)	0.0358	(0.8117)
Leverage	−0.1145	(−0.4998)	−0.1351	(−0.5706)	−0.1427	(−0.6020)
Founded Age	−0.0035*	(−1.8921)	−0.0032*	(−1.7237)	−0.0032*	(−1.7160)
Constant	yes		yes		yes	
Industry dummies	yes		yes		yes	
Year dummies	yes		yes		yes	
No. of observations	3678		3678		3678	
Sq-Root of Sum of squared Resid.	15.5326		15.4909		15.4834	
Akaike info. crit.	0.5016		0.5003		0.5007	

This table represents logit regressions of the ownership structure, board characteristics and company controls on the dummy variable indicating if there is a woman among the management board members. All variables used are described in the appendix. The sample is described in Table 1. We report Huber/White (QML) robust z-values in parentheses. The symbols ***, ** and * indicate significance at the 1%-, 5%- and 10%-level, respectively *companies* and *strategic investors* do not have any significant effect on the probability of having at least one woman among the management board members. Hence, hypotheses H2b and H2c, which stated that male-dominated banks and corporations mainly support male managers, cannot be confirmed. Moreover, the signs of both coefficients are positive, and not negative as expected. However, since the coefficients are not significant in any model, we were not able to show a positive effect of either *banks and insurance companies* or *strategic investors*.

The effect of *institutional investors* on the probability of having at least one woman among the management board members in model 1.2 is significantly positive. That is to say, hypothesis H2d can be confirmed: active owners positively affect the strategic decisions concerning the management board's composition. This result is consistent with the studies by Carleton et al. (1998) and Farrell and Hersch (2005).

The separate consideration of national and foreign active investors can be found in model 1.3. The regression demonstrates that the positive effect of active owners on the probability of having at least one woman among the management board members only holds for owners based abroad, and not for the German ones. The variable *institutional investors foreign* has a significantly positive coefficient, whereas the positive coefficient of *institutional investors national* is not significant. This results in a confirmation of hypothesis H3.

The results for our control variables are the following: the size of the management board has a positive effect on the probability of having a woman on the management board. This is feasible since the possibility to enhance diversity is higher in larger groups. We also find a positive effect of codetermination on the probability of having a woman on the management board. This might be caused by the presence of union representatives who increase the companies' awareness of the importance of equality. For the average tenure of the management board members we find a significant negative effect on the probability of having at least one woman on the management board. This result can be explained via the stability of the board composition, at which the high tenure can be seen as an approximation for stability. The more fluctuation a board has, the higher the possibility to also appoint a woman at some point of time.

Additionally the company control variables support the idea of young and small companies having women on the management board more frequently: the company size has a significantly negative coefficient also the influence of the founded age is significantly negative.

5.3 Model quality and robustness tests

To challenge the model quality, we paid attention to the potential problems of heteroscedasticity and multi-collinearity. To resolve the heteroscedasticity problem, we used Huber/White (QML) standard errors (Freedman 2006). Multi-collinearity is not of concern since, apart from codetermination and company size, the variance inflation factors (VIFs) do not exceed 3. The VIFs for model 1.3 are displayed in Table 4.

To examine the robustness of our results, we considered the following three dimensions: selection bias, choice of endogenous variable and choice of exogenous variables.[10] All robustness tables can be found in the appendix.

To eliminate any concerns about a selection bias driven by the lower availability of ownership data, we used a Heckit regressions model that includes a Heckman correction term. Following Sigelman and Zeng's (1999) example, we took a two-step approach to build a Heckit model (Siegelman and Zeng 1999). In the first step we performed a logit regression model with the existence of ownership data as the binary dependent variable. We used year dummies as explanatory variables within this model and a HDAX dummy and an event variable to explain the probability of missing ownership data. The year dummies should control for time effects, the HDAX-dummy[11] for potential size effects and the event variable for events such as delisting, insolvency, etc. that could lead to missing data. The event variable is a count variable (with a maximum value of ten), which counts the number of company years for which data are available within the *Hoppenstedt Aktienführer*. Because the *Hoppenstedt Aktienführer* is supposed to cover all German-listed companies, we expect that missing years are an appropriate proxy for special events such as delistings or insolvencies. In the second step, we used the results of the logit regression to calculate the inverse Mills ratios. We then expanded our regression models 1.1–1.3 by including the inverse Mills ratio as an additional independent variable. As Table 7 in the appendix shows, our results remain qualitatively identical. Therefore, we exclude sample selection biases within our regression models.

To consider the robustness of the endogenous variable, we replaced the dummy variable *female manager* with *number of female managers*. Since we thereby replaced a binary variable with a count variable, changes in terms of methodology were also necessary. Models explaining count variables are calculated using a poisson regression (Farrell and Hersch 2005). Our results are also qualitatively stable for this change (see Table 8 in the appendix). The results are therefore robust concerning the choice of the endogenous variable.

With respect to the choice of exogenous variables, we made two changes: First, we calculated our models without the variable codetermination. Second, we included a performance measure in our models. Tables 9 and 10 in the appendix show that neither of these two changes had an effect on our results. Our results can therefore be considered as robust in relation to the choice of exogenous measures.

6 Discussion

This paper analyses the impact of ownership structure on the presence of women on management boards. In 2007, just 2.47% of the management board members of German companies were female. In other words, German companies do not use nearly 50% of the country's intellectual capacity in management positions. The purpose of our study was to investigate if ownership concentration and the specific type of owner have had an influence on this percentage.

We arrived at the following results. We did not find any evidence that ownership concentration influences the presence of women on management boards. As argued in our hypotheses strong owners have the power to influence the composition of the management board and thereby as the case may be disturb the reproduction of same types of managers over generation. Our results however do not show any significantly positive impact on the presence of women among management board members. This means that the power to have the possibility for change is not enough. Owners also need a special interest to favor female managers. We therefore distinguished between different types of investors and we found significant positive effects on the presence of women on management boards; the concentration of individual as well as institutional owners positively affects the probability of having female management board members. However our results do not show any evidence for a negative effect of banks and insurance companies or strategic investors on the presence of women on management boards. The demographic reflection of the social network of the deciders in banks and strategic investors seems to be non-existent for the case of management board compensation. A further separation of the institutional owners into national and foreign owners illustrates that only the foreign institutional owners drive the positive effect. It is not only important to be an institutional owner but it is also of relevance what kind of institutional experiences the active owner bases its behaviour on. German-based funds are directly confronted with a family policy that detracts female careers, and thus they do not dare to force women into management positions. In contrast, foreign investors know that careers are possible for females and therefore they actively support them.

This research study adds to the recent public and political discussion in the following way: We have shown that specific corporate governance institutions exist—blockholders and in particular families and foreign institutional owners—who act in favour of women on management boards. However, it is unclear if their effect is strong enough to enable the country's regulators to relinquish on further actions. One specific measure that is often discussed in this regard is a binding quota regulation as already implemented for example in Norway (Ahern and Dittmar 2010; Bøhren and Strøm 2010; Gregoric et al. 2010). Whether this is an effective measure was not part of our investigation and has to be critically debated by politicians. In this debate, legislators should contrast the many disadvantages of quota regulations with the alleged advantage of increasing the number of female board members. By forcing companies to recruit a specific number of women onto their boards, the numbers will grow. But will the situation of women in management positions improve sustainably? Actions against discrimination quite often result in reinforcement of prejudices and stereotypes (Coate and Loury 1993; Franck and Jungwirth 1998). Women who have achieved management positions as a result of the quota regulation will be exposed to the general suspicion of being a "quota woman". Moreover, many opportunities remain for male managers to exclude women from important decisions, such as through informal meetings that the legislator cannot regulate.

For a sustainable reform of female career opportunities, the legislator is strongly dependent on the commitment and the will of the companies. Instead of implementing the hard law of a quota, soft laws might be a possibility to boost the companies' commitment (Aguilera et al. 2008). One possibility of a soft law would be the following extension of the Corporate Governance Codex: companies could be forced to publish the percentage of women included in the first three management levels. As a result, an external social pressure could be created for companies with few or no women among their managers and directors. The resulting disadvantages of this social pressure for the companies would include negative profiling on the labour market for young female talent and the possible loss of image amongst female customers. Currently, the German Corporate Governance Codex only stresses adequate consideration in management and supervisory boards (Weber-Rey 2009).

For companies our research results have the following consequences. The evaluation of the company by the capital market is of high relevance. Since there is actually no type of owners that is acting against the favour of women in management position, they do not have to fear penalisation of the capital market of measurements to increase career opportunities of women in their company.

7 Study limitations and future research suggestions

This paper is not without limitations: First, we used only publically available data. Using data originating from databases such as *Datastream* and annual reports, we were able to model good indicators for owners' behaviour concerning the support of women in top management positions. However, we did not concretely measure their preferences at an individual level. To do so, in-depth interviews with representatives of the owners would be necessary. Admittedly, this kind of data often affiliates with strong selection biases. Only persons who are affected by the issue of interest, or are actively interested in the topic of the interview, are willing to participate. In summary, neither of the two methods might be able to extract the pure investors' preferences and behaviour without any measurement issues. We decided to suspend the bias due to the willingness to participate in interviews, and in return to accept the high level of abstraction of the publically available data on company level. Nevertheless, interview-based investigations in this field of research might be an interesting extension to our study and provide a direction for future research. Second, our analyses investigated which factors explain the presence of women on management boards (the probability of having been appointed and not having been dismissed). Another possible investigation could be the analysis of concrete appointment decisions. However, to have a representative number of cases, a larger sample would be necessary. Extending the given sample to the future would probably result in biases due to the recently intensified public discussion on quota regulations. But this could also be an advantageous opportunity to measure and investigate quota effects. This brings us to the third limitation: While we provide further insights on the mechanisms that increase the percentage of women on management boards, we do not answer the question of whether a quota regulation could be effective and whether it is needed. One way to approach this research question would be the extension of the analysis over more countries, covering some societies that have already introduced a quota regulation. Such investigation of an international sample would also enable researchers to identify institutional drivers, such as the impact of a country's family policy on the presence of women in top management positions. Research of this kind might also enable evaluating family political mechanisms and give answers on the question why Germany still has very few women in management positions though housekeeping expenses are deductable from income tax. Fourth, in our study, we only focused on the highest possible management positions—the management board. An analysis of drivers—institutional or organisational—of women in middle management positions would supplement our research and give companies concrete advice on how to increase the percentage of women at every hierarchical level.

Beyond that, our paper provides possible directions for future research on board diversity: For example, our analyses could be extended to include other diversity dimensions. The gender variable used in our study is only one demographical category (Randel 2002) and could be extended to include age or nationality. Investigation of diversity in terms of educational and professional background would also further broaden our knowledge of the drivers and impacts of diversity in top management teams. In particular, research covering more than one diversity dimension simultaneously would be of high relevance. The underlying theoretical concept might hereby be the theory of faultlines (Tuggle et al. 2010).

Endnotes

1. http://www.welt.de/wirtschaft/article12923472/Ministerin-lobt-Frauenfoerderung-deutscher-Firmen.html, 15.06.2011.
2. Compare e.g. Elston and Goldberg (2003) and Rapp and Wolff (2010) on the influence of owners on aspects of management compensation (Elston and Goldberg 2003; Rapp and Wolff 2010) or Carleton et al. (1998) and Chizema and Kim (2010) on the impact of owners on the board composition (Carleton et al. 1998; Chizema and Kim 2010).
3. Our empirical research is based on a German sample. The German corporate governance system is a two-tier system. It distinguishes between management board members—comparable to the executive board members in the Anglo-Saxon one-tier system used in the U.S.—and supervisory board members—the outside board members in the U.S. system (Baums and Scott 2005; Douma 1997). Our empirical investigation focuses on management board members.
4. Most of the papers cited analyse the drivers for women on boards or women in top management teams. The majority of papers analysing women on boards are based on US data. Since the US has a one-tier corporate governance system, in contrast to Germany, no further separation into management and supervisory board members can be achieved.
5. For the consideration of non-financial companies as strategic investors also compare with Andres (2008).
6. British studies showed that banking was 2007 with 14% women among all board members the 5th out of ten industries concerning female representatives on board (Sealy et al. 2007). For German numbers compare Table 2 of this article. 2007 only two percent of the management board members of banks and five percent of insurance management board members were female.
7. The CDAX is the Composite Deutscher Aktien Index, which includes all companies fulfilling the Prime or General Standard at the Frankfurt Stock Exchange. In Europe, companies can generally choose between two different points of access to equity capital markets. Beside an EU-regulated market, most exchanges offer a market regulated by itself. The two markets differ with respect to legal basis and status, but also with respect to differences in transparency requirements. Within the EU-regulated market, the Frankfurt Stock Exchange (FWB—Frankfurter Wertpapierbörse), which is the most important German stock exchange, allows companies to be listed in one of two different market segments. While companies willing to fulfil the EU-regulated minimum transparency level only have to be listed in the General Standard, companies opting for a listing in the Prime Standard must fulfil additional transparency requirements. Accordingly, the Prime Standard is the market segment with the highest reporting and disclosure level at the most important German stock exchange.

8 An additional supply-driven argument bases on the age of companies: In young companies the hierarchies are still flat. The probability for a woman working in this young company to become a member of the management is therefore greater. This explains e.g. the relatively high percentage of women on management boards in the software industry.

9 The German law imposes some restrictions concerning the size of the supervisory board. The maximum size allowed depends on the equity capital: for more than ten millions in equity the maximum number of supervisory board members is 21, for between 1,5 and ten million, it is 15 members and for less than 1,5 nine members are allowed at maximum (§ 95 AktG). For codetermined companies there are additional rules depending on the number of employees in Germany: in the case of more than 20.000 employees the company has to have more ten shareholder representatives (and ten employee representatives), between 10,000 and 20,000 the imposed number of shareholder representatives is eight (and eight employee representatives) and for between 2,000 and 10,000 employees companies must have six shareholder and six employee representatives (§ 7(1) MitbestG.). However, the variance inflation factors (Table 4) show that multi-collinearity due to the close relation to firm size is not a problem and does not affect our empirical model quality.

10 To challenge the robustness of the used method, a logit regression, we additionally conduct a propensity score matching according to Becker and Ichino (2002). We first determined a control group for the companies with women on their management boards based on the control variables used in model 1.3 and calculated the t-values for the important ownership variables (Becker and Ichino 2002) using the nearest neighbourhood approach (Ivanov and Xie 2010). With t-values of 1.55 for *individual investor* 1.53 for *institutional investor*, and 1.89 for *institutional investor foreign* the first two variables are almost significant and the third is significant to a level of 10%. Our results can therefore be considered as robust regarding the choice of method.

11 The HDAX-dummy takes the value of one if the company was listed in the HDAX-Index, which is a combination of the three important German indices DAX, MDAX. After the index restructuring, this index also included the TecDAX.

Appendix

Table 6: Definition of variables and data sources

Variable	Description	Source
Ownership Structure		
Freefloat	Percentage of shares that are not owned by blockholder	Thomson Datastream/Worldscope, annual reports
Individual investors	Percentage of shares that are owned by individual and family owners	Thomson Datastream/Worldscope, annual reports
Banks and Insurance companies	Percentage of shares that are owned by banks and inssurance companies	Thomson Datastream/Worldscope, annual reports
Strategic investors	Percentage of shares that are owned by other non-financial corporations or governemental organizations	Thomson Datastream/Worldscope, annual reports
Institutional investor	Percentage of shares that are owned by institutional owners	Thomson Datastream/Worldscope, annual reports
Institutional investor national	Percentage of shares that are owned by institutional owners based in Germany	Thomson Datastream/Worldscope, annual reports
Institutional investor foreign	Percentage of shares that are owned by institutional owners based abroad	Thomson Datastream/Worldscope, annual reports
Board Characteristics		
Size management board	Number of management board members	Hoppenstedt Aktienführer, annual reports
Size supervisory board	Number of supervisory board members (shareholder representatives)	Hoppenstedt Aktienführer, annual reports
Codetermination (0,0.5,1)	Variable that indicates the kind of codetermination existing in the company; equals zero in case of no codetermination, 0.5 in case of one-third codetermination and 1 in case of parity codetermination	Hoppenstedt Aktienführer, annual reports
Tenure	Average tenure of supervisory board members (shareholder representatives) in years	Hoppenstedt Aktienführer, annual reports

Table 6: (continued)

Variable	Description	Source
Firm Characteristics		
Size	Natural logarithm of total employees	Thomson Datastream/Worldscope
Diversification	Number of business segments the firm is operating in	Thomson Datastream/Worldscope
Performance	Return on invested capital	Thomson Datastream/Worldscope
Leverage	Debt-equity-ratio	Thomson Datastream/Worldscope
Founded-Age	Age since foundation	Annual reports, IR requests
Industrie Affiliation	Dummy variables that indicated industry affiliation	German Stock Exchange

This table describes the set of variables used for our analyses

Table 7: Robustness: Selection Bias

Dependent variable Method	Model 2.1 Female manager (0,1) Logit		Model 2.2 Female manager (0,1) Logit		Model 2.3 Female manager (0,1) Logit	
	Coefficient	z-Statistic	Coefficient	z-Statistic	Coefficient	z-Statistic
Ownership Structure						
Freefloat	−0.2203	(−0.7759)				
Individual investors			0.0059	(1.6301)	0.0058	(1.5956)
Banks and Insurance companies			0.0110	(0.8602)	0.0112	(0.8869)
Strategic investors			0.0001	(0.0238)	0.0000	(0.0158)
Institutional investor			0.0119**	(2.4813)		
Institutional investor national					0.0087	(1.1789)
Institutional investor foreign					0.0144***	(2.6587)
Board Characteristics						
Size management board	0.1804***	(4.0771)	0.1765***	(3.9298)	0.1766***	(3.9293)
Size supervisory board	0.0067	(0.1537)	0.0053	(0.1183)	0.0034	(0.0766)
Codetermination (0,0.5,1)	0.5627*	(1.9098)	0.6159**	(2.1244)	0.6016**	(2.0684)
Tenure	−0.0894**	(−2.3447)	−0.0891**	(−2.3018)	−0.0864**	(−2.2003)
Firm Characteristics						
Size	−0.2349***	(−4.6703)	−0.2463***	(−4.7750)	−0.2446***	(−4.7689)
Diversification	0.0522	(1.1123)	0.0457	(0.9650)	0.0475	(0.9954)
Leverage	−0.0904	(−0.3969)	−0.1156	(−0.4899)	−0.1230	(−0.5208)
Founded Age	−0.0033*	(−1.7617)	−0.0031	(−1.6394)	−0.0030	(−1.6293)
Constant	yes		yes		yes	
Inverse Mills ratio	yes		yes		yes	
Industry dummies	yes		yes		yes	
Year dummies	yes		yes		yes	
No. of observations	3678		3678		3678	
Sq-Root of Sum of squared Resid.	15.5307		15.4954		15.4860	
Akaike info. crit.	0.5015		0.5005		0.5009	

This table represents the robustness check for the sample selection. The models are extensions of models 1.1 – 1.3 and include the inverse Mills ratio as the Heckman correction term. All variables used are described in the appendix. The sample is described in Table 1. We report Huber/White (QML) robust z-values in parentheses. The symbols ***, ** and * indicate significance at the 1%-, 5%- and 10%-level, respectively

Table 8: Robustness: Endogenous variable

Dependent variable	Model 3.1 Number of Female managers Poisson		Model 3.2 Number of Female managers Poisson		Model 3.3 Number of Female managers Poisson	
Method	Coefficient	z-Statistic	Coefficient	z-Statistic	Coefficient	z-Statistic
Ownership Structure						
Freefloat	−0,0017	(−0.6300)				
Individual investors			0,0051	(1.5683)	0,0050	(1.529)
Banks and Insurance companies			0,0110	(0.8230)	0,0111	(0.8371)
Strategic investors			−0,0005	(−0.1503)	−0,0005	(−0.1627)
Institutional investor			0,0101**	(2.2768)		
Institutional investor national					0,0079	(1.2592)
Institutional investor foreign					0,0114**	(2.2089)
Board Characteristics						
Size management board	0,1781***	(3.6862)	0,1726***	(3.5285)	0,1729***	(3.5313)
Size supervisory board	0,0103	(0.2502)	0,0100	(0.2376)	0,0086	(0.2056)
Codetermination (0,0.5,1)	0,5473*	(1.9162)	0,5881**	(2.0485)	0,5771**	(2.0065)
Tenure	−0,1019***	(−3.0209)	−0,0949***	(−2.7885)	−0,0933***	(−2.7298)
Firm Characteristics						
Size	−0,2239***	(−4.5015)	−0,2322***	(−4.5653)	−0,2308***	(−4.5324)
Diversification	0,0398	(1.0207)	0,0373	(0.9460)	0,0382	(0.9666)
Leverage	−0,0640	(−0.2416)	−0,0791	(−0.2896)	−0,0843	(−0.3076)
Founded Age	−0,0035*	(−1.9574)	−0,0033*	(−1.7955)	−0,0033*	(−1.7896)
Constant	yes		yes		yes	
Industry dummies	yes		yes		yes	
Year dummies	yes		yes		yes	
No. of observations	3678		3678		3678	
Adjusted R-squared	0,0471		0,0528		0,0537	

This table represents the robustness check for the choice of the endogenous variable. Compared to the models 1.1 – 1.3, the endogenous dummy variable FEMALE MANAGER is exchanged with the count variable NUMBER OF FEMALE MANAGERS. The methodology must be changed as well. It is a poisson regression and all used variables are described in the appendix. The sample is described in Table 1. We report Huber/White (QML) robust z-values in parentheses. The symbols ***, ** and * indicate significance at the 1%-, 5%- and 10%-level, respectively

Table 9: Robustness: Exogenous variables—1

Dependent variable	Model 4.1 Female manager (0,1) Logit		Model 4.2 Female manager (0,1) Logit		Model 4.3 Female manager (0,1) Logit	
Method	Coefficient	z-Statistic	Coefficient	z-Statistic	Coefficient	z-Statistic
Ownership Structure						
Freefloat	−0.2504	(−0.8806)				
Individual investors			0.0061*	(1.7058)	0.0059*	(1.6745)
Banks and Insurance companies			0.0134	(1.0566)	0.0136	(1.0789)
Strategic investors			0.0004	(0.1174)	0.0003	(0.1078)
Institutional investor			0.0122***	(2.6130)		
Institutional investor national					0.008778	(1.2331)
Institutional investor foreign					0.0150***	(2.8071)
Board Characteristics						
Size management board	0.1842***	(4.1981)	0.1790***	(4.0290)	0.1792***	(4.0301)
Size supervisory board	0.0177	(0.4311)	0.0176	(0.4105)	0.0151	(0.3548)
Tenure	−0.1065***	(−3.0750)	−0.1005***	(−2.8650)	−0.0982***	(−2.7807)
Firm Characteristics						
Size	−0.1976***	(−4.3400)	−0.2026***	(−4.3539)	−0.2021***	(−4.3620)
Diversification	0.0499	(1.1200)	0.0488	(1.0927)	0.0503	(1.1207)
Leverage	−0.1242	(−0.5367)	−0.1421	(−0.5949)	−0.1527	(−0.6378)
Founded Age	−0.0025	(−1.4440)	−0.0022	(−1.2411)	−0.0022	(−1.2373)
Constant	yes		yes		yes	
Industry dummies	yes		yes		yes	
Year dummies	yes		yes		yes	
No. of observations	3678		3678		3678	
Sq-Root of Sum of squared Resid.	15.5435		15.5037		15.4938	
Akaike info. crit.	0.5019		0.5008		0.5012	

This table represents logit regressions of ownership structure, board characteristics and company controls on the dummy variable, indicating if there is a woman among the management board members. Compared to the models 1.1–1.3, the endogenous variable CODETERMINATION is excluded. All variables used are described in the appendix. The sample is described in Table 1. We report Huber/White (QML) robust z-values in parentheses. The symbols ***, ** and * indicate significance at the 1%-, 5%- and 10%-level, respectively

Table 10: Robustness: Exogenous variables—2

Dependent variable Method	Model 5.1 Female manager (0,1) Logit		Model 5.2 Female manager (0,1) Logit		Model 5.3 Female manager (0,1) Logit	
	Coefficient	z-Statistic	Coefficient	z-Statistic	Coefficient	z-Statistic
Ownership Structure						
Freefloat	−0.1955	(−0.6857)				
Individual investors			0.0059*	(1.6582)	0.0058	(1.6242)
Banks and Insurance companies			0.0113	(0.8919)	0.0115	(0.9162)
Strategic investors			−0.0004	(−0.1173)	−0.0004	(−0.1288)
Institutional investor			0.0118**	(2.4957)		
Institutional investor national					0.00865	(1.1959)
Institutional investor foreign					0.0143***	(2.6545)
Board Characteristics						
Size management board	0.1873***	(4.2091)	0.1813***	(4.0153)	0.1816***	(4.0187)
Size supervisory board	0.0040	(0.0926)	0.0047	(0.1043)	0.0027	(0.0614)
Codetermination (0,0.5,1)	0.5535*	(1.8940)	0.6086**	(2.1137)	0.5951**	(2.0623)
Tenure	−0.1167***	(−3.3560)	−0.1111***	(−3.1517)	−0.1091***	(−3.0743)
Firm Characteristics						
Size	−0.2494***	(−4.7999)	−0.2605***	(−4.8770)	−0.2591***	(−4.8783)
Diversification	0.0381	(0.8740)	0.0348	(0.7950)	0.0363	(0.8243)
Performance	0.0032	(1.0985)	0.0034	(1.1209)	0.0034	(1.1443)
Leverage	−0.0918	(−0.4021)	−0.1125	(−0.4778)	−0.1202	(−0.5098)
Founded Age	−0.0036*	(−1.9179)	−0.0033*	(−1.7513)	−0.0033*	(−1.7432)
Constant	yes		yes		yes	
Industry dummies	yes		yes		yes	
Year dummies	yes		yes		yes	
No. of observations	3678		3678		3678	
Sq-Root of Sum of squared Resid.	15.5320		15.4894		15.4811	
Akaike info. crit.	0.5018		0.5005		0.5009	

This table represents logit regressions of ownership structure, board characteristics and company controls on the dummy variable, indicating if there is a woman among the management board members. Compared to the models 1.1–1.3, the endogenous variable PERFORMANCE is included. All used variables are described in the appendix. The sample is described in Table 1. We report Huber/White (QML) robust z-values in parentheses. The symbols ***, ** and * indicate significance at the 1%-, 5%- and 10%-level, respectively

Open Access: This article is distributed under the terms of the Creative Commons Attribution Noncommercial License which permits any noncommercial use, distribution, and reproduction in any medium, provided the original author(s) and source are credited.

References

Adams RB, Ferreira D (2009) Women in the boardroom and their impact on governance and performance. J Finan Econ 94:291–309. doi:10.1016/j.jfineco.2008.10.007
Aggarwal R, Klapper L, Wysocki PD (2005) Portfolio preferences of foreign institutional investors. J Bank Financ 29:2919–2946. doi:10.1016/j.jbankfin.2004.09.008
Aguilera RV, Filatotchev I, Gospel H, Jackson G (2008) An organizational approach to comparative corporate governance: costs, contingencies, and complementarities. Organ Sci 19:475–492. doi:10.1287/orsc.1070.0322
Ahearne AG, Griever WL, Warnock FE (2004) Information costs and home bias: an analysis of US holdings of foreign equities. J Int Econ 62:313–336. doi:10.1016/S0022-1996(03)00015-1
Ahern KR, Dittmar AK (2010) The changing of the boards: the value effect of a massive exogenous shock. Mendeley 1001:49
Anderson RC, Reeb DM (2003a) Founding-family ownership and firm performance: evidence from the S & P 500. J Financ 58:1301–1327. doi:10.1111/1540-6261.00567
Anderson RC, Reeb DM (2003b) Founding-family ownership, corporate diversification, and firm leverage. J Law Econ 46:653–684. doi:10.1086/377115
Andres C (2008) Large shareholders and firm performance—an empirical examination of founding-family ownership. J Corp Financ 14:431–445. doi:10.1016/j.jcorpfin.2008.05.003
Aretz H-J, Hansen K (2003) Erfolgreiches Management von Diversity. Die multikulturelle Organisation als Strategie zur Verbesserung einer nachhaltigen Wettbewerbsfähigkeit. Z Personalforschung 17:9–36
Arfken DE, Bellar SL, Helms MM (2004) The ultimate glass ceiling revisited: the presence of women on corporate boards. J Bus Ethics 50:177–186
Barclay MJ, Holderness CG, Sheehan DP (2009) Dividends and corporate shareholders. Rev Financ Stud 22:2423–2455. doi:10.1093/rfs/hhn060
Barth E, Gulbrandsen T, Schone P (2005) Family ownership and productivity: the role of owner-management. J Corp Financ 11:107–127. doi:10.1016/j.jcorpfin.2004.02.001
Baums T, Scott KE (2005) Taking shareholder protection seriously? Corporate governance in the United States and Germany. Am J Comp Law 53:31–75
Becker GS (1985) Human capital, effort, and the sexual division of labor. J Lab Econ 3:33–58
Becker SO, Ichino A (2002) Estimation of average treatment effects based on propensity scores. Stata J 2:358–377
Bennedsen M, Nielsen KM, Pérez-Gonzàlez F, Wolfenzon D (2006) Inside the family firm: the role of families in succession decisions and performance. Quart J Econ 122:647–691
Berle AA, Means GC (1968) The modern corporation & private property. Transaction Publishers, New Brunswick
Berrone P, Cruz C, Gomez-Mejia LR, Larraza-Kintana M (2010) Socioemotional wealth and corporate responses to institutional pressures: do family-controlled firms pollute less? Adm Sci Q 55:82–113. doi:10.2189/asqu.2010.55.1.82
Brammer S, Millington A, Pavelin S (2009) Corporate reputation and women on the board. Br J Manag 20:17–29. doi:10.1111/j.1467-8551.2008.00600.x
Broome LL (2008) The corporate boardroom: still a male club. J Corp Law 33:665–680
Böhler D, Rapp MS, Wolff M (2010) Foreign investors as a mechanism to resolve domestic director networks—evidence from the Germany Inc. Networks
Bøhren Ø, Strøm RØ (2010) Governance and politics: regulating independence and diversity in the board room. J Bus Financ Account 37:1281–1308. doi:10.1111/j.1468-5957.2010.02222.x

Carleton WT, Nelson JM, Weisbach MS (1998) The influence of institutions on corporate governance through private negotiations: evidence from TIAA-CREF. J Financ 53:1335–1363

Carter DA, Simkins BJ, Simpson WG (2003) Corporate governance, board diversity, and firm value. Financ Rev 38:33–53. doi:10.1111/1540-6288.00034

Chaganti R, Damanpour F (1991) Institutional ownership, capital structure, and firm performance. Strateg Manag J 12:479–491

Chizema A, Kim J (2010) Outside directors on korean boards: governance and institutions. J Manag Stud 47:109–129. doi:10.1111/j.1467-6486.2009.00868.x

Coate S, Loury GC (1993) Will affirmative-action policies eliminate negative stereotypes? Amer Econ Rev 83:1220–1240

Conyon MJ, Schwalbach J (2000) Executive compensation: evidence from the UK and Germany. Long Range Plan 33:504–526. doi:10.1016/S0024-6301(00)00052-2

Cucculelli M, Micucci G (2008) Family succession and firm performance: evidence from Italian family firms. J Corp Financ 14:17–31. doi:10.1016/j.jcorpfin.2007.11.001

Daily CM, Certo ST, Dalton DR (1999) A decade of corporate women: some progress in the boardroom, none in the executive suite. Strateg Manag J 20:93–99

Deeg R (2005) The comeback of modell Deutschland? The new German political economy in the EU. Ger Politics 14:332–353. doi:10.1080/09644000500268795

Denis DJ, Denis DK, Sarin A (1997) Agency problems, equity ownership, and corporate diversification. J Financ 52:135–160. doi:10.2307/2329559

Dharwadkar R, Goranova M, Brandes P, Khan R (2008) Institutional ownership and monitoring effectiveness: it's not just how much but what else you own. Organ Sci 19:419–440. doi:10.1287/orsc.1080.0359

Dittmann I, Maug E, Schneider C (2010) Bankers on the boards of german firms: what they do, what they are worth, and why they are (still) there. Rev Financ 14:35–71. doi:10.1093/rof/rfp007

Douma S (1997) The two-tier system of corporate governance. Long Range Plan 30:612–614. doi:10.1016/S0024-6301(97)00047-2

Edwards JSS, Nibler M (2000) Corporate governance: banks versus ownership concentration in Germany. Econ Policy 15:239–267

Edwards JSS, Weichenrieder AJ (2004) Ownership concentration and share valuation. Ger Econ Rev 5:143–171. doi:10.1111/j.1465-6485.2004.00100.x

Elston JA, Goldberg LG (2003) Executive compensation and agency costs in Germany. J Bank Finance 27:1391–1410. doi:10.1016/S0378-4266(02)00274-1

Fama EF, Jensen MC (1983) Separation of ownership and control. J Law Econ 26:301–325

Farrell KA, Hersch PL (2005) Additions to corporate boards: the effect of gender. J Corp Financ 11:85–106. doi:10.1016/j.jcorpfin.2003.12.001

Ferreira D (2010) Board diversity. In: Baker HK, Anderson R (eds) Corporate governance: a synthesis of theory, research, and practice. Wiley, Hoboken, pp 225–242

Forbes DP, Milliken FJ (1999) Cognition and corporate governance: understanding boards of directors as strategic decision-making groups. Acad Manag Rev 24:489–505

Franck E, Jungwirth C (1998) Vorurteile als Karrierebremse? Ein Versuch zur Erklärung des Glass Ceiling-Phänomens. Z Betriebswirtschaftliche Forschung 50:1083–1097

Franks J, Mayer C (2001) Ownership and control of German corporations. Rev Financ Stud 14:943–977

Freedman DA (2006) On the so-called "Huber Sandwich Estimator" and "Robust Standard Errors." Am Statistician 60:299–302

Fryxell GE, Lerner LD (2009) Contrasting corporate profiles: women and minority representation in top management positions. J Bus Ethics 8:341–352

Goodstein J, Gautam K, Boeker W (1994) The effects of board size and diversity on strategic change. Strateg Manag J 15:241–250

GovernanceMetrics International (GMI) (2011) 2011 Women on Boards Report

Gregoric A, Oxelheim L, Randoy T, Thomsen S (2010) How diverse can you get? Gender quotas and the diversity of nordic boards. Center for corporate Governance, Copenhagen Business School: Workingpaper

Harrigan KR (1981) Numbers and positions of women elected to corporate boards. Acad Manage J 24:619–625

Henrekson M, Stenkula M (2009) Why are there so few female top executives in egalitarian welfare states? Independent Rev 14:239–270

Hillman AJ, Shropshire C, Cannella AA (2007) Organizational predictors of women on corporate boards. Acad Manag J 50:941–952. doi:10.2307/20159898

Himmelberg CP, Hubbard GR, Palia D (1999) Understanding the determinants of managerial ownership and the link between ownership. J Finan Econ 53:353–384. doi:10.1016/S0304-405X(99)00025-2

Hoetker G (2007) The use of logit and probit models in strategic management research: critical issues. Strateg Manag J 28:331–343. doi:10.1002/smj

Hollingshead AB, Fraidin SN (2003) Gender stereotypes and assumptions about expertise in transactive memory. J Exp Soc Psychol 39:355–363. doi:10.1016/S0022-1031(02)00549-8

Holst E, Wiemer A (2010) Zur Unterrepräsentanz von Frauen in Spitzengremien der Wirtschaft—Ursachen und Handlungsansätze. Biol Cell 103:1–17. doi:10.1042/BC20100104

Ivanov VI, Xie F (2010) Value to start-up firms? Evidence from IPOs and acquisitions of VC-backed companies. Finan Manag 39:129–152

Jehn KA, Northcraft GB, Neale MA (1999) Why differences make a difference: a field study of diversity, conflict, and performance in workgroups. Adm Sci Q 44:741–763. doi:10.2307/2667054

Jensen MC (1986) Agency cost of free cash flow, corporate finance, and takeovers. Am Econ Assoc 76:323–329. doi:10.2139/ssrn.99580

Jensen MC (1993) The modern industrial revolution, exit, and the failure of internal control systems. J Financ 48:831–880. doi:10.2307/2329018

Jensen MC, Meckling WH (1976) Theory of the firm: managerial behavior, agency costs and ownership structure. J Finan Econ 3:305–360

Kalev A, Dobbin F, Kelly E (2006) Best practices or best guesses? Assessing the efficacy of corporate affirmative action and diversity policies. Am Sociol Rev 71:589–617

Kilduff M, Angelmar R, Mehra A (2000) Top management-team diversity and firm performance: examining the role of cognitions. Organ Sci 11:21–34

Kim H, Kim H, Lee PM (2008) Ownership structure and the relationship between financial slack and r&d investments: evidence from Korean firms. Organ Sci 19:404–418. doi:10.1287/orsc.1080.0360

Krell G (2008) Programme und Maßnahmen zur Realisierung von Chancengleichheit in deutschen Großunternehmen von Mitte der 1990er Jahre bis 2006—Befragungen der Mitglieder des "Forum Frauen in der Wirtschaft". Chancengleichheit durch Personalpolitik -Gleichstellung von Frauen und Männern in Unternehmen und Verwaltungen. Rechtliche Regelungen—Problemanalysen—Lösungen

Kronborg D, Thomsen S (2009) Foreign ownership and long-term survival. Strateg Manag J 30:207–219. doi:10.1002/smj

La Porta R, Lopez-de-Silanes F, Shleifer A, Vishny RW (2000) Agency problems and dividend policies around the world. J Financ 55:1–33. doi:10.1111/0022-1082.00199

Lederle S (2007) Die Einfuehrung von Diversity Management in deutschen Organisationen-Eine neoinstitutionalistische Perspektive. Z Personalforschung 21:22–41

Leuz C, Lins KV, Warnock FE (2009) Do foreigners invest less in poorly governed firms? Rev Financ Stud 22:3245–3285. doi:10.1093/rfs/hhn089

Lynall MD, Golden BR, Hillman AJ (2003) Board composition from adolescence to maturity: a multitheoretic view. Acad Manag Rev 28:416–431. doi:10.2307/30040730

McPherson M, Smith-Lovin L (1987) Homophily in voluntary organizations: status distance and the composition of face-to-face groups. Am Sociol Rev 52:370–379

McPherson M, Smith-Lovin L, Cook JM (2001) Birds of a feather: homophily in social networks. Annual Rev Sociol 27:415–444. doi:10.1146/annurev.soc.27.1.415

Morck R, Shleifer A, Vishny RW (1988) Management ownership and market valuation: an empirical analysis. J Finan Econ 20:293–315

Noe RA (1988) Women and mentoring: a review and research agenda. Acad Manag Rev 13:65–78

Oehmichen J (2010) Frauenquoten in Deutschland?—Wer Symptome lindert adressiert nur selten die Grundursache des Problems. ifo-Schnelldienst 63:10–12

Pearce JL, Xu QJ (2010) Rating performance or contesting status: evidence against the homophily explanation for supervisor demographic skew in performance ratings. Organ Sci (forthcoming). doi:10.1287/orsc.1100.0585

Pelled LH (1996) Demographic diversity, conflict, and work group outcomes: an intervening process theory. Organ Sci 7:615–631

Randel AE (2002) Identity salience: a moderator of the relationship between group gender composition and work group conflict. J Organ Behav 23:749–766. doi:10.1002/job.163

Rapp MS, Wolff M (2010) Determinanten der Vorstandsvergütung-Eine empirische Untersuchung der deutschen Prime-Standard-Unternehmen. Z Betriebswirtschaft 80:1075–1112

Renneboog L (2000) Ownership, managerial control and the governance of companies listed on the Brussels stock exchange. J Bank Financ 24:1959–1995

Sealy R, Singh V, Vinnicombe S (2007) The Female FTSE Report 2007. Cranfield University

Shleifer A, Vishny RW (1997) A survey of corporate governance. J Financ 52:737–783. doi:10.2307/2329497

Siegelman L, Zeng L (1999) Analyzing censored and sample-selected data with tobit and heckit models. Polit Anal 8:167–182

Simons T, Pelled LH, Smith KA (1999) Making use of difference: diversity, debate, and decision comprehensiveness in top management teams. A Manag J 42:662–673

Simpson A, Smith T, Kvam A (2008) Should capital be socially responsible? Yale Q4 43–53

Sraer D, Thesmar D (2007) Performance and behavior of family firms: evidence from the french stock market. J Eur Econ Assoc 5:709–751. doi:10.1162/JEEA.2007.5.4.709

Straub C (2007) A comparative analysis of the use of work-life balance practices in Europe: do practices enhance females' career advancement? Women Manag Rev 22:289–304. doi:10.1108/09649420710754246

Süß S (2008) Diversity-Management auf dem Vormarsch. Eine empirische Analyse der deutschen Unternehmenspraxis. Z betriebswirtschaftliche Forsch 60:406–430.

Terjesen S, Singh V (2008) Female presence on corporate boards: a multi-country study of environmental context. J Bus Ethics 83:55–63. doi:.1007/s10551-007-9656-1

Tharenou P (2008) Disruptive decisions to leave home: gender and family differences in expatriation choices. Organ Behav Hum Decis Process 105:183–200. doi:10.1016/j.obhdp.2007.08.004

Thomsen S, Pedersen T (2000) Ownership structure and economic performance in the largest European companies. Strateg Manag J 21:689–705.

Tsui AS, Egan TD, O'Reilly CA (1992) Being different: relational demography and organizational attachment. Adm Sci Q 37:549–579. doi:10.2307/2393472

Tuggle CS, Schnatterly K, Johnson RA (2010) Attention patterns in the boardroom: how board composition and processes affect discussion of entrepreneurial issues. Acad Manag J 53:550–571

Weber-Rey D (2009) Änderungen des Deutschen Corporate Governance Kodex 2009. Z Wirtsch Bankenrecht—Wertpapiermitteilungen 63:2255–2264

Westphal JD, Milton LP (2000) How experience and network ties affect the influence of demographic minorities on corporate boards. Adm Sci Q 45:366–398. doi:10.2307/2667075

GRUNDSÄTZE UND ZIELE

Die Zeitschrift für Betriebswirtschaft (ZfB) ist eine der ältesten deutschen Fachzeitschriften der Betriebswirtschaftslehre. Sie wurde im Jahre 1924 von Fritz Schmidt begründet und von Wilhelm Kalveram, Erich Gutenberg und Horst Albach fortgeführt. Sie wird heute von 11 Universitätsprofessoren, die als **Department Editors** fungieren, herausgegeben. Dem **Editorial Board** gehören namhafte Persönlichkeiten aus Universität und Wirtschaftspraxis an. Die Fachvertreter stammen aus den USA, Japan und Europa.

Die ZfB verfolgt das Ziel, die **Forschung auf dem Gebiet der Betriebswirtschaftslehre** anzuregen sowie zur Verbreitung und Anwendung ihrer Ergebnisse beizutragen. Sie betont die Einheit des Faches; enger und einseitiger Spezialisierung in der Betriebswirtschaftslehre will sie entgegenwirken. Die Zeitschrift dient dem **Gedankenaustausch zwischen Wissenschaft und Unternehmenspraxis**. Sie will die betriebswirtschaftliche Forschung auf wichtige betriebswirtschaftliche Probleme in der Praxis aufmerksam machen und sie durch Anregungen aus der Unternehmenspraxis befruchten.

In der ZfB können auch englischsprachige Aufsätze veröffentlicht werden. Die Herausgeber begrüßen die Einreichung englischsprachiger Beiträge von deutschen und internationalen Wissenschaftlern. Durch die Zusammenfassungen in englischer Sprache sind die deutschsprachigen Aufsätze der ZfB auch internationalen Referatenorganen zugänglich. Im Journal of Economic Literature werden die Aufsätze der ZfB zum Beispiel laufend referiert.

Die Qualität der Aufsätze in der ZfB wird durch die Herausgeber und einen Kreis renommierter Gutachter gewährleistet. Das **Begutachtungsverfahren** ist doppelt verdeckt und wahrt damit die Anonymität von Autoren wie Gutachtern gemäß den international üblichen Standards. Jeder Beitrag wird von zwei Fachgutachtern beurteilt. Bei abweichenden Gutachten wird ein Drittgutachter bestellt. Die Department Editors entscheiden auf der Grundlage der Gutachten eigenverantwortlich über die Annahme und Ablehnung der von ihnen betreuten Manuskripte. Sie können Beiträge auch ohne Begutachtungsverfahren ablehnen, wenn diese formal oder inhaltlich von den Vorgaben der ZfB abweichen.

Die ZfB veröffentlicht im Einklang mit diesen Grundsätzen und Zielen:

- **Aufsätze** zu theoretischen und praktischen Fragen der Betriebswirtschaftslehre einschließlich von Arbeiten junger Wissenschaftler, denen sie ein Forum für die Diskussion und die Verbreitung ihrer Forschungsergebnisse eröffnet,
- **Ergebnisse der Diskussion** aktueller betriebswirtschaftlicher Themen zwischen Wissenschaftlern und Praktikern,
- **Berichte** über den Einsatz wissenschaftlicher Instrumente und Konzepte bei der Lösung von betriebswirtschaftlichen Problemen in der Praxis,
- **Schilderungen von Problemen** aus der Praxis zur Anregung der betriebswirtschaftlichen Forschung,
- „**State of the Art**"-Artikel, in denen Entwicklung und Stand der Betriebswirtschaftslehre eines Teilgebietes dargelegt werden.

Die ZfB informiert ihre Leser über **Neuerscheinungen** in der Betriebswirtschaftslehre und der Management Literatur durch ausführliche Rezensionen und Kurzbesprechungen.

IMPRESSUM/HINWEISE FÜR AUTOREN

Zeitschrift für Betriebswirtschaft
Journal of Business Economics
Springer Gabler | Springer Fachmedien Wiesbaden GmbH,
Abraham-Lincoln-Straße 46 | 65189 Wiesbaden,
http://www.springer-gabler.de, http://www.zfb-online.de
Amtsgericht Wiesbaden, HRB 9754, Ust-IdNr. DE8 11148419
Geschäftsführer: Dr. Ralf Birkelbach (Vors.) | Armin Gross | Albrecht F. Schirmacher
Verlagsbereichsleitung: Andreas Funk
Gesamtleitung Anzeigen und Märkte: Armin Gross
Gesamtleitung Marketing und Individual Sales: Rolf-Günther Hobbeling
Gesamtleitung Produktion: Christian Staral
Editor-in-Chief:
Professor Dr. Dr. h.c. Günter Fandel
FernUniversität in Hagen
Fakultät für Wirtschaftswissenschaft
58084 Hagen
Tel: 0 23 31/9 87-2625, Fax: 0 23 31/9 87-2575
E-Mail: ZfB@FernUni-Hagen.de
Administration Manuscript Central™
Sebastian Bartussek, Tel.: 0 23 31/9 87-2652,
Fax: 0 23 31/9 87-2575, E-Mail: Sebastian.Bartussek@FernUni-Hagen.de
Produktion: Dagmar Orth, Tel: 0 62 21-4 87-8902
E-Mail: dagmar.orth@springer.com
Kundenservice: Springer Customer Service Center GmbH, Service Gabler Verlag, Haberstr. 7, 69126 Heidelberg,
Telefon: +49 (0)6221/345-4303, Fax: +49 (0)6221/345-4229,
Montag bis Freitag 8.00 Uhr bis 18.00 Uhr,
E-Mail: gabler-service@springer.com
Produktmanagement: Kristiane Alesch
Tel.: 06 11/78 78-359, Fax: 06 11/78 78-78359,
E-Mail: Kristiane.Alesch@springer.com
Gesamtverkaufsleitung Fachmedien: Britta Dolch
Mediaberatung: Yvonne Guderjahn, Tel.: 0611/78 78-155,
Fax: 06 11/78 78-430, E-Mail: Yvonne.Guderjahn@best-ad-media.de
Anzeigendisposition: Monika Dannenberger,
Tel.: 06 11/78 78-148, Fax: 06 11/78 78-430,
E-Mail: Monika.Dannenberger@best-ad-media.de
Anzeigenpreise: Es gelten die Mediainformationen vom 1.1.2011
Bezugsmöglichkeiten: Die Zeitschrift erscheint monatlich. Das Abonnement kann jederzeit zur nächsten erreichbaren Ausgabe schriftlich mit Nennung der Kundennummer gekündigt werden. Eine schriftliche Bestätigung erfolgt nicht. Zuviel gezahlte Beträge für nicht gelieferte Ausgaben werden zurückerstattet. Jährlich können 1 bis 6 Special Issues hinzukommen. Jedes Special Issue wird den Abonnenten mit einem Nachlass von 25% des jeweiligen Ladenpreises gegen Rechnung geliefert.

Preise Abonnement Inland/Ausland*

Studenten-**/Emeritus-Abo:	98,-Euro
ausgewählte Verbände:***	195,-Euro
Privat-Abo:	229,-Euro
Lehrstuhl-Abo:	259,-Euro
Bibliotheks-/Unternehmensabo:	449,-Euro

*Versand ins Ausland: 26,-Euro / Airmail 58,-Euro
** Studienbescheinigung, *** auf Anfrage beim Verlag
Einzelheft 44,- zzgl. Versand Inland und Ausland
©Springer Gabler | Springer Fachmedien Wiesbaden
Alle Rechte vorbehalten. Kein Teil dieser Zeitschrift darf ohne schriftliche Genehmigung des Verlages vervielfältigt oder verbreitet werden. Unter dieses Verbot fällt insbesondere die gewerbliche Vervielfältigung per Kopie, die Aufnahme in elektronische Datenbanken und die Vervielfältigung auf CD-ROM und allen anderen elektronischen Datenträgern.
Satzherstellung: Crest Premedia Solutions, Pune, Indien
Gedruckt auf säurefreiem und chlorfrei gebleichtem Papier.
ISSN: 0044-2372 (Print)
ISSN: 1861-8928 (Online)
Springer Gabler ist eine Marke von Springer DE. Springer DE ist Teil der Fachverlagsgruppe Springer Science+Business Media

Hinweise für Autoren

1. Bitte beachten Sie die „Grundsätze und Ziele" der ZfB.

2. Einreichungen werden bei der ZfB ausschließlich über ein Online-Verfahren abgewickelt. Manuskripte – in deutscher oder englischer Sprache – können vom Autor unter http://mc.manuscriptcentral.com/zfb direkt in das Manuskriptverwaltungssystem hochgeladen werden. Hierbei ist insbesondere auf die Wahrung der Anonymität der zur Begutachtung eingereichten Vorlagen zu achten. Der Autor verpflichtet sich mit der Einsendung des Manuskripts nicht unwiderruflich, das Manuskript bis zur Entscheidung über die Annahme nicht anderweitig zu veröffentlichen oder zur Veröffentlichung anzubieten. Diese Verpflichtung erlischt nicht durch Korrekturvorschläge im Begutachtungsverfahren.

3. Um die eingereichten Manuskripte in den Begutachtungsprozess geben bzw. diese im Manuskriptlauf zügig behandeln zu können, wird um Beachtung der folgenden Punkte gebeten: Gesamtlänge des Manuskriptes darf 25 DinA4 nicht überschreiten (bei ca. 3800 Zeichen pro Seite), Schriftart „Times New Roman", Schriftgröße 12, einfacher Zeilenabstand, jeweils 2,5 cm Außenrand, Angabe von Abbildungs- und Tabellenüberschriften (Abb. 1: Text; Tab. 1: Text etc.), eingebundene Objekte (insbes. Bild-, .ppt-, .xls-Dateien etc.) auch separat in Dateiform beifügen, das Hauptdokument muss in **anonymer** Form eingereicht werden, d. h. alle Autorennamen, Autoreninformationen und evtl. Danksagungen sind für die Begutachtung restlos zu streichen. Einhaltung der Gliederungssystematik: **1 Überschriftsebene 1** (12pt, fett, 2 Zeilen Abstand davor, 1 Zeile danach), *1.1 Überschriftsebene 2* (12pt, kursiv, 1 Zeile Abstand davor, 1 Zeile danach), 1.1.1 Überschriftsebene 3 (12pt, kursiv, 1 Zeile Abstand davor, 1 Zeile danach), **Spitzmarke:** (12pt, fett mit Doppelpunkt zu Beginn des Absatzes, 1 Zeile Abstand davor). Harvard-Zitierweise, keine End- oder Fußnoten: Ein Autor: (vgl. Meier 2007) bzw. (Meier 2007, S. 30); Zwei Autoren: (vgl. Meier/Müller 2007) bzw. (Meier/Müller 2007, S. 30); Drei oder mehr Autoren: (vgl. Meier et al. 2007) bzw. (Meier et al. 2007, S. 30); Eventuelle Erläuterungen zu Textpassagen können weiterhin als Endnoten angehängt werden, sollten aber – soweit möglich – vermieden werden. Das Literaturverzeichnis muss in *Harvard Stil* bzw. *Basic Springer Reference Style* aufgebaut sein. Bei einer Wiedereinreichung eines Beitrags muss eine Stellungnahme zu den Gutachten beigelegt werden. Einreichung der Beitragsdatei als **Microsoft Word®-Datei** oder in einem Word®-kompatiblen Format; **kein (La)TeX.** PDF-Dateien sind generell nicht geeignet und können auch nicht ins Onlinesystem Manuscript Central™ hochgeladen werden. Der Beitrag muss in folgender Reihenfolge aufgebaut sein: Erste Seite: prägnanter Beitragstitel in deutscher bzw. in englischer Sprache (max. 80 Zeichen; bei Bedarf: Angabe eines Untertitels), dem Beitrag vorgestellt die einleitende „Zusammenfassung" bzw. einleitender „Abstract" (Fließtext, max. 15 Zeilen bzw. 1100 Zeichen), deutsche „Schlüsselwörter" (max. 5 Angaben) bzw. englische Keywords (max. 5 Angaben), JEL-Klassifikation (max. 5 Angaben); Ab Seite 2: Beitragstext, falls nötig: „Anmerkungen" als Endnoten (keine Fußnoten im Text), „Literaturverzeichnis", letzte Seite: (nur bei deutschsprachigen Beiträgen, bei englischsprachigen Beiträgen) prägnanter Beitragstitel in englischer Sprache (max. 80 Zeichen; bei Bedarf: Angabe eines Untertitels), „Abstract" in englischer Sprache (Fließtext, max. 15 Zeilen bzw. 1100 Zeichen). Zusätzlich sollten auch Autorenfotos in digitaler Form, 300dpi, mind. 640×480 Pixel) als auch die Autorenangaben (Titel, Name, Institut, Lehrstuhl, Adresse, Land, ggf. Arbeitsgebiete, E-mailadresse und URL; insgesamt pro Autor max. 4 Zeilen) in separaten Dateien eingereicht werden. **Alle Kopf- und Fußzeilen sowie Seitenzahlen sind zu entfernen!**

4. Der Autor verpflichtet sich, die Korrekturfahnen innerhalb einer Woche zu lesen und die Mehrkosten für Korrekturen, die nicht vom Verlag zu vertreten sind, sowie die Kosten für die Korrektur durch einen Korrektor bei nicht termingerechter Rücksendung der Fahnenkorrektur zu übernehmen.

5. Der Autor ist damit einverstanden, dass sein Beitrag außer in der Zeitschrift auch durch Lizenzvergabe in anderen Zeitschriften (auch übersetzt), durch Nachdruck in Sammelbänden (z. B. zu Jubiläen der Zeitschrift oder des Verlages oder in Themenbänden), durch längere Auszüge in Büchern des Verlages auch zu Werbezwecken, durch Vervielfältigung und Verbreitung auf CD-ROM oder anderen Datenträgern, durch Speicherung auf Datenbanken, deren Weitergabe und dem Abruf von solchen Datenbanken während der Dauer des Urheberrechtsschutzes am Beitrag sowohl im In- und Ausland vom Verlag und seinen Lizenznehmern genutzt werden.

HERAUSGEBER/EDITORIAL BOARD

Editor-in-Chief

Prof. Dr. Dr. h.c. Günter Fandel ist Universitätsprofessor und Inhaber des Lehrstuhls für Betriebswirtschaft, insbesondere Produktions- und Investitionstheorie an der FernUniversität in Hagen. Seine Hauptarbeitsgebiete sind Industriebetriebslehre, Produktionsmanagement und Hochschulmanagement.

Department Editors

Prof. Dr. Hans-Joachim Böcking ist Universitätsprofessor und Inhaber der Professur für Betriebswirtschaftslehre, insbesondere Wirtschaftsprüfung und Corporate Governance, an der Goethe-Universität Frankfurt am Main. Seine Forschungsschwerpunkte sind Wirtschaftsprüfung, Corporate Governance, nationale und internationale Rechnungslegung sowie Unternehmensbewertung.

Prof. Dr. Wolfgang Breuer ist Universitätsprofessor und Inhaber des Lehrstuhls für Betriebswirtschaftslehre, insb. Betriebliche Finanzwirtschaft, an der Rheinisch-Westfälischen Technischen Hochschule Aachen. Seine Hauptarbeitsgebiete sind Finanzierungs- und Investitionstheorie sowie Portfolio- und Risikomanagement.

Prof. Dr. Oliver Fabel ist Universitätsprofessor und Inhaber des Lehrstuhls für Personalwirtschaft mit Internationaler Schwerpunktsetzung am Institut für Betriebswirtschaftslehre der Universität Wien. Seine Hauptarbeitsgebiete sind Personal-, Organisations- und Bildungsökonomik.

Prof. Dr. Dr. h.c. Günter Fandel, s.o.

Prof. Dr. Armin Heinzl ist Universitätsprofessor und Inhaber des Lehrstuhls für Allgemeine Betriebswirtschaftslehre und Wirtschaftsinformatik an der Universität Mannheim. Seine Hauptarbeitsgebiete sind Wirtschaftsinformatik, Organisationslehre sowie Logistik.

Prof. Dr. Harald Hruschka ist Universitätsprofessor und Inhaber des Lehrstuhls für Betriebswirtschaftslehre mit dem Schwerpunkt Marketing an der Universität Regensburg. Sein Hauptarbeitsgebiet bezieht sich auf Marktreaktionsmodelle unter Einschluss semiparametrischer und hierarchischer Bayes'scher Ansätze.

Prof. Dr. Jochen Hundsdoerfer ist Universitätsprofessor und Inhaber der Professur für Betriebswirtschaftslehre, insb. Betriebswirtschaftliche Steuerlehre, an der Freien Universität Berlin. Seine Hauptarbeitsgebiete sind Unternehmensbesteuerung und Steuerwirkungsforschung.

Prof. Dr. Dr. h.c. Hans-Ulrich Küpper ist Universitätsprofessor und Direktor des Instituts für Produktionswirtschaft und Controlling der Universität München. Seine Hauptarbeitsgebiete sind Unternehmensrechnung, Controlling und Hochschulmanagement.

Prof. Dr. Joachim Schwalbach ist Universitätsprofessor und Inhaber des Lehrstuhls für Internationales Management an der Humboldt-Universität zu Berlin.

Prof. Dr. Stefan Winter ist Universitätsprofessor und Inhaber des Lehrstuhls für Human Resource Management an der Ruhr-Universität in Bochum. Seine Hauptarbeitsgebiete sind die Analyse von Anreizstrukturen in Unternehmen, Gestaltung von Vergütungssystemen für Führungskräfte sowie die Institutionenökonomische Analyse von Personal- und Organisationsproblemen.

Prof. Dr. Peter Witt ist Universitätsprofessor und Inhaber des Lehrstuhls für Technologie- und Innovationsmanagement an der Bergischen Universität Wuppertal. Seine Hauptarbeitsgebiete sind Innovationsmanagement, Entrepreneurship und Familienunternehmen.

Editorial Board

Prof. (em.) Dr. Dr. h.c. mult. Horst Albach (Chairman)
Prof. Alain Burlaud
Prof. Dr. Dr. Dr. h.c. Santiago Garcia Echevarria
Prof. Dr. Lars Engwall
Dr. Dieter Heuskel
Dr. Detlef Hunsdiek
Prof. Dr. Don Jacobs
Prof. Dr. Eero Kasanen
Dr. Bernd-Albrecht v. Maltzan
Prof. Dr. Koji Okubayashi
Hans Botho von Portatius
Prof. Dr. Oleg D. Prozenko
Prof. (em.) Dr. Hermann Sabel
Prof. Dr. Adolf Stepan
Dr. med. Martin Zügel

Wolfgang Weber / Rüdiger Kabst
**Einführung
in die Betriebswirtschaftslehre**
8., akt. u. überarb. Aufl. 2012.
XXIV, 498 S. Br. EUR 29,95
ISBN 978-3-8349-1994-6

Dieses Lehrbuch gibt eine kompakte und sehr gut verständliche Einführung in die Betriebswirtschaftslehre. Es macht in didaktisch einprägsamer Form mit den Grundbegriffen sowie den wichtigsten Problemen der Betriebswirtschaftslehre und ihrem Denken vertraut. Ein umfangreiches Glossar mit den wichtigsten Begriffen ergänzt die Ausführungen.

Der Inhalt
- Gegenstand der Betriebswirtschaftslehre
- Gesellschaftliches, wirtschaftliches, rechtliches und technologisches Umfeld
- Strategische Planung
- Organisation
- Beschaffung und Materialwirtschaft
- Produktionswirtschaft
- Absatzwirtschaft
- Finanzwirtschaft
- Rechnungswesen
- Personalwirtschaft
- Informationsmanagement
- Internationale Unternehmenstätigkeit
- Glossar

Die Autoren
Prof. Dr. Dr. h.c. Wolfgang Weber war Gründungsdekan der Fakultät Wirtschafts- und Sozialwissenschaften an der Universität Hamburg und hatte an der Universität Paderborn einen Lehrstuhl für Betriebswirtschaftslehre, insbesondere Personalwirtschaft inne.

Prof. Dr. Rüdiger Kabst ist Inhaber des Lehrstuhls für Betriebswirtschaftslehre, insbesondere Personalmanagement, Mittelstand und Entrepreneurship an der Justus-Liebig-Universität Gießen.

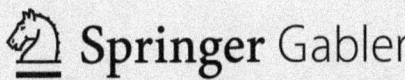

Einfach bestellen: SpringerDE-service@springer.com
Telefon +49(0)6221/345 – 4301

GPSR Compliance

The European Union's (EU) General Product Safety Regulation (GPSR) is a set of rules that requires consumer products to be safe and our obligations to ensure this.

If you have any concerns about our products, you can contact us on

ProductSafety@springernature.com

In case Publisher is established outside the EU, the EU authorized representative is:

Springer Nature Customer Service Center GmbH
Europaplatz 3
69115 Heidelberg, Germany

www.ingramcontent.com/pod-product-compliance
Lightning Source LLC
LaVergne TN
LVHW010343260326
834688LV00036B/858